Sociology of Diversity series

Series Editor: **David G. Embrick**,
University of Connecticut, US

The Sociology of Diversity series brings together the highest quality sociological and interdisciplinary research specific to ethnic, racial, gender and sexualities diversity.

Forthcoming in the series:

Race, Diversity and Humanitarian Aid
Black Ecologies and the Problem of Whiteness in New Orleans
Diana Harvey

Racial Diversity in Contemporary France
Rethinking the French Model
Marie Neiges Léonard

Out now in the series:

Southern Craft Food Diversity
Challenging the Myth of a US Food Revival
Kaitland M. Byrd

Beer and Racism
How Beer Became White, Why It Matters, and the Movements to Change It
Nathaniel Chapman and **David Brunsma**

The Death of Affirmative Action?
Racialized Framing and the Fight Against Racial Preference in College Admissions
J. Scott Carter and **Cameron Lippard**

Find out more at
bristoluniversitypress.co.uk/sociology-of-diversity

Sociology of Diversity series

Series Editor: **David G. Embrick**,
University of Connecticut, US

Advisory board:

David L. Brunsma, Virginia Tech, US
Sharon S. Collins, University of Illinois at Chicago, US
Enobong Anna Branch, University of Massachusetts at Amhurst, US
Vessula Misheva, Uppsala Universitet, Sweden
J.T. Thomas, University of Mississippi, US
Peter Wade, University of Manchester, UK

Find out more at
bristoluniversitypress.co.uk/sociology-of-diversity

DISPROPORTIONATE MINORITY CONTACT AND RACISM IN THE US

How We Failed Children of Color

Paul R. Ketchum and B. Mitchell Peck

First published in Great Britain in 2023 by

Bristol University Press
University of Bristol
1-9 Old Park Hill
Bristol
BS2 8BB
UK
t: +44 (0)117 374 6645
e: bup-info@bristol.ac.uk

Details of international sales and distribution partners are available at bristoluniversitypress.co.uk

© Bristol University Press 2023

British Library Cataloguing in Publication Data
A catalogue record for this book is available from the British Library

ISBN 978-1-5292-0240-3 hardcover
ISBN 978-1-5292-0245-8 paperback
ISBN 978-1-5292-0242-7 ePub
ISBN 978-1-5292-0241-0 ePdf

The right of Paul R. Ketchum and B. Mitchell Peck to be identified as authors of this work has been asserted by them in accordance with the Copyright, Designs and Patents Act 1988.

All rights reserved: no part of this publication may be reproduced, stored in a retrieval system, or transmitted in any form or by any means, electronic, mechanical, photocopying, recording, or otherwise without the prior permission of Bristol University Press.

Every reasonable effort has been made to obtain permission to reproduce copyrighted material. If, however, anyone knows of an oversight, please contact the publisher.

The statements and opinions contained within this publication are solely those of the authors and not of the University of Bristol or Bristol University Press. The University of Bristol and Bristol University Press disclaim responsibility for any injury to persons or property resulting from any material published in this publication.

Bristol University Press works to counter discrimination on grounds of gender, race, disability, age and sexuality.

Cover design: blu inc, Bristol
Front cover image: istockphoto.com - FOTOKITA

Contents

List of Figures and Tables		vi
About the Authors		ix
Acknowledgments		x
Series Editor Preface		xii
1	Introduction: Policy Born Out of Racist Myth	1
2	Occam's Razor: Racial/Ethnic Inequality Throughout Society	34
3	Law Enforcement Contact with Juveniles: Arrests and Citations	55
4	The Juvenile Justice System: Intake Decisions and Outcomes	74
5	Juvenile Self-Reports of Deviant and Criminal Behavior	101
6	Data Issues and the Case for Self-Report Data	123
7	Police, Juvenile Court and Juvenile Specialist Interviews	144
8	Conclusion and Discussion	175
Appendix A: Juvenile Self-Report Questionnaire		184
Appendix B: Interview Guide for Judges, Police Officers and Juvenile Specialists		190
Bibliography		196
Index		224

List of Figures and Tables

Figures

1.1	Data triangulation to examine DMC	17
3.1	Typical progression through the juvenile justice system	56
3.2	Summary of arrests and tickets/citations	63
3.3	Arrests and tickets/citations by race/ethnicity	64
3.4	Unadjusted risk ratios of arrest by race/ethnicity	65
3.5	Summary of types of offense	67
3.6	Types of offense by race/ethnicity	68
3.7	Offenses that ended in arrest by race/ethnicity	69
3.8	Adjusted risk ratios of arrest by race/ethnicity	70
4.1	Summary of intake decisions	86
4.2	Intake decisions by race/ethnicity	87
4.3	Risk ratios of declined referral by race/ethnicity	89
4.4	Risk ratios of referral to informal probation by race/ethnicity	89
4.5	Risk ratios of referral petition filed by race/ethnicity	90
4.6	Summary of intake decisions by race/ethnicity	91
4.7	Summary of disposition of referrals	92
4.8	Disposition of referred cases by race/ethnicity	93
4.9	Risk ratios of referral dismissed by race/ethnicity	95
4.10	Risk ratios of referral placed on court-ordered probation by race/ethnicity	95
4.11	Risk ratios of referral placed in OJA custody by race/ethnicity	96
4.12	Risk ratios of referral convicted and sentenced as adults by race/ethnicity	97
4.13	Juvenile justice decision points	98
5.1	Risk ratios of being detained or transported by the police for non-White juveniles	118
5.2	Detained and transported and criminal behavior by race	119
6.1	Comparison of juvenile self-reports of offenses committed at school and school disciplinary data	129

6.2	Comparison of juvenile self-report of physical violence committed at school and school disciplinary data of physical violence by race	130
6.3	Comparison of juvenile self-report of physical violence committed at school and school disciplinary data of physical violence by gender	131
8.1	Depiction of DMC	176

Tables

3.1	Summary descriptions of the study group characteristics	59
3.2	Distribution of individual youths in the dataset	61
3.3	Comparison of percentages by race in Oklahoma and in the study group	62
4.1	Summary descriptions of the study group characteristics	81
4.2	Summary of referred offenses	83
4.3	Summary of referred offenses by race	84
4.4	Summary of referred offenses by White/non-White race categories	85
5.1	Summary of characteristics of the schools in the study	103
5.2	Comparison of the sample and population data from the urban school	107
5.3	Comparison of the sample and population data from the suburban school	108
5.4	Comparison of the sample and population data from the rural school	109
5.5	Summary descriptions of the characteristics of the study group	110
5.6	Summary of self-reported deviant and criminal behaviors	112
5.7	Self-reported deviant and criminal behaviors by race	113
5.8	Self-reported deviant and criminal behaviors by race (non-White/White)	114
5.9	Mean number of self-reported deviant and criminal behaviors by race	115
5.10	Mean number of self-reported deviant and criminal behaviors by race (non-White/White)	115
5.11	Summary of self-reported interactions with police	116
5.12	Summary of self-reported interactions with police by race	116
5.13	Summary of self-reported interactions with police by race (non-White/White)	117
5.14	Summary of deviant and criminal behavior differences by White and non-White race categories	120

6.1	Demographic comparisons of juvenile self-report of offenses committed at school and school administrative disciplinary report	128
6.2	Comparisons of odds ratios of arrest for race by location in Oklahoma	132
6.3	Comparisons of referred offenses by location in Oklahoma	134
6.4	Comparisons of intake decision to decline by race and location in Oklahoma	135
6.5	Comparisons of intake decision for informal probation by race and location in Oklahoma	136
6.6	Comparisons of intake decision to file petition by race and location in Oklahoma	136
6.7	Comparisons of disposition of referrals by location in Oklahoma	137
6.8	Comparisons of odds ratios of the case dismissed by race and location in Oklahoma	137
6.9	Comparisons of odds ratios of being placed on probation by race and location in Oklahoma	138
6.10	Comparisons of odds ratios of being placed in OJA custody by race and location in Oklahoma	138
6.11	Comparisons of odds ratios of being convicted and sentenced in adult criminal court by race and location in Oklahoma	139
6.12	US juvenile arrest rate ratios compared with White juveniles per 100,000 juveniles, 2019	140
7.1	Categories of responses to the one thing juvenile justice professionals would change to minimize the need for the justice system	148
7.2	Is there a culture of violence in barrio and ghetto neighborhoods?	162
7.3	Are members of some races more prone to gang membership?	164
7.4	Perceptions of being prone to gang membership for specific race groups	165
7.5	Importance of a juvenile's prior record in determining how juvenile justice officials deal with the juvenile	170
7.6	Does direct or overt discrimination play a role in juveniles ending up in the juvenile justice system?	171
7.7	Is disproportionate minority contact a problem?	171

About the Authors

Paul R. Ketchum is Assistant Professor of Criminal Justice at the University of Oklahoma. He earned his PhD in Sociology at Texas A&M University with an emphasis on race and ethnicity and criminology. His teaching and research focus on race and ethnicity, criminology and the intersection of the two. Before earning his PhD, he taught high school for Los Angeles Unified School District in the community of Watts. He has created a transition program for a residential treatment facility and has taught college classes in prisons and juvenile detention facilities. When not researching disproportionate minority contact, he has spent much of the last seven years creating and growing a small program that prepares kids from a Title I school, at no cost to the students, for admission to R-1 institutions. The Title I school had 54 percent of its last senior class accepted to at least one four-year school and 8–18 percent of each of the last five senior classes accepted to the University of Oklahoma. He lives with his wife Heather, seven dogs, eight horses, one miniature donkey, two cats that they claim and two to seven others that show up fairly regularly.

B. Mitchell Peck is Associate Professor of Sociology at the University of Oklahoma. He is a quantitative sociologist whose research focuses on race and the intersection of individuals and social institutions. He has examined officers in the military, doctor and patient interactions in the medical encounter, and interactions of adults and juveniles in the justice system.

Acknowledgments

There are many people we need to recognize and thank for making this book possible. We are very grateful to the juvenile justice professionals who shared their views about the juvenile justice system, race issues and disproportionate minority contact in the juvenile system. As you will see, we spoke with many police officers, attorneys, judges and juvenile probation officers. Our conclusions about the juvenile justice system are generally not flattering and in some cases are downright critical. We are not, however, critical of the fine folks who have dedicated their professional lives trying to make a difference for juveniles. We are indebted to them all for their input for this book and their service to the juvenile justice system—a difficult and often thankless job. We would also like to thank the superintendents, principals, teachers, administrators and staff members at the various schools where we collected data on students. It is not a simple task to collect data from students. We appreciate the effort of all the school personnel who not only allowed us to collect data in their schools but facilitated the process in many ways. We also owe a huge debt to the juveniles—the kids—who are the primary focus of this book. We collected data on over 500 juveniles from all walks of life and from different backgrounds. The kids answered questions (anonymously, of course) about difficult topics—their own deviant and criminal behavior. The kids at all the schools took the project seriously and provided excellent information and data. We hope those data will help begin the process of change in the juvenile justice system.

We also must recognize our professional colleagues and academic departments. Thank you to our academic department administrators Martha Banz (Dean, College of Professional and Continuing Studies at the University of Oklahoma) and Loretta Bass (Chair, Department of Sociology at the University of Oklahoma). Thank you to our colleagues who read drafts of chapters, answered questions about methodology and analysis, and provided general support. Thanks to Shannon Powers. She helped with the qualitative data, which was no small task. Her work in digging through the transcriptions of 84 hour-long interviews was immensely helpful. Professor John Duncan helped with the data collection from students and helped us categorize and code offenses in the police reports. Special thanks to Sebastian "Sam" Davis.

Sam was instrumental in helping us get access to the data that make up the bulk of the quantitative analyses presented in the book. His understanding and expertise of the juvenile justice system was invaluable. Thank you, Sam.

Finally, we both owe untold thanks to our families, especially our wives. More than once, we have commented to one another that we are married to the same woman—or at least the same type of woman. The similarities between our spouses are uncanny. It's likely because they are both professors, both smarter than we are and both generally more capable than either of us. They also both live and put up with insufferable husbands. To Heather and Jennifer: much love, thanks and gratitude. This would not have been possible without you.

Series Editor Preface

The attack on critical race theory (CRT) is not new, but it has certainly taken on a life of its own since I wrote this editor's preface. While arguments within and outside academia abound with ideas about how best to understand CRT, the reality is that the attack on this over 40-year-old concept is not only an attack on CRT itself but is also a façade for rendering silent both the deep legacies of racism in the United States and attempts at better understanding how systemic racism continues to affect Blacks and other minoritized groups in our society. Saying we are a post-racial society does not make it true, and ignoring the ugly truths about our history of racial and ethnic oppressions does not mean that those histories are not part of the fabric of the United States. Teaching about the history of racism allows us better insights into understanding modern phenomena such as housing and neighborhood segregation, the racial wealth gap, institutional racism and disproportionate minority contact, for example. The Bristol University Press Sociology of Diversity series challenges the ridiculous notion that discussing racism will only fuel racism, or that it is divisive and anti-patriotic, or that it is an unfair attack on White people. In many instances, diversity ideology and the ambiguity of similar language only serve to undermine real attempts at getting to the truth about past and existing inequalities in our society. To that end, books in the series open up readers' eyes beyond the often-disguised public presentations that promote our institutions, public policies and even daily lives as ideal, honest, fair or equal. The previous books in this series have dutifully and meticulously interrogated the concepts of affirmative action, Whiteness and White supremacy in the craft beer industry, and the co-optation and myth of a US food revival. In each book, the authors challenge readers to re-examine how they understand the world by guiding them behind closed curtains in order to dismantle and deconstruct myths in the affirmative action debates, the beer industry and the world of Southern craft foods.

In this fourth book to be published in the Sociology of Diversity series, *Disproportionate Minority Contact and Racism in the US: How We Failed Children of Color*, Paul R. Ketchum and B. Mitchell Peck challenge readers on their current understanding of law enforcement, the juvenile justice system and the realities of minority overrepresentation in that system. Through the lens of structural racism and its impact on minoritized youth, the authors painstakingly guide readers into dismantling and debunking current (and past) myths surrounding the aforementioned topics, and in particular the intersections between disproportionate minority contact, police and the juvenile courts. Their central argument, weaved through eight chapters, is that minoritized youth are over-policed because of a racialized system (both institutional racism and actors) that has consistently overgeneralized (incorrectly) high rates of violent crimes of a small proportion of minoritized youth to the larger population. The result is a long history of not only false misconceptions about minoritized youth, but also the promotion of a viewpoint (or viewpoints) to the general public about the best way to understand the phenomenon of disproportionate minority contact. By pulling aside the curtain, the authors open up new questions about what is really going on but also provide some insights into how best to move forward.

David G. Embrick
University of Connecticut

1

Introduction: Policy Born Out of Racist Myth

> In effect, the juvenile justice labeling process works to single out adolescents from groups culturally alien to those in power. Those singled out, because of their powerlessness, are ill-equipped to stop the process or to intervene in it effectively to prevent themselves from having various and sundry tags imposed upon them by police, judges, probation officers, psychiatrists, and others who are employed as agents of the juvenile justice system.
> John McCullough Martin (1970)

Fifty years later, Martin's quote is still an eerily accurate description of the juvenile justice system in the United States. In Oklahoma City, Oklahoma, Native American juveniles are two and a half times as likely as White youth to be arrested rather than cited, Black juveniles are more than twice as likely to be arrested as are White juveniles, and Latinx juveniles are almost twice as likely. Our data—from Oklahoma City—are consistent with national levels of overrepresentation by race and ethnicity in the juvenile justice system. This overrepresentation has been relatively consistent since it was first studied. In 1970, four years before the 1974 Juvenile Justice and Delinquency Prevention Act, Black juveniles were 2.3 times as likely as White juveniles to be arrested nationally (Racial Disparities in Youth Commitments and Arrests, 2016). In almost 50 years, we have done little to lessen the impact of disproportionate minority contact (DMC).

This book examines how structural racism dramatically impacts the lives of non-White youth through their interactions with the juvenile justice system. Specifically, we aim to answer the question: To what extent is minority overrepresentation in the juvenile justice system due to differential involvement/behavior (i.e., non-White youth commit crimes at a higher rate) and to what extent is minority overrepresentation attributable to differential treatment (i.e., racism/racial bias within the system)? We hypothesize that non-White youth are over-policed, with the rationalization of over-policing resting upon juvenile justice officials incorrectly overgeneralizing the high rates of violent crime among a small number of non-White youth to include all or most non-White youth.

Our results can quickly be summarized in the statement that differential treatment is the cause of DMC and that researchers and policy makers (purposely) confound two issues, (a) DMC and (b) racial/ethnic gang violence, which is statistically rare in scope and limited to a very few individuals, yet all Black, Latinx and Native American youth (and most or all adults) are treated as if they may be part of that very small group. The same cannot be said for White youth.

We would like to take a moment to address some of the terms used in this book and explain the reasons for our choices. We use the term "non-White" to describe the treatment of racial/ethnic minorities. This term can be problematic as it suggests a generalized other, those who are simply not White, ignoring racial, cultural and social differences between racial/ethnic groups. We have chosen to use this term for that very reason, not in support of the generalized "othering" on racial/ethnic minorities, but because the juvenile justice system treats racial/ethnic minorities as a monolithic "other." We use this term because it better explains the *intent* of the treatment of racial/ethnic minorities, to treat them as less than White. Minority youth are not treated based on what they have done or not done, but based on who they are not. Blacks, Latinx and Native Americans, in the juvenile justice system and elsewhere in society, are treated differently simply because they are not White, and we do not want to minimize the intent behind the treatment of minority juveniles.

We also use the phrase "differential treatment" rather than the more common "differential selection" used in most writings on DMC as it has a legal meaning, consistent with how DMC operates. If an employer were to make it difficult for disabled workers to complete their job duties, that would be a potentially illegal form of differential treatment. Differential selection, however, has primarily biological or genetic connotations, which makes the authors uncomfortable given that race is socially constructed, despite many efforts over the centuries to argue that race is biological or genetic. We are also concerned that "differential selection" sounds too compartmentalized, whereas "differential treatment" better reflects process, and DMC is very much a multi-point process. This book was written to disseminate conclusions from a study of DMC, but it is also a narrative of both how we came to do this research and how we drew our conclusions.

This book is a story of our intellectual journey to our conclusions. One of the authors (Ketchum) grew up in Southern California in the very White Orange County, adjacent to Los Angeles. After completing a BA and an MA in political science as well as a years' worth of graduate school in education, he found himself looking for a career change, for a year or two, before continuing to a PhD. An application to substitute teach for Los Angeles Unified School District (LAUSD) led, instead, to a full-time position as a biology teacher in the South-Central Los Angeles community of Watts. Ending up as a biology teacher without having a degree (or even a minor) in biology is really where the first roots of awareness of systemic racism took hold. Unlike his own high school experience where his physics teacher was a retired aerospace engineer with a PhD in engineering, his biology teacher had an MSc in biology and returned to complete his PhD in biology at one of the University of California schools, and his chemistry teacher had a master's degree, suddenly being one of the more qualified teachers in an urban high school science department was a bit of a shock.

Forgive me dropping into first person, but in a world of racial equality, I should never have been a biology teacher at any high school. Social science? Absolutely! Biology? I simply don't know the subject well enough to do much good in teaching it. A teacher needs to have a solid understanding of the area they are teaching. Being a chapter ahead, having a slightly better understanding of the details than the students, is not conducive to quality education. I walked into a second-floor classroom, about a month and a half into the fall semester. The room was a traditional high school science lab: long black countertops with wooden, locking drawers and cabinets below; tall metal stools for the students to sit on; and sinks, air and gas outlets (all turned off at a point outside the classroom). The long-term substitute was sitting at his desk, reading a newspaper. Students were mostly talking among themselves, with a few sitting on the windowsill, dropping textbooks out the window. The destruction of textbooks really bothered me, until I realized that the biology textbooks were almost 20 years old and predated the inclusion of DNA. The knowledge in these books stopped at Mendelian genetics.

The high school's principal was motivated, creative and dealing with ridiculous limitations. She would hire any new faculty with potential, knowing that most would develop their teaching skills and move on to a suburban high school or middle school. There were actually a number of us with non-education master's degrees, none of whom were in their actual field. This was not because the principal was inattentive, but because she had to plug teaching area holes with what she could find. She also had to deal with her school being one of two unofficial "must place" high schools, where teachers who had severe issues or limitations, but were not problematic enough to have their employment terminated, were sent. This was, apparently, also a reason for hiring anyone with potential as quickly as possible, so that there were fewer open positions for "must places." The result was an odd mix of a very few experienced and remarkably talented teachers doing their best to make a difference (many with real, measurable success), as well as a fairly large group of experienced but ineffective teachers who showed films every day or resorted to a stack of mimeographed worksheets. The senior science teacher who taught honors biology, physics and chemistry showed PBS science shows in each and every class. He did not even try to make them course specific. He would show the same film to every class on a given day. We had a state-of-the-art, commercial photocopier and unlimited copies, which I used to copy an entire biology textbook for each student, yet we still had an old mimeograph machine, the kind that used a template to make copies, in purple ink, of old worksheets, unchanged over the decades. The final group was also large, made up of teachers with less than three years' experience, frequently recent college graduates and mostly without teaching credentials, who struggled to become good teachers. The principal did dedicate a lot of resources to helping students who were motivated to seek help. The school had many students passing advanced placement exams in a few areas and a very talented counselor dedicated to college placement, who was great at her job.

Anyone who has read Kozol's "Savage Inequality" (1991) or one of the many other works describing the state of urban, Title I schools (where students are eligible for the federal government's subsidized meal program) would recognize many aspects of this school. I was like many other well-meaning teachers, seeing myself and my experiences as superior and assuming I could change students' lives by exposing them to my life, experience and knowledge. I was fortunate to be called out on this by a very bright young student, who simply asked why I acted like I was doing them a favor by being there. The realization that she was correct did not immediately alter my actions and motivations, but it started me on a path toward recognizing the extent of structural racism. As I look at the transcribed interviews in this study, I empathize a bit with the misunderstandings and stereotypes expressed, as I recognize that I, too, would have once said many of the very same things expressed by the police, judges, lawyers and juvenile specialists who were gracious enough to participate in our interviews.

Non-White kids are typically presumed to be "broken." They are presumed to be more criminalistic, less interested in education and less deserving of the same treatment and opportunities we offer to most White kids. Black, Native American and Latinx children are expected to fail, with the burden of proof being on the child to somehow show they are an exception and will not fail. White kids, on the other hand, are treated as if they are successful, and they will be treated as such until they give evidence to the contrary. This very different starting point is key to understanding DMC. This differential starting point between White and non-White kids first became clear to me while teaching for the LAUSD. Despite a very well educated and progressive principal's best efforts to minimize the effects of systemic racism, that racism is so deeply rooted, and tacitly supported by society, that efforts at progressive change are limited to individuals or small groups. Students found themselves, time and again, in a position where they had to prove themselves to be worthy of a better education.

While teaching for the LAUSD, it became clear to me that education was not the only area of systemic racism that impacted my students. The neighborhood they lived in was a high crime area. Kids would be robbed of jewelry while playing sports on the athletic field, as our school had an adjoining wall with a large housing project. Kids would frequently be "jumped" (robbed) on their way to school. The crime was real and all too common. However, those committing the violent crimes were few in number compared with the rest of the community of juveniles. We would have police searches of students every few months. Faculty were not involved in the searches and were excused from the room while they were conducted. Searches were only announced to faculty in the morning on the day they were to occur. I did not know the students well before the first search, but we discussed it a bit afterward. I was surprised to learn that students often carried weapons to stave off being "jumped" on the way to or from school. The defensive weapon of choice was almost always a screwdriver, as my students explained that carrying a knife would typically lead to an arrest, but it could be argued that a screwdriver was necessary for a school project or that it had been accidentally carried to school after working on a project at home that morning. There were many surprising parts of this story for me, but the oddest, based on my White experiences, was that these very normal and good kids, no different than myself and my friends at their age in most ways, were stopped on a regular basis by police to be searched. They always agreed to be searched because not doing so was seen as leading to further problems. I had been pulled over and given well-deserved speeding tickets in my youth, but I had never been stopped by the police for no reason. This was simply part of their experience. On one occasion I was driving an academic decathlon student, a high school senior, home after practice. As I approached a four-way stop, a Los Angeles Police Department (LAPD) car pulled up to the intersection from my right. I arrived at the stop first and proceeded through the intersection after a complete stop. I was pulled over immediately. An officer got out and came to the driver's side of my car with his hand on his holster. His partner took the male student out of the car from the other side and moved him away from the car. The officer speaking to me asked if I was okay, or if I was under any duress. I explained the situation and, after searching my student, but not me, I was wished a good day and left to continue on my travels. I had not committed any traffic violation. My student was unhappy but largely unfazed. He even expressed a bit of sympathy for the officers as he was a large, Latinx young man and he could see why they might have suspected a kidnapping. In fact, the last I heard from this student, he was just completing his bachelor's degree and was applying to the LAPD. To this day, I still think about this experience and how all hell would have broken loose if the same had happened to me or one of my affluent White high school friends.

After almost a decade teaching in the LAUSD, a job I thoroughly enjoyed, I moved, with my now wife, to Texas, where she started work on her PhD. During my first year in Texas, I ran a program at a residential treatment program and taught college classes inside juvenile detention facilities and state prisons. Again, a pattern of overrepresentation was clear. Few older White boys (it was a boys-only facility) were at the residential treatment facility. Despite Blacks making up less than 14 percent of the state population, Black boys made up over 80 percent of the 14–18-year-old residents, with Latinx and White making up the remainder. White kids were a bit more prevalent in the younger kids' housing. The same was true of the juvenile detention facility. Non-Whites were significantly overrepresented, except in my college classes. In the college classes, Whites made up the majority of my students.

These experiences led me to purse a PhD; my dissertation focused on DMC in juvenile courts in Harris County, Texas. One observation/experience from my dissertation research is worth noting here. Harris County has a larger Black population by percentage than the state does, about 20 percent according to court records at the time. Non-Latinx Whites make up just under 30 percent of the county population, and the largest single group is Latinx, at almost 50 percent. I was able to observe hundreds of cases over a summer. There are multiple courts running at the same time, with a large number of folks milling about in the area outside the courtrooms. I was surprised to observe no more than a dozen juveniles I would identify as "White." We would expect in a county with about a 70 percent non-White population for most kids in juvenile court to be non-White. However, I observed more than 500 cases in the courtrooms, and there were even more folks waiting in the hallways going in and out of the other juvenile courtroom, so I would estimate that I observed more than 1,000 kids. My notes indicate that I was only able to identify 12 juveniles as phenotypically, to my view, White. We will address colorism and skin tone later in this book, but it is significant that all but a handful of the kids in the juvenile courthouse were phenotypically non-White.

This research and the resulting book are an outgrowth of my observations of differential racial treatment in the juvenile justice system as well as my frustration with most major criminological theories as a basis for understanding DMC. There are simply no valid arguments for the current nonexistence of a truly color-blind juvenile justice system. This research is simply our attempt to explain why a racialized juvenile justice system is still in existence. My friend and co-author, B. Mitchell Peck, became equally interested in DMC over the last decade, though his interest came about differently. I am a qualitative researcher while Peck is a quantitative researcher. Over the years, I would ask for his input or further explanation on quantitative data, which quickly piqued his interest, which then turned into a simmering anger at the obvious inequality. More than once, we have discussed the idea that this book should not be necessary. Even without our data and analysis, the assumptions necessary to ignore the differential treatment of juveniles, by race, are astounding.

This first chapter will offer a short historical overview of DMC, including a brief summary of our findings, an overview of our methodology and an introduction to the following chapters. We propose that DMC can be attributed to systemic racism. The overrepresentation of minorities in the juvenile justice system is part of an informally choreographed social drama highlighting a perception of minority failure. Differential treatment is masked as differential involvement, creating a false image of the justice system being used by Whites to fix all that is wrong with non-White America. Within this social drama, overt racism is (mostly) publicly unacceptable, yet little more than lip service is paid to equality of opportunity or treatment. Within the framework of color-blind racism, one can see a system designed to induce, if not assure, failure for minority youth while maintaining a smooth veneer of denial of involvement. To top it off, the actual victims are accused of being more criminalistic, which allows the use of the very system that limits opportunity, the justice system, to be portrayed as the morally necessary means of stopping the imagined criminalism of non-Whites. The juvenile justice system can then confirm this failure while establishing its own importance. All the while, the larger (White, middle-class) community can pat itself on the back for trying to help out the incorrigible Black and Brown children. We conclude that DMC *is not* (a) reducible to higher crime rates committed by minority youth, (b) limited to racial bias on the part of overzealous police officers and/or racist juvenile justice personnel, (c) merely a reflection of class-based discrimination, (d) the result of differing cultural values (e.g., culture of violence or culture of poverty) or even (e) attributable to lower levels of intelligence among minorities, as some have suggested (Herrnstein and Murray, 1994). DMC *is* the differential treatment of non-White youth, utilizing circular logic, in which non-White youth are policed much more harshly, resulting in non-White youth having significantly higher rates of arrest and conviction, which in turn is used as a reason to police non-White youth even more.

One final point we would like to make is that the "old-fashioned" racism of the slavery and Jim Crow eras was based upon the presumed biological inferiority of Blacks, Native Americans, Latinx and other groups. Few scholars openly admit to a belief in biological inferiority these days; this perspective, however, seems alive and well among the public (Villarosa, 2019). All too often, interview data have included suggestions or even overt statements about biological differences. While mainstream criminological theories have moved away from explaining racial/ethnic differences in crime in terms of biology, the ghost of Cesare Lombroso is alive and well among the field practitioners of juvenile justice.

A brief history of the juvenile justice system

Prior to the 1820s, US criminal law clearly differentiated only between infants and adults. Those who were six years of age or younger were considered "infants" and legally incapable of committing crime with "vicious will" (Bernard, 1992). Industrialization and urbanization created the first identifiable population of "at risk" juveniles, those youth who were seen as potentially at risk of not becoming contributing members of society. Up to that point, children over the age of seven who committed crimes were seen as choosing their actions based on "free will." As with the adult poor, pauper children were considered inherently evil, their poverty caused by their own wickedness, corruption and unacceptable behavior. According to Bernard (1992), "juvenile delinquent" was originally a term meaning "potential pauper." These delinquents were believed to be the cause of many of the problems in large cities.

Eventually the perception of free will began to change. Those who were 14 years of age or older were still considered adults, capable of understanding their own actions. These individuals were eligible for all potential punishments applied to adults. This created a third group, children between the ages of six and 14. For these children, before being charged with a crime, it first had to be determined if the child understood the difference between right and wrong. If the individual did, then he or she was tried and punished as an adult and was even eligible for the death sentence for a capital offense. Records show this to have been carried out on children at least as young as 12 (Feld, 1999b).

With time it became impossible to ignore the social forces that resulted in many children begging or stealing simply to survive. Two changes in public perception occurred around 1820. First, children were now seen as malleable, unlike adults who were still seen as set in their ways. This concept suggested the possibility to intervene in the lives of children with the intent to change their ways. The second was the rise of the positivist school of criminology, which contended that delinquent behavior was caused by forces outside the control of the juvenile, as opposed to individual choice. In this climate, Progressive groups, typically consisting of conservative upper- and middle-class White women, began to demand change in how the state treated juvenile delinquents (McShane and Williams, 2003).

The Progressive movement was the second major reform movement in this country. The first occurred in the years preceding the Civil War and consisted of social activists working to reform issues such as workplace conditions and the treatment of the mentally ill and prisoners. The second reform era, the Progressive movement, which ran from the Reformation Era to World War I, was a loose-knit coalition of activist groups, largely held together by their rejection of Social Darwinism and their belief in the possibility of bettering the lives of all people (Feld, 1999a). Though Progressives never spoke with one voice, the values of the movement remained consistent. Women's rights and the temperance movement were among the first efforts of the Progressives, followed shortly by the populist movement, designed to take political control away from party bosses. Much of their success in challenging social conditions resulted from newspaper accounts of poverty, factory conditions, child labor, urban slums and other social ills. The newspaper stories led to popular outrage, creating an opportunity for change.

Prior to the Progressive movement, juvenile justice did not really exist. In its place was an all-or-nothing system that based treatment on the ability of a child to determine right from wrong. For those deemed capable of discerning the difference, the result was often harsh punishment for a young child. For those not yet able to determine the difference, children were completely released from state control. Sentencing children to years in prison or even death was often seen as too extreme, yet preteens committing minor crimes frequently escaped formal sanctions altogether. To address this issue, in the early to mid-1800s, the houses of refuge, the first age-segregated institutions, began to appear. Legislation governing these houses of refuge created certain legal distinctions for youths. First, there was a clear age-based distinction between juvenile and adult offenders. Second, the use of indeterminate sentences, allowing for professional judgment as to what would work best for reforming a child, was introduced to allow for the necessary rehabilitation of minors. Finally, the concept of parens patriae began to be applied, which allowed the state to assume control of a juvenile in place of the parent in the case of young criminal offenders, neglected children or those deemed "incorrigible" by the state. By the middle of the century, the country was dotted with reformatories and youth institutions serving most cities.

Cook County, Illinois, created the first juvenile court in 1899, and others followed in a relatively short time. Early juvenile courts embraced the legal distinctions first given to houses of refuge. These courts were informal civil hearings that were closed to the public to protect the reputation of the youths. In these early courts, neither a prosecutor nor a defense attorney was present. Consistent with the Progressives' belief in the power of the state to regulate society, control of the life of the youth rested with the judge and his advisors, predecessors to the modern social worker (Humes, 1996). The original goal of the juvenile justice system, through the allowance for discretion at each level, was individualized justice, emphasizing prevention and rehabilitation of juvenile offenders (Hendricks and Byers, 2000). Juvenile courts were simply a specialized version of civil court, as opposed to a juvenile criminal court.

The Progressives envisioned a country where all Americans were to enter the ranks of the middle class. Everyone was to respect private property, send their children to school and give up whatever vices that they may have brought with them as they immigrated, so that they might become hard-working and law-abiding. The juvenile courts, along with schools and other governmental agencies, were used to Americanize, assimilate and acculturate immigrants (Feld, 1999b). Giving the state the right and responsibility to substitute its own control over children for that of the natural parents when the latter appeared unable or unwilling to meet their responsibilities, or when the child posed a problem for the community, proved a powerful tool for imposing assimilation. In essence, the legal concept of parens patriae provided the formal justification to intervene in the lives of immigrants and the poor. It was a tool to control "other people's children," a theme continued by the juvenile courts today.

In 1838, the Pennsylvania Supreme Court rejected legal challenges to the pre-emptory incarceration of "troublesome" youths in *Ex parte Crouse*, citing that the incarceration was in the best interest of the juvenile and merely an opportunity to rehabilitate an individual when the parents had proven unable to do so. "Troubled" children could be removed from their parents against the wishes of the parents or children and placed in a house of refuge for the good of both the children and the community. Because houses of refuge, and later juvenile courts, were charged with decriminalizing youths' behaviors, reformers were allowed great latitude in controlling children. Smoking, idleness, immorality and most significantly sexual activity could be regulated by the state. In fact, girls who were either sexually active or deemed "at risk" of becoming sexually active received the most severe treatment by juvenile courts, often much more severe than boys who had committed criminal acts. Judges and those in assorted social work positions had the power to decide what was in the "best interest" of the child.

Probation became the favored first choice of treatment for a juvenile in the Progressive Era. Juvenile probation officers took on the task of reporting a child's actions to the court as well as supervising the juvenile's return to the community. Unfortunately, the vast majority of juvenile courts of the time had little success in rehabilitating minors, due mostly to poor training and minimal funding of courts and probation departments (Feld, 1999b). The almost limitless discretion given to juvenile courts began to change in the 1960s with a number of cases that appeared before the US Supreme Court. The first of these, in 1966, was *Kent v. United States*. The 14-year-old male defendant, who had a fairly long criminal record, admitted to raping and robbing a woman when confronted with fingerprint evidence. His lawyer filed a motion to get the boy psychiatric evaluation and treatment, but the judge ignored the motion and waived the juvenile to be tried in adult criminal court without a hearing. The Supreme Court found that the juvenile court erred in not allowing a hearing on the matter and further chastised the court for leaving juveniles with the "worst of both worlds," no legal protection as afforded adults and no rehabilitative role as had been traditionally promised in the juvenile justice system.

A year after the Kent case, a 15-year-old boy from Arizona was convicted of making an obscene phone call to a neighbor. This boy, who was on probation at the time for stealing a wallet, was taken into custody by the police. The police neglected to even leave a note for his parents about the incident. The police simply took the boy into custody, leaving his parents to wonder, for hours, what had happened to him. Neither the boy nor his parents were ever notified of the specific charges against him. No record of the hearing was made. No witnesses were ever called. The boy was sentenced to a state institution until he turned 21. This meant a possible six-year term for a crime that, should he have been tried as an adult, would have carried a maximum sentence of up to two months in jail and a $50 fine. His parents contended that due process had been denied their son. The US Supreme Court agreed with the parents, handing down their decision that due process must be followed for juveniles, in the case that had the most significant impact upon juvenile courts, *In re Gault* (1967).

In re Winship (1970) chipped away further at both the discretion afforded juvenile courts and their non-criminal status. This time the US Supreme Court found that a "preponderance of evidence" was not a strict enough standard to convict a juvenile. Instead, the criminal court standard of "beyond a reasonable doubt" must be applied. This change was significant because it signaled an official shift from a juvenile civil court ("preponderance of evidence" is the typical standard in civil court) toward a juvenile criminal court.

This shift toward forming a juvenile criminal court was limited just a year later, however, when the court found, in *McKeiver v. Pennsylvania* (1971), that a juvenile was not entitled to a "trial by jury." This suggests that the US Supreme Court was reluctant to give up on the original concept of the juvenile court as a place of rehabilitation, while at the same time acknowledging the failure of the court to live up to its original goal.

In many ways we have come full circle. Prior to the changes made by early reformers, a 14-year-old would have been tried as an adult. In 1998, the US Congress passed the Violent Predator Act, which (a) allows the federal government to impose the death penalty on children as young as 16, (b) requires states to try juveniles as adults in certain circumstances and (c) in an interesting case of historical déjà vu, allows 14-year-olds to be tried as adults. Despite the ethnocentric beliefs of the Progressives, in many ways their rationalizations for controlling other peoples' children seem farsighted by today's more putative standards.

Recognition of DMC

In 1974, Congress passed the Juvenile Justice and Delinquency Prevention Act (JJDP Act), which had two key components. First, states and other organizations receiving federal funding were required to deinstitutionalize juveniles convicted of status offenses (behavior that is typically legal for adults but illegal for minors). Status offenders as well as deprived/neglected youth (juvenile victims of parental neglect) could no longer be held in training or reform schools. Second, juveniles could not be held in institutions where they had regular contact with adult offenders. This resulted in juveniles who were tried as adults serving time in juvenile facilities and then possibly being transferred to adult institutions, usually between the ages of 18 and 21.

In 1988, the Disproportionate Minority Contact mandate (originally known as Disproportionate Minority Confinement) was implemented as part of the reauthorization of the JJDP Act. In 1992, state-level studies of DMC became mandatory to receive federal funding through the Title II Formula Grants Program (Bishop, 2005; Leiber et al, 2011).

From Progressives to Black criminals

How did we, as a country, move from training other people's children to be assimilated members of society (perhaps not a pleasant starting point, but arguably the lesser of two evils) to characterizing crime as a Black phenomenon and young Black males as "super-predators?" The movement to try juveniles as adults in this country has been largely fueled by the explosion of juvenile gangs and the use of guns by juvenile offenders, although the historical roots of the movement run deep. A March 1965 *Newsweek* article entitled "Crime in the streets" pointed out that although Blacks made up only about 10 percent of the US population at the time, 53 percent of those arrested for violent crime were Black. Up to that point, most media attention regarding Blacks and violence focused on the civil rights movement. The *Newsweek* article began to transform the view of Blacks from victims to predators. *Newsweek* referred to the "high rate of Negro crime" and "the high rate of juvenile crime" as the harsh facts represented in crime reports (Barlow, 1998). This set the stage to transform the more sympathetic image of the young Black male from a group battered by difficult social conditions (or even biologically limited abilities in the eyes of those still tethered to the idea of biological differences) to an unsympathetic individual supremely capable of and willing to choose criminal behavior. As further testimony to the impact of this particular article, it also seems to be the source of the first mainstream media reference to the "war on crime," further describing crime as an epidemic (Barlow,

1998). The imagery of young Black males as the enemy and Black culture as a disease in need of a cure proved to be so compelling that it remains with us more than 50 years later.

At about the same time, the Moynihan Report (1965), titled "The Negro Family: The Case for National Action," argued that the Black family in America was facing a crisis. According to the report, this family breakdown was rooted in four issues: (a) the legacy of slavery, (b) rapidly growing urbanization, (c) a matriarchal family structure and (d) discrimination in education and employment. Moynihan painted a rather dejected picture of the future for Black youth: in a word, the report claimed that most Negro youth were in danger of being caught up in the tangle of pathology that affected their world, and probably a majority were so entrapped. Many of those who escaped did so for one generation only: as things stood, their children might have to run the gauntlet all over again.

Politicians at the time were attempting to generate public panic about crime. In 1964, Barry Goldwater tried to make fear of Black crime resonate with voters, only to have Lyndon Johnson mitigate that fear by suggesting his Great Society program would deal with the root causes of crime (Chambliss, 1995). Johnson appeared to have a better read on public opinion, as polls consistently showed that crime was not identified as a major social problem (Barlow, 1998). Conservative politicians continued to link crime with minority urban unrest in an attempt to roll back political and social reforms recently achieved by minorities (Omi and Winant, 1994). By the 1970s, Goldwater's warnings had found an audience. For the first time in two decades, 1968 public opinion polls identified fear of crime as a major social problem (Chamblis, 1995). In 1970, *Time* magazine ran an article entitled "Cops vs. crime." This article blamed the "universal fear" across the US of "violent crime and vicious strangers" on young Black males, who typically committed the most common form of interracial crime, armed robbery (Barlow, 1998). Militant Black organizations, such as the Black Panthers, were viewed by both law enforcement and the general public as a violent threat to the public (Barlow, 1998). These groups (incorrectly) gave White America a clear vision of the enemy, forever cementing the image of the angry young Black male as the potential source of harm.

The 1980s brought a whole new wrinkle to the concept of racialized criminal behavior. The Reagan and Bush years saw the launch of the "war on drugs." Based on data from the Reagan/Bush era, according to the US Dept. of Heath and Human Services, National Institute on Drug Abuse (1991), Blacks were no more likely than Whites ever to have used commonly abused drugs. In 1978, at a time when the Black population hovered at about 10 percent of the US population, 21 percent of those arrested for drug-related offenses were Black and 78 percent were White. By 1989, fully

42 percent of those arrested for drugs were Black and only 57 percent were White (US Department of Justice, 1993). Given that rates of drug use for both Blacks and Whites have consistently been equal, Blacks were being arrested at twice the rate of Whites for relatively equal levels of offending in the 1970s (Tonry, 1994).

Interestingly, by 1990 Blacks were being arrested at a rate of almost four times that of Whites. Of course, if the war on drugs was actually having the effect of minimizing illicit drug use, an argument, albeit a racially biased one, could be made for the greater good. However, there is no evidence that the almost three-decade-long war on drugs has had any discernable effect upon drug use (Tonry, 1994). The reason for this growing disparity in arrest rates appears to be one of convenience. According to Tonry (1994), drug dealers in poor Black communities have greater relative economic incentives to deal drugs to strangers, while White, middle-class drug dealers are better able to deal to people they know. Poor Black drug dealers are also forced to deal drugs in public settings, while Whites are more likely to sell drugs in private settings. Tonry (1994) and Chambliss (1995) argue that the "convenience" issue was actually premeditated and racially motivated, citing evidence such as Ronald Reagan's attack on gains made from the civil rights movement, first voiced nationally in his 1964 speech supporting Goldwater's presidential campaign, and George H. W. Bush's infamous "Willie Horton" campaign ads, which used the Black convict as a depiction of the consequences of being "soft on crime."

While the Republicans may have begun the war on minorities (arguably a more accurate title than war on crime or war on drugs) as an attempt to gain mainstream votes, the Democrats, rather than opposing Reagan and Bush, tried to outdo the Republican leaders. Democratic Speaker of the House from 1977 to 1987 and longtime liberal Tip O'Neill was an outspoken advocate for the war on drugs, especially after the death of college basketball phenomenon Len Bias from a drug overdose, who coincidentally had been drafted by the professional team in O'Neill's district (Barlow, 1998). Later, President Bill Clinton actually escalated the war on minorities by pushing for harsher sanctions for drug offenders (Tonry, 1994).

After looking at rising rates of violent juvenile crime, Princeton political scientist (and future director of the White House Office of Faith-Based and Community Initiatives for George W. Bush's administration) John Dilulio and his colleagues published a book in which they detected a new criminal concern for the American public. Throughout the book, it is made clear that the young men Dilulio is concerned with are young men of color. "Based on all we have witnessed, researched and heard from people who are close to the action ... here is what we believe: America is now the home to thickening ranks of juvenile 'super-predators'—radically impulsive, brutally remorseless youngsters, including ever more pre-teenage boys, who murder, rape, assault, burglarize, deal deadly drugs, join gun-toting gangs and create serious communal disorders" (Bennett et al, 1996, p. 27).

According to the Office of Juvenile Justice and Delinquency Prevention's February 2000 report entitled "Challenging the myths," the serious violent crime rate among juveniles (all sexual assaults, robbery and aggravated assault) remained relatively consistent from 1973 until 1989, ranging from 25 to 32 victimizations by juveniles per 100 persons aged 10–17. This number spiked to 43 in 1993 but declined again to pre-1990 levels by 1995. This spike was enough to convince Dilulio that some type of evolutionary change had occurred in US ghettos, transforming resource-poor, disenfranchised young Black men into amoral monsters. The Brothers Grimm would, no doubt, approve of his tale of Black terror, but in a largely unnoticed interview (with his co-author William Bennett) he apologized for his mistake. However, the damage was done, and his apology received little press compared with his initial, incorrect claim (Pizarro et al, 2007), leaving a lingering legacy of an idea that, just maybe, super-predators really do exist. It is an image that has been difficult for the Black community to live down precisely because it feeds on those fears stoked by politicians and the media for so long. This is evidenced by the post-1995 juvenile arrest rates for violent crime. In 1997, the arrest rate for juvenile violent crime was still almost one third higher than the rate in the 1980s, despite similar crime rates (Snyder and Sickmund, 2006). By 1997, the frightening image of the Black (or Hispanic) super-predator was sufficient to override the statistical evidence and cause the public to demand ever-harsher penalties for these monsters. Yet again, society wants to treat them not as children but as fully formed sociopathic criminals.

The current image of the Black male super-predator is not that different than the slavery and Jim Crow eras' image of the angry "young buck" out to rape White women (an irony, given the reality of slave owners routinely raping slaves). The juvenile court has mimicked popular opinion through the years, alternating between treating and controlling other peoples' children. All our talk about how to deal with these problem children has really been a discussion about how to deal with these young men of color. Until the recent Black Lives Matter movement, little had changed in how we see non-White youth in the last two decades.

Summary of findings

DMC is not about Black, Latinx or Native American kids' behavior. DMC is about a racialized social system treating non-White kids as if they are broken and a problem to be solved unless they, individually, prove themselves to be an exception to that rule. DMC is best described as collapsing two very different variables into a single category: (a) high crime individuals, who are few in number but active in crime; and (b) juveniles participating in criminal or deviant activity at a very normal rate, but who happen to be Black, Native American or Latinx. Despite overwhelming evidence of racism in American society, the starting point for differential involvement as the primary cause of DMC begins with the assumption that non-White kids are somehow different, ignoring the fact that they have always been treated differently. Worse, sometimes we acknowledge that they have been treated differently but claim that this is now the cause of differential involvement, such as the strain theory perspective. Most of the major criminological theories, including choice/rational choice/classical, social control, social learning, strain, positivists and, perhaps to a lesser extent, life course, rest upon arrest and conviction rates being an accurate reflection of criminality, while critical and conflict theories challenge those assumptions. We find that police arrests are an accurate reflection of arrests but an extremely inaccurate reflection of criminality.

DMC negatively impacts all youth of color, as they are presumed to be super-offenders despite that fact that almost all non-White youth are criminally indistinguishable from their White counterparts. A study in Orange County found that 8 percent of juveniles committed most of the severe crimes (Shumacher and Kurz, 2001). As a nation, we are reacting to the actions of 8 percent and applying that to about 40 percent of the nation's kids. It is the equivalent of requiring all male drivers to have an ignition interlock breathalyzer device (IID) installed on any vehicle they drive. According to the National Highway Traffic Safety Administration (NHTSA), male drivers are responsible for 80 percent of drunk driving accidents ("Drunk driving," 2018. Similarly interpreting the data and assuming all male drivers are likely drunk and forcing them to prove that they are not through the use of an IID is no more absurd than treating all Black children as criminals and expecting them to prove otherwise.

To test our hypothesis of the criminal actions of a few non-White youth being generalized to all non-White youth, we utilized multiple sources and types of data to triangulate the causes of DMC. The data sources and approach we used are presented in Figure 1.1. We did this with an eye toward teasing out what Wilbanks frames as the following: "the question of whether the criminal justice system is racist must not be confused with that of whether Blacks commit crimes at a higher rate than Whites because of discrimination in employment, housing, education, and so forth" (1987, p. 7).

All understanding of DMC revolves around how much of it is attributable to differential involvement and how much is attributable to differential treatment. Differential involvement presumes that DMC is an accurate reflection of criminality by race and ethnicity and assumes police and court

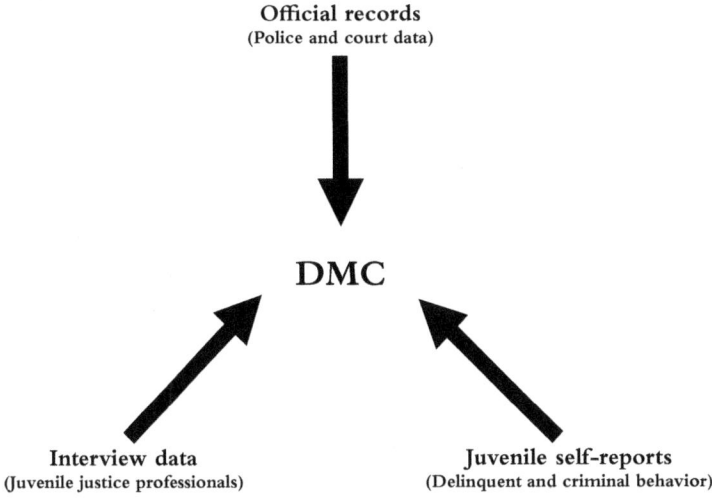

Figure 1.1: Data triangulation to examine DMC

data are correct in asserting that non-Whites commit crimes at a higher rate than do Whites. Differential treatment, on the other hand, presumes that non-White youth are treated differently by race and ethnicity throughout the justice system. To examine both differential involvement and differential treatment, we broke the issue apart, first looking at the official police and court data, which gave us the extent of DMC. To determine the cause(s) of DMC, we then conducted anonymous self-report surveys of criminal activity and police interactions among juveniles from one metropolitan area to determine any differences in criminality (we are defining "criminality" as the propensity to engage in criminal activity) by race and ethnicity. We used anonymous self-report surveys from juveniles. Methodologically, this is stronger than most research on DMC as police data are also self-report but are not anonymous, resulting in possible motivations to manipulate the data when reporting them. The surveys of juvenile criminal activity and police interaction had no identifiers, and students placed their survey responses through a slot into a locked container, assuring anonymity. While this is an imperfect guarantee of participant accuracy, there is little motivation to lie as there can be no real credit claiming or other benefit of dishonesty. Police, however, are subject to a number of social, career and political forces that could influence their self-report police reports.

Unless otherwise noted, all data used in this study originate from a single county. Because of the rural nature of much of the state, we were able to include urban, suburban and rural students in the self-report data. Our participants were 77 percent White and 23 percent non-White, which is a slight oversampling of non-Whites as the state's population is 74 percent

White. Whites were, as expected, significantly underrepresented in the urban settings and were overrepresented in the suburban and rural settings. Essentially, in the self-report data, we are comparing the criminality of largely non-White urban juveniles to largely White suburban and rural juveniles. We used anonymous self-report surveys specifically to (a) determine the extent and type of criminal activity, (b) determine the extent and type of police and further juvenile justice decision points by race and ethnicity, and (c) compare those two areas to determine if there is a discrepancy by race and ethnicity. We found that White and non-White juveniles self-report similar levels of deviant and criminal behaviors. Where there were significant differences in criminal behavior, the differences were mostly in the direction of White juveniles offending more.

After determining (a) the extent of overrepresentation through official data and (b) the cause of overrepresentation as differential treatment rather than differential involvement through self-report data, we (c) interviewed 83 juvenile justice professionals working in one county, including police officers, juvenile court judges, and lawyers and juvenile probation professionals. We chose this methodology for a few reasons. A longitudinal study was simply not possible given our budget and time frame, though this would be our chosen methodology given adequate time and resources. An analysis of police and court data is the accepted means to determine the extent of DMC. We used police and court data only to determine the extent of DMC, rather than the cause, because police and court data are not well suited to the task of determining the cause. Police data, the entry point for DMC, provide an excellent report on the numbers of arrests and so forth, but they are not an accurate measure of crime or who commits crime. They report who has been arrested for crime. Police data are self-report data. We often pretend they are not, but they are simply self-report data that not only are not anonymous, but where those reporting the data are often called upon to answer for what they have recorded. For that reason, we utilized anonymous self-report data from juveniles from area high schools. It is an imperfect sample, but it is anonymous, and it does show that White and non-White kids commit crimes at pretty much the same rate, and that they commit similar types of crimes. It also shows that within this sample, non-White kids were treated differentially in the juvenile justice system. Finally, we interviewed juvenile justice professionals to determine their views, beliefs and ideas on DMC to get an idea of the reason for differential treatment of non-White youth. Taken together, we know the extent of DMC, we know that most or all of DMC is due to differential treatment rather than differential involvement, and we know how juvenile justice professionals explain the differential treatment of non-White youth.

We conclude that (a) differential treatment is the cause of DMC and (b) race and ethnicity are of no use in predicting the criminality of juveniles. White and non-White youth commit crimes at essentially the same rate (we will circle back to this when addressing the limitations of our study). Finally, (c) stereotyping is used to both create and explain overrepresentation in the juvenile justice system. As a result of our analysis, we hypothesize that these findings are not unique to the area studied or the years the study was conducted and we look forward to others critiquing, replicating, building upon and utilizing this study.

Review of literature

There has long been a divide among those who research DMC. One camp argues that most or all of DMC is attributable to differential involvement. Proponents of this perspective argue that differential involvement in crime is a result of individual traits or choices either (a) independent of social problems or (b) attributable as a result of social problems. This split in the differential involvement camp is significant, as those seeing differential involvement as independent of social problems see criminality as an individual choice, suggesting intervention that is designed to "fix" the individual.

D'Sousa (1995) aligned himself with the first possibility when he stated that those who are especially cautious of young Black men are simply employing rational discrimination based on prudent statistics that use racial or ethnic identity combined with gender, demeanor and other factors to avoid interaction with young Black men when possible because we know that these individuals commit more crimes, especially violent and drug-related crimes. A number of scholars have suggested that young, angry men of color actually commit more crimes than do other individuals (Wilson and Herrnstein, 1985; Wilbanks, 1986; Herrnstein and Murray, 1994; D'Sousa, 1995). Overrepresentation in the justice system is perceived as a fallacy from this point of view, as observed inequities in the justice system reflect the realities of which individuals commit crimes rather than focusing on social problems that lead certain groups to be more or less likely to commit a crime. This concept assumes (a) that each individual has the ability to choose whether or not to commit a crime, (b) that social forces take a back seat to individual choice and (c) that measurement of crime/criminality is accurate. One would be hard pressed to find research that is relatively current that is rooted in old-fashioned racism, yet we still find many individuals who have these beliefs.

A few years back, one of the authors was teaching large (100-plus) classes on Introduction to Sociology and Social Problems. As an icebreaker for discussion of the social construction of race, the professor asked for anonymous responses, on a sheet of paper, asking if any racial or ethnic group was overrepresented in high-salaried professional athletics and why or why not. The expectation was that a few students would argue that selective breeding during slavery resulted in an overrepresentation of Blacks in football, basketball and baseball. Unexpectedly, in class after class for three years, a small group of students, just less than 7 percent, explained that Black people have an extra muscle in their legs. This was not a study, so we have no idea if the students who gave this answer were from different parts of the country or if this idea was unique to a region, or perhaps it was a rumor started by a single student at a single high school. What is clear is that there are people who still believe there are biological differences between the races. Even if a new version of *The Bell Curve* is never written, the belief in biological differences is alive and well.

Much of our theoretical understanding of juvenile justice is rooted in an understanding of non-White youth as being more criminalistic than White youth, based upon arrest and conviction rates. Control theories assume that crime will occur unless prevented by strong social and personal controls. Proponents of control theories argue that only personal controls (guilt, religion, etc.) and social controls (punishment, public ridicule, etc.) stop most of us from committing crimes (Agnew, 2002). In this view, stronger controls lead directly to a lower crime rate. Hirschi's (1969) social bonding theory is the most developed of the control theories. By incorporating four values (attachment to others, commitment, involvement and belief), Hirschi proposed that the more an individual was invested in (a) attachment (to parents, school and peers), (b) commitment (investing time, energy and effort in conventional values), (c) involvement (of time and effort in conventional activities, which minimizes idle time) and (d) belief (in society's laws, institutions and customs), the less likely that individual was to commit a deviant act. As we will see in the interviews in Chapter 7, a belief in greater social control over non-White kids is seen as necessary, as their parents are seen as unable or unwilling to exert control over their children. Given the extent of DMC, we have two possible explanations utilizing control theories. A) that lower levels of control are a feature of Black, Latinx and Native American culture. This is explained by describing racial/ethnic inequality as loosening these values related to social control. Using Hirschi's social bonding as an example, non-Whites would be expected to have lower levels of attachment to parents, school and peers. As we will detail in Chapter 7, most of the juvenile justice professionals interviewed for this study firmly believe that Latinx, Black and Native American families are characterized by weaker connections between parents and children, lower value given to education and attachment to deviant rather than mainstream peers. One would also have to assume, as do a majority of our interview participants, that race/ethnicity is tied to commitment to conventional values and that minorities have too much idle time. Finally, one would have to assume that there is a lower valuation, among minorities, of society's norms and institutions and that they are therefore more likely to commit deviant or criminal acts. Or B) that Control Theory has no application in understanding the cause of DMC.

For decades, residents of non-White neighborhoods have claimed that they are treated much more harshly than their White neighbors (Hinton, 2017). Much of the literature has suggested that over-policing is the result of more crime being committed by persons of color and that over-policing is due to differential involvement based upon stereotyped images on the part of non-Whites (Gottfredson and Hirschi, 1990; Martinez, 2002). A number of mainstream criminological theories have been used to frame DMC from a differential involvement perspective. A common and problematic theme is the reliance upon the assumption that official crime rates are an accurate measurement of crime by race/ethnicity. Rooted in Merton's strain theory, Agnew's general strain theory has been used to explain crime as a product of race/ethnicity, class and community differences (Agnew, 2002; Eitle and Turner, 2003). If it were not for the overwhelming evidence of the inaccuracy in using arrest rates as a measurement of crime, general strain theory might be useful in understanding DMC. However, contrary to self-report crime data, general strain theory is only helpful in understanding DMC if non-White kids actually commit crimes at a higher rate than do White juveniles.

There is clearly empirical support for the contention that strain has a measurable impact upon crime rates, yet not only is crime not class based (Reinarman et al., 2000), but "class" and "community" are often used as code for "race" (Bonilla-Silva, 2003. Strain/anomic theory appears to better explain a rather narrow group of offenders, without being effective for explaining the much more common over-policing of non-White youth.

Gottfriedson and Hirschi (1990) developed their self-control theory, which claims that individual self-control is at the heart of all actions. High levels of self-control will likely lead to socially acceptable behavior. Low levels of self-control are much more likely to lead to deviant or criminal behavior. Gottfriedson and Hirschi found that the congruence between victim data and arrest rates for all racial and ethnic groups was so strong, it suggests that DMC is a result of disproportionate involvement rather than a system biased against minority youths. For those who subscribe to the differential involvement perspective, criminal activity is often a result of what Gottfredson and Hirschi (1990) refer to as the personality trait of "low self-control," in which family childrearing practices and the attractiveness of criminal events coalesce somewhere along the negative end of a continuum from a law-abiding child of high self-control to a likely criminal with low self-control. This suggests that a large part of criminality lies at the feet of inadequate parenting (resulting from teaching poor standards of individual choice). Taken a step further, minority overrepresentation in the criminal justice system may be argued as largely attributable to poor parenting by Black and Hispanic parents, as these groups are most overrepresented in both the criminal and juvenile justice systems. This echoes Daniel Patrick Moynihan's (1965) work *The Negro Family: The Case for National Action*. Interestingly, this is a reoccurring theme among the juvenile justice professionals we interviewed for this study.

The obvious problem with self-control theory, as with other theoretical perspectives, is its assumption that arrest rates are an accurate reflection of crime by race/ethnicity. As noted in the previous paragraph, Gottfriedson and Hirschi found that the congruence between victim data and arrest rates for all racial and ethnic groups was so strong … which implies that victim and arrest data support each other and are, therefore, both accurate. However, the fact that police data are self-report data, which are not anonymous, and that officers must answer for their self-report data implies that police data may not be accurate. As we will address in the next chapter, there exists ample research data and video evidence to support the contention that police data are biased.

The suggestion that non-White families are somehow more broken and have different values is a theme that appeared often in the interviews of juvenile justice professionals conducted for this study. There simply is not much to support this, however. We suspect that the work of Elijah Anderson (1999), Ramiro Martinez Jr. (2002) and others is being misinterpreted. Anderson's and Martinez's relevant work (for DMC) deals with racial/ethnic minority neighborhoods that are among the poorest. Neither author attempts to generalize their findings to all members of a racial/ethnic minority community. The kids from the neighborhoods studied by Martinez and Anderson make up a very small part of the minority youth impacted by DMC. In fact, Black fathers tend to be more involved in their children's lives, compared to all other racial/ethnic groups, whether they live with them or not. This remains true for both younger and older children (Jones and Mosher, 2013).

All in all, this information suggests that Black and other non-White families are not very different from White families, except when racialized institutions, such as mass incarceration of non-Whites, force structural differences. The claim that non-White families cause DMC and other criminality becomes a feedback loop where family structure is claimed to be the cause of crime, which results in children from those families being brought into the justice system, which in turn shows that there is a problem with these non-White children who are overrepresented in the system, which suggests the family is somehow the problem … and on, and on, and on the self-replication goes, despite it being based on false assumptions from the beginning.

There is support for differential involvement that focuses on a specific subgroup of DMC, that is, criminal behavior by the young living in poor, minority neighborhoods, where DMC may be rooted environmental factors

(Anderson, 1999; Martinez, 2002). This perspective suggests that issues such as poverty, disrupted home life, relative disadvantage, limited economic and educational opportunities, disenfranchisement and limited community policing are among those factors that influence both the prevalent types of crime as well as the crime rate. From this point of view, minorities' differential involvement in crime is due to environmental factors encouraging or otherwise rewarding criminal behavior. However, this cannot be generalized to all minority youth, and it appears to often be incorrectly attributed to all minority youth. Both Anderson and Martinez drive home that higher rates of crime in poor non-White areas are not universal but are the result of systemic racism. To summarize, racism is the cause of differential treatment, which results in DMC, with the exception of a small subset of DMC, revolving around a small number of minority juveniles who live in the harshest conditions in the US, and this small subset are more criminalistic due to the social forces resulting from systemic racism. To further illustrate this point, the Oklahoma Office of Juvenile Affairs (Charish et al, 2004) found that Black and Hispanic youths committed more crime than did White youth, however once environmental condition were controlled for, that difference disappeared.

Juvenile arrest records from Office of Juvenile Justice and Delinquency Prevention (OJJDP) clearly and consistently show significant overrepresentation of Black male youths in almost every category of juvenile court records, including arrests. However, the discrepancy in arrest and conviction rates for Black and White youth cannot be easily explained as different rates of offending between White and Black juveniles (Snyder and Sickmund, 1999). For example, Wordes and Bynum (1995), in their study of the juvenile justice system in Michigan, based on official police records and interviews with officers, found that race or race-related factors, such as being in the wrong neighborhood or hanging out on the street, heavily contributed to a decision by officers to initiate contact. Many of the officers interviewed also noted that boys need a father figure in their lives and that single mothers cannot adequately control delinquent behavior. Similarly, in Pennsylvania, Kempf-Leonard et al (1995) discovered that "offense-related, system-related, and social history factors are accorded different weight depending on race" (p. 120).

Differential involvement is ideologically grounded in blame for DMC assigned either fully (individual choice) or partially (rooted in social problems) based on arrest and conviction rates. It further assumes that arrest and conviction rates of minorities compared with Whites are reflective of actual rates of commission of delinquent and criminal acts. From the perspective of differential involvement, if minorities actually commit delinquent and criminal acts at rates well above those of Whites, the only rational course is to address how to limit minorities' involvement in delinquent and criminal acts.

Differential involvement, be it dependent on or independent of social problems, is not the only potential explanation for DMC. The other major option is differential treatment, which suggests that minorities receive disproportionate punishment for crime. Potential causes of differential treatment-induced DMC range from indirect racial effect to overt racism. Indirect racial effect could be caused by juvenile justice officials focusing on factors that are strongly correlated to race, such as socioeconomic status (SES), demeanor, family structure and school status, resulting in racialized outcomes (Pope and Feyerhern, 1990a; Pope and Snyder, 2003).

Along these lines, Wordes and Bynum (1995) found that police officers sometimes formed decisions based on expectations tinged with racial and ethnic stereotypes. Bridges and Steen (1998) found the same of court officials. In fact, a number of studies have found that while the type of current offense and prior record explain much of the observed minority overrepresentation in the juvenile justice system, these do not explain all the racial differences (McCarthy and Smith, 1986; Fagan et al, 1987; Krisberg et al, 1987; Austin, 1995). Feld (1999b) argues that "a system of justice in which the most powerful explanatory legal variables—present offense and prior record—account for only about 25 percent of the variance in sentencing remains a highly discretionary and perhaps discriminatory one" (p. 94).

Differing rates of official placement of juvenile offenders itself creates de facto segregation as (a) Latinos are more likely to be placed in public facilities, (b) Blacks and Latinx are more often placed in private residential care and (c) White offenders are most likely to be placed in privately run group homes and private drug and alcohol treatment centers (Kempf-Leonard et al, 1995). Another cause of differential treatment is what Feld (1999b) refers to as "justice by geography." Feld (1999b) notes that "individualized discretion is often synonymous with racial disparities in sentencing juveniles" (p. 72). Urban and, to a lesser degree, suburban courts tend to be more formalized in structure, allowing less judicial discretion. According to Feld, this is due to the larger caseloads found in urban courts, which in turn forces reliance upon standardized bureaucratic measures (1999b).

It is likely that Blacks are not the only group significantly affected by racial (or ethnic) profiling. Latinx are probably often subjected to racial/ethnic profiling as well, although the rate at which this happens is not easy to determine. Surprisingly, minority overrepresentation is likely substantially underreported in the OJJDP data (Snyder and Sigmund, 1999) and FBI reports (Steffensmeier and Demuth, 2000) as not all police and court agencies separate ethnic groups, resulting in an often inaccurate, hodgepodge method of counting Latinos in the criminal and juvenile justice systems. Often only the race of those in the justice system, rather than their ethnicity, is recorded.

This has led to numerous cases of Latinos being categorized as White, making it seem as if the system is less discriminatory by overcounting White arrest and conviction rates through the inclusion of Hispanics (Steffensmeier and Demuth, 2000).

By any measurement, minorities are overrepresented in the juvenile justice system. This overrepresentation has remained fairly constant since the 1990s. Figures from the FBI dated 1993 show that African Americans, though only 12 percent of the general population (about 15 percent of the juvenile population), accounted for 27 percent of all juvenile arrests, 49 percent of juvenile arrests for violent crime and 26 percent of arrests for property crime (Joseph, 1995). Significantly, the further they move through the system, the greater their disproportionate representation (Leonard et al, 1995). At the juvenile court level, in 1993, about 20 percent of all youths referred to juvenile court were detained. Of that 20 percent, however, judges detained about 18 percent of White juveniles and 26 percent of Black juveniles (Feld, 1999b).

The OJJDP has concluded that institutional bias or racism occurs from the initial contact the juvenile makes with law enforcement up through the juvenile court system itself (Lardiero, 1997). Other evidence similarly suggests that race is frequently a factor at different points throughout the juvenile justice system. Bishop and Frazier (1996), using both analysis of case histories and interviews with officials at all levels of the juvenile justice system, concluded that race is the dominant factor at every stage of processing, but that it is most important at the initial arrest stage. Free (1996) found that African Americans were less likely than whites to be released by the police. Both the case history analysis and the interviews support the idea that race is more of a determining factor for the police than in any other part of the juvenile system, likely due to a lack of public oversight as officers have significant latitude in deciding to commit to initial contact and then whether to make the contact official, such as a citation or arrest (Leonard et al, 1995).

The practice of racial profiling also makes African American youth more susceptible to initial contact (Jackson and Pabon, 2000). The concepts of differential treatment and differential involvement collide most publicly with the issue of racial profiling. Key to the mistrust of the justice system for many minorities is the concept of racial profiling or the "out-of-place" doctrine. Kathryn Russell (1998) points out that the "out-of-place" doctrine, which a number of courts have upheld as legal, gives police a legal justification for stopping and questioning Blacks when they are in a predominantly White neighborhoods. Studies indicate that Black males are stopped and questioned by the police at a rate much higher than any other racial or ethnic group. According to Russell, this creates a problem in that Black males are stopped and questioned at a rate much higher than the level of Black involvement in crime. Of course, racial targeting for the purpose of enhancing the efficiency of the criminal justice system (racial profiling) has effects upon the minority community well beyond the scope of the justice system. For instance, as Coates (2007, p. 223) explains:

> How racial nonelites respond to racial profiling may be the difference between life and death. In cities across the nation, increased levels of incarceration, fear, and even death have resulted as these nonelites have found their opportunities for freedom and security impaired. ... Repeated episodes of racial intimidation, profiling, and discrimination may produce increased levels of stress, hypertension, and other related health conditions.

Racial profiling targets minorities and damages their lives, yet many Whites see it as, at worst, a necessary evil, while programs with the goal of enhancing Black lives are seen negatively by Whites (Bobo and Kluegel, 1993).

There is evidence to suggest that many minority youths and their parents may not fully understand their options in juvenile court or trust those representing their interests (Joseph, 1995; Leonard et al, 1995). This may be related to research that shows that Blacks are significantly more likely to be represented by public defenders rather than private attorneys, which may in turn play a role in the overrepresentation of minority youth in detention facilities (Hendricks and Byers, 2000). However, a lack of private attorneys does not explain overrepresentation of minority juveniles at other stages of the juvenile justice system, such as initial police contact or arrest. Within the juvenile justice continuum, beginning with initial police contact as the least severe end and ending with juvenile certification/waiver (moving juvenile cases to criminal court to be tried as an adult) as the most severe end, there is a constant growth in overrepresentation of Black youths, with the greatest level of disproportional representation in juvenile waivers to criminal court (Leonard et al, 1995). Interestingly, there is no rational evidence to support the disparities in sentencing or in waivers between minority and White offenders (Joseph, 1995; Leonard et al, 1995; Free, 1996; Hendricks and Byers, 2000).

Bridges and Steen (1998) found, during their interviews with juvenile court judges, a disturbing tendency for judges to decide that it was in the best interest of many minority youths to place them in a detention facility as it was considered preferable to their home life, though they did not extend this same decision to White (non-Hispanic) youths (Leonard et al, 1995). The specter of single-parent families, or more specifically of Black women raising children alone, appears to play a significant role in the juvenile justice decision-making process. The problem with these stereotypes and assumptions, particularly those involving parental ability and involvement, is that, in an overworked system, shortcuts, in the form of decisions made using stereotypes rather than factual information, may be used (Singer, 1996; Feld, 1999b).

Few juvenile court judges believe racial disparities in confinement to be racially based (Bridges and Steen, 1998). Instead, most judges (Leonard et al, 1995; Secret and Johnson, 1997; Bridges and Steen, 1998) attributed the disparities to Blacks' and other minorities' "substantial ethnic and racial differences in criminal behavior" (institutionalized discrimination) or the fact that youths from wealthier families have access to non-adjudicated facilities that the poor do not (contextual discrimination). Essentially, judges may use extralegal characteristics such as race to create "a mental map of the accused person's underlying character" (Secret and Johnson, 1997) and to predict his/her future behavior. Alternatively, the harsher treatment of African American and Latinx juveniles may reflect both class and race biases on the part of juvenile court judges (Secret and Johnson, 1997). In other words, "the individual's economic and social class and the color of his skin ... determine his relationship to the legal system" (Feld, 1999b, p. 94).

Bridges and Steen's (1998) study of probation officers examined 233 narrative reports written by juvenile probation officers in three different counties in the state of Washington in 1990 and 1991. Each narrative included the probation officer's description of the crime and an assessment of the factors that motivated the crime, as well as an evaluation of the youth's background and an assessment of his or her likelihood of recidivism. The probation officers:

> tended to attribute crimes committed by whites to negative environmental factors (poor school performance, delinquent peers, dysfunctional family, use of drugs or alcohol) ... [yet] ... they tended to attribute crimes committed by Black youths to negative personality traits and 'bad attitudes' (refusal to admit guilt, lack of remorse, failure to take offense seriously, lack of cooperation with court officials). They also found that P.O.'s (probation officers) judged Black youth to have a significantly higher risk of reoffending than white youth. (Bridges and Steen, 1998, p. 174)

We draw our conclusions on DMC utilizing a critical race theory perspective as it gives a clearer understanding of DMC than do the major criminological theories. We also utilize both quantitative and qualitative data to better triangulate our understanding of DMC. In order to give the reader an overview of "where we are going, and how we get there," a brief explanation of each subsequent chapter is included here.

Chapter 2: Occam's razor: racial and ethnic inequality throughout society

In Chapter 2, we argue that looking at DMC as an issue of crime rather than an issue of racism results in an overreliance on circular logic in which non-Whites are arrested at a higher rate, causing police to focus their attention more on non-White juveniles. This greater focus (over-policing) then results in non-Whites being arrested, proportionately, more often. If, on the other hand, DMC is just another part of a racialized social system that consistently treats non-Whites as somehow lesser and in need of control, then the criminological theories used to explain DMC are of no use for the vast majority of DMC.

As noted earlier, despite a wealth of previous literature on DMC, there is no clear consensus on its causes, specifically whether it is primarily explained by differential involvement (i.e., non-White youth are more criminally active) or by the fact that non-White youth experience unique and unequal treatment in the juvenile justice system when compared with their White counterparts. However, in other areas of social life, there is a well-established and continually growing body of empirical evidence that shows racialized differences are, in fact, the result of a deeply entrenched racialized social system that routinely and systemically privileges Whites, often at the expense of non-Whites (Bonilla-Silva, 2018). This is important to note because DMC, as a phenomenon, does not take place in a vacuum but rather exists within the context of a larger racialized criminal justice system (Alexander and West, 2012) that is part of an even larger social, political and economic world that is highly racialized and skews heavily toward disproportionately negatively impacting non-Whites ((Sears & Henry, 2003; Bonilla-Silva, 2001).

Prior literature has intricately linked racial difference with racial discrimination in the following areas, to name just a few: the Black–White wealth gap (Oliver and Shapiro, 2006); economic immobility of African Americans compared with their White counterparts (Mazumder, 2014); residential segregation and housing searches (Massey and Denton, 1993; Ross and Turner, 2005); the placement of Blacks into racialized and often stagnant career trajectories (Collins, 1996); hiring decisions (Kirschenman and Neckerman, 1991; Pager, 2003; Bertrand and Mullainathan, 2004); non-Whites being more likely to obtain higher interest rate, subprime mortgage loans despite full economic history such as income, length of income and credit (Oliver and Shapiro, 2006; Bond and Williams, 2007; Pager and Shepherd, 2008; Casey, Glaberg and Beeman, 2011); and wages (Western and Pettit, 2005). Prior literature has also shown the racial difference–racial discrimination link in school funding and the uneven provision of school resources in non-White schools (Kozol, 1991); predominantly non-White communities of color being disproportionately exposed to higher levels of environmental toxins (Taylor et al, 2014); the unequal administration of dosages for medical pain relief by medical professionals to non-White and White youth (Goyal et al, 2015); as well as a long record of vast racial disparities in the areas of general medicine and surgical care, coronary artery disease, HIV/AIDS, stroke, various forms of cancer, and renal disease and kidney transplantation (Smedley et al, 2003).

This chapter explores the differential treatment of non-Whites in multiple areas of society and asks, short of evidence that race operates differently in the juvenile justice system, that we presume differential treatment is the most likely cause until research shows significant evidence to the contrary. While this may sound simplistic, historically non-Whites have been blamed for their social problems.

Chapter 3: Law enforcement contact: juvenile arrest data

For many juveniles, their first encounter with the juvenile justice system involves police contact. To assess racial differences in contact with police, we examined differences in arrests and citations from police report data. The data come from more than 40,000 police reports from the Oklahoma City metropolitan area involving juveniles for multiple years between 2006 and 2014. Law enforcement contact data provide information about the number of law enforcement contacts with juveniles as well as the outcome of the encounter, that is, whether the encounter ended in an arrest or citation. Police contact data provide important information about the totality of law enforcement contacts with juveniles during a given time frame within a given jurisdiction. These data provide information about the race of juveniles in contact with law enforcement, the nature or type of incident that initiated the contact and the outcome of the incident. Central to the current project, these data will allow us to assess whether there are differential rates of contact with law enforcement for White and minority juveniles and the outcome of that contact.

Chapter 4: Intake and detention: the disposition of referred cases

After initial police contact, the next step in the juvenile justice process is intake and detention decisions. To assess race differences in decisions at intake and detention, we use data from the same metropolitan area (Oklahoma City) from the same years. The data come from two sources: the Oklahoma Office of Juvenile Affairs Juvenile On-Line Tracking System (JOLTS) and records from the juvenile proceedings in Oklahoma City municipal court. JOLTS is an extensive source of information on juvenile crime, combining police and court data. We also use municipal court data because some juvenile cases in Oklahoma City are processed through the city court, not the statewide juvenile system. The municipal court data contain similar information to the JOLTS system as described previously. The primary difference in the two data sources is that the JOLTS system is a statewide database, while the municipal data are for a single city.

JOLTS is an extensive and statewide transactional juvenile justice information system with participation by local county juvenile bureaus, the statewide network of statutorily designated nonprofit Youth Services agencies, the secure detention centers and the Community Intervention Centers (CICs). JOLTS incorporates information uniquely identifying juveniles and their referrals to the state- and county-based juvenile justice system, reflecting reports from a variety of individuals and agencies including law enforcement. Each offense associated with each referral for each juvenile and each related intake decision by the Office of Juvenile Affairs or bureau staff and district attorneys is recorded, as is each related court petition, adjudication and disposition; every in-home and out-of-home placement including detention stays; and each related referral for programs and services.

These data provide information about the race of juveniles and the outcomes associated with intake and detention decisions. The data allow us to assess whether race is associated with the decision to decline or file a petition in a specific case.

Chapter 5: Juvenile self-report of criminality and deviance data

We conducted 520 anonymous, self-report surveys of criminal or delinquent behavior at multiple area high schools. We included urban, suburban and rural high schools in our study, as the "metro" area includes a significant rural component. We utilized self-report surveys as one of our "points" in our triangulation of the topic. Police reports are self-report, but they are not anonymous. In fact, the opposite is true. Police reports are subject to scrutiny and may be relevant to an officer's career success. The justice system depends upon transparency to instill trust in the system, and without trust, the system simply does not work (Frankel, 2019). Unfortunately, there are numerous examples of police misrepresenting or manipulating the facts to better suit the story they want to tell (Kaur, 2020; Miracle, 2020).

The self-report surveys show differential treatment, with non-White kids having negative police and court contact that is more severe and more frequent than their White peers, despite no meaningful difference in White and non-White youth offending. The official police and court data show us the extent of DMC. The self-report data show us the cause of DMC. In the next chapter, we learn the "why."

DMC is calculated at contact points in the juvenile justice system. Social scientists measure criminal behavior in three general ways. The oldest, and frequently considered best, way to measure it is from official data collected by various criminal justice agencies. Typical of this approach is the use of data on arrests or convictions. The other two ways are to use data from victims of crime or from perpetrators of crime. Both these methods typically rely on survey data. In the former case, individuals are asked if they have been victims of crime. In the other case, people are asked to self-report their own criminal and deviant behaviors.

Chapter 6: The case for self-report data: self-report vs. arrest/conviction data

Official agency data (e.g., arrest data) are most commonly used and are considered by many to be the gold standard. Official agency data have known advantages. For example, arrests and criminal case processing are recorded at specific points in time, they are collected in similar fashion across time and location, and there are generally agreed-upon definitions of what activities constitute criminal or deviant behavior (Farrington et al, 2003). Criminologists and other social scientists have long noted the limitations of official records, however. The most obvious revolve around issues of underestimation of the true volume of crime (Kirk, 2006). Citation, arrest and conviction rates are simply that: a record of the times each of those incidents occurred. Crime rates use official records as a proxy for the extent of crime. However, police are not always objective, either at the individual or institutional level, allowing for institutional, systemic and individual racism to influence the data (Bolton and Feagin, 2004). Victimization surveys consistently show that victims of crime often do not report incidents, with reporting rates varying by crime type. Self-report surveys also indicate that most crimes are not detected by law enforcement personnel (Thornberry and Krohn, 2003).

Perhaps most important in questioning the accuracy of official data is the growing body of video evidence suggesting that, at least some of the time, police reports and actions or events do not always line up.

Chapter 7: Police, juvenile court and juvenile specialist interviews

We conducted, transcribed and coded 83 interviews with Oklahoma City area juvenile professionals, at an average of about 1.5 hours each. Of that total, we interviewed 63 police officers, one juvenile court judge, eight district attorneys and/or public defenders and 12 juvenile specialists (juvenile probation officers). There were three general categories of interview questions: (a) background/demographics, (b) generalized questions on the justice system and their job in particular, and finally (c) questions specific to DMC.

Background/demographic questions included the self-identified race and ethnicity of the participant, gender, and questions on race and ethnicity and class for both their childhood and current neighborhoods. Questions about friendships, those outside of work as well as those from their childhood, were included to help identify the extent of White habitus and/or interracial/ interethnic balance in their life, outside of work. Finally, we asked a number of questions about DMC, both in general and with specific reference to Blacks, Latinos, Whites, Native Americans and Asians.

We found that most of the participants believed in stereotypes regarding non-White families having significantly different value systems and involvement of parents, neither of which is supported by research. There was also a tendency for those who live and/or were raised in White, segregated communities to state a strong belief in racial/ethnic family differences. However, those who were raised in less segregated communities also tended to share the same stereotypes, though they were much more likely to point out that there were exceptions to these stereotypes. This suggests the need for a structural interpretation of racism in the juvenile justice system, as the interview responses on DMC tended to closely follow the four frames of color-blind racism as described by Bonilla-Silva (2001, 2003): abstract liberalism, naturalization, cultural racism and minimization of racism were all present throughout the interviews.

Chapter 8: Discussion and conclusions

Our final chapter brings together the component studies used to triangulate the primary cause of DMC. The longstanding differential treatment of non-Whites throughout the justice system, so much of it involving small and seemingly minor instances of casual racism—in traffic stops, healthcare, shopping, travel, education and every other facet of everyday social life— shows systemic differential treatment due to racism. These small injustices shape the landscape that allows the greater injustices. The tragedies that are the deaths of so many non-Whites at the hands of police, the Trayvon Martins, the Eric Garners, the Breonna Taylors, whose deaths created a need for groups such as Black Lives Matter and Say Her Name, are rooted in the casual racism of treating a Black person as a suspect when shopping or driving, instead of being treated as a customer or a driver. This is the slippery slope that creates a society that allows White supremacists to work in the White House and in police departments.

DMC is not an accurate category but rather two very different groups merged together to support the inaccurate contention that non-White youth are more criminalistic than are White kids. The bulk of those individuals who make up the "disproportionate" part of DMC are criminally no different than their White counterparts. DMC is about applying findings about a small group, who are from the poorest minority neighborhoods in the US, not only to all minorities in those high poverty neighborhoods but to every other non-White kid, regardless of their criminal record, social class, education and so forth. DMC is about painting *every* non-White youth as a dangerous criminal who must prove otherwise. This is despite the fact that White and non-White youth commit crimes at the same rate, and White youth are presumed to be non-criminal until proven otherwise. DMC simply changes the starting point for juveniles based upon their race/ethnicity.

2

Occam's Razor: Racial/Ethnic Inequality Throughout Society

> Occam's Razor is used as a heuristic, or "rule of thumb" to guide scientists in developing theoretical models. The term "razor" refers to the "shaving away" of unnecessary assumptions when distinguishing between two theories.
>
> Susan Borowski (2012)

Introduction

In this chapter, we look at two opposing explanations for DMC. One, differential involvement, states that DMC is due to minority youth committing crimes at a much higher rate than White youth, which, in turn, means DMC is simply a reflection of higher rates of criminality, rather than systemic racism. The other explanation is differential treatment, which, consistent with both historical and current treatment of non-White youth, suggests that differential treatment is the cause of DMC, just as differential treatment impacts non-White youth in all areas of American society. Borowski's definition of Occam's Razor best describes the focus of this chapter, in which we outline that DMC appears strikingly similar to all other areas of racism, and differential treatment should be presumed the likely cause of DMC according to the principle of removing unnecessary assumptions when distinguishing between two theories.

According to the US Census, the following percentages of the population in 2019 identified as the following racial/ethnic categories:

- Latinx/Hispanic 18.5 percent
- Black/African American alone 13.4 percent

- Asian alone 5.9 percent
- Native American alone 1.3 percent
- White alone 76.3 percent
- Nat. Hawaiian/Pac Islander alone 0.2 percent
- Two or more races 2.8 percent
- White alone, not Hispanic/Latinx 60.1 percent
  These percentages represent those who identified solely as one of the racial/ethnic groups.

If race does not matter, we would expect about 13 percent of CEOs to be Black, 19 percent to be Latinx, 6 percent to be Asian, 1 percent to be Native American, 76 percent to be White (because of rounding, this totals more than 100 percent) and, for ethnicity, 19 percent to be Latinx. We would expect 13 percent of lawyers, medical doctors, warehouse workers, nurses, delivery drivers, PhDs, those in poverty, those who are the wealthiest, those in the middle class, those with a high school degree as their highest level of education, those who own a home and so forth to be Black. We would expect to see the same proportional representation for all racial/ethnic groups throughout both the "good" and "bad" elements of society. If race really does not matter, then we would expect proportional distribution throughout society. We, of course, do not find that. Instead, we find racial/ethnic minorities overrepresented in "bad" areas of society and underrepresented in "good" areas.

The late Devah Pager, in her seminal 2003 work *The Mark of a Criminal Record*, while not specific to disproportionate minority contact (DMC), makes two major points that help to understand the causes of DMC. Pager's study sent young men, both Black and White, to apply for entry-level jobs, while varying their criminal history in the applications. First, she found that White applicants were *much* more likely to get a callback for a job, with Whites without a criminal record getting a callback more than one third of the time (34 percent). Black applicants without a criminal record only received a callback 14 percent of the time, significantly less than half as often as White applicants. Her second major finding is even more striking. White applicants *with* a criminal record were given callbacks more often (17 percent) than were Black applicants *without* a criminal record (14 percent). Blacks with a criminal record received callbacks only 4 percent of the time. Pager's study shows, at least in entry-level job hiring, that Whiteness is the key factor in hiring. Being Black, on the other hand, is a major penalty in hiring, and being Black with a criminal record results in great difficulty in securing an entry-level job.

DMC is two issues masquerading as one. This is the cause of a 50-year logjam preventing us from reaching a consensus on the cause of DMC. For more than two and a half decades, dueling perspectives have been unable to offer an agreed upon cause. Without a cause of DMC to rectify, it is not surprising to find that the extent of DMC has not really changed since the 1970s. As noted in Chapter 1, one potential explanation offered for DMC is differential involvement, where non-White juveniles are more criminalistic. Most research following this line assumes that societal pressures limit choices or make criminal options more desirable. The other explanation is differential treatment, where non-Whites are treated differently by the justice system. This would include over-policing and harsher treatment in the court and probation system. It is also possible that the cause lies somewhere on this continuum between the two extremes. More than a decade ago, Piquero (2008) suggested that it was time to move on from this endless disagreement as to the cause of DMC as, he suggests, it simply cannot be determined. We appreciate his frustration regarding the issue; however, the cause of DMC must be both known and acknowledged through policy in order for a meaningful reduction of DMC to be possible. Again, DMC has not really changed in over 50 years, resulting in minor changes being celebrated at the state level. Our data clearly shows DMC is due to differential treatment, yet many programs to combat DMC focus on changing the behavior of non-White kids, which is meaningless in terms of reducing DMC. Demanding that non-White kids be significantly better behaved, in terms of criminality, than White kids simply in order to be treated the same within the juvenile justice system is indefensible and incredibly racist. DMC resulting from differential treatment requires significant changes in how society polices and prosecutes non-White youth.

Utilizing self-report data from youth, we find no significant difference in criminal and deviant behavior between White and non-White youth. Using interviews with police, juvenile court professionals and juvenile probation officers, we also find that juvenile justice professionals see non-White youth and their families as somehow "broken," which broadly explains why they are, in their eyes, more criminalistic. Most of the kids impacted by DMC are criminally no different than their White counterparts. There are outliers. These are the youth who are much more likely to commit the most serious crimes. Comparatively few non-White kids are chronic offenders and/or violent gang members, and just over one half of 1 percent of the US population (0.6 percent) is responsible for half of the violent crime in the United States (National Network for Safe Communities at John Jay College, 2021). The cause of differential treatment is that society tends to treat non-White youth as potential criminals who must prove (over and over) that they are worthy to walk in our society, whereas White youth are treated as if they belong, unless they prove otherwise. Analysis of our data suggests two things regarding the outliers: (a) they are a small enough group that their behavior should not be generalized to all non-White youth, and (b) their behavior is clearly, all too often, generalized to all non-White youth. Simply put, we take the behavior of a small number of violent, non-White juvenile offenders and treat the much larger group of non-White youth as if they belonged in that very rare scenario.

This much larger population who make up the overrepresentation measured in DMC are non-White kids who are no different criminally than their White counterparts. Their experiences differ, but their actions, goal and aspirations are strikingly similar. DeLuca et al (2016) refer to these non-White kids as "On Track" youth. White and non-White kids commit crimes. White and non-White kids are very similar in their illegal/deviant activities, both in type and frequency. As a society, we have taken the stories of outliers and used them as an excuse that maybe, just maybe, other non-White kids are also dangerous. We treat all Black, Latinx and Native American youth as dangerous, simply because we can find examples of dangerous Black, Latinx and Native Americans. We may not always consciously discriminate, but we give rationalizations for differential treatment based upon our fears so that we may discriminate without having to acknowledge it.

If researchers and policymakers focus only on official police and court data, the cause of DMC seems clear. Utilizing police and court data, it appears that DMC must be caused by differential involvement. Non-White juveniles are arrested and sentenced proportionally more often than are White youth simply because they commit crime at a higher rate. Court data are very precise. Court data give a very accurate record of courtroom results. There is much about inequality that these data do not address, but they paint an accurate picture of the results. Unlike court data, the primary concern with police data is that they may be neither precise nor accurate. Initial police contact typically has no record unless the contact becomes official. Until there is a written warning, citation or arrest, only those involved in or witnessing an individual event know the details. Records are created, and police departments typically have very extensive records; however, an officer's written report is simply self-report data. Not only is it self-report data, but it is not even anonymous. The officers who create these self-report police data are held accountable for those data, which may place pressure on them to manipulate what the data state. There exist few controls over the accuracy of police data. It has been said that the justice system only works if the members of society believe in the system. Perhaps we have placed too much belief in the objectiveness of police officers. Using police data as a means of determining juvenile criminality by race/ethnicity is racism masquerading as science. It is unfathomable that so much control over the lives of non-White juveniles is based upon data with so little objectivity.

The argument for differential involvement is strongly supported by official police and court data. Non-Whites are arrested more frequently than Whites. Non-Whites are stopped by police more often than Whites. The problem with utilizing arrest and conviction data as a proxy for criminality is that it is nothing more than an attempt to promote racism as scientifically proven.

We propose that looking at criminality on the less severe end of the justice system gives us a much more broadly applicable picture of race and crime than does the most severe end. Comparatively few extremely violent crimes occur, in contrast to lesser crimes. There are few murders compared with the number of incidents of drug or alcohol use. It is on that less severe and much more common end where data show the vast majority of crime resides. Black kids, Latinx kids and Native American kids commit crimes of lesser severity at much the same rate as Whites, but they are treated as if they are criminals. White kids use illegal substances a bit more often than Black kids, while Black kids commit violent crimes a bit more often than White kids (Farrington, Barnes et al, 1996), but neither group commits substance abuse or violent crimes often enough to objectively subject either group to increased suspicion or differential treatment. Despite there being no significant difference in the type or frequency of crime between races/ethnicities, society treats non-White youth as suspected criminals and White youth as kids.

Before going into the analysis of the different parts of our study, we first want to question why differential treatment is not the presumptive cause of DMC before examining differential involvement. This sounds like an odd statement, yet, given the overwhelming evidence of race-based differential treatment of non-Whites throughout US society, we might logically expect that the starting point for examining DMC is to determine if the cause is, somehow, different from that of other racial inequalities in society. Differential involvement as the cause of DMC suggests that non-White youth are more criminalistic than their White counterparts. This unsupported assumption not only denies centuries of racial discrimination, it also pretends that the criminal justice system—the same justice system that has enforced racial inequality—is somehow now color-blind and unbiased. It is simply unclear why anyone would start assuming racial neutrality in the treatment within the justice system, given both our history and current experiences. Barring something unique to DMC, the evidence of differential treatment of non-Whites is abundant. With sincere respect to Piquero's (2008) work in understanding DMC, we argue, in response to his suggestion that researchers and policymakers may never know to what degree differential treatment drives DMC, that DMC is an absurd category that mostly or fully measures racism rather than criminality.

As we were making our final edits to submit this book, perhaps the perfect illustration of differential treatment for Whites and non-Whites was televised to the entire planet. We will include information from major news sources for this part as details are only beginning to come to light as we write this. On January 6, 2021, a mob of angry, devoted Trump supporters, made up of often overlapping members of subgroups of racists (e.g., Proud Boys), conspiracy theory lovers (QAnon), some fundamentalist Christians and even a few elected politicians, stormed the Capitol building in an attempt to thwart the legal certification Joe Biden's presidency. This attempted coup (Hart, 2021) resulted in six deaths, including two Capitol Police officers, and was instigated by the sitting president, Donald Trump (BBC News, 2020). Only 52 arrests were made on the day of the attack (Hart, 2021), with most of the terrorists being allowed to walk away from the attack unchallenged. *Time* described the scene:

> One video appears to show a Capitol Police officer taking selfies with the rioters. Another featured several officers removing metal barriers to let the mob freely pass toward the Capitol. In yet another video, an officer appeared to hold a door open so [sic] a handful of rioters, apparently allowing them to exit the Capitol building without being arrested or charged. (Hennigan and Bergengruen, 2021)

The angry White male rage was directed, full force, at police officers. Given the deaths, including those of two officers, it is somewhat surprising that they were not more prepared for the riot, which was preplanned weeks in advance, with plans to attack police and others broadcast ahead of time. "'You can go to Washington on Jan 6 and help storm the Capital,' said one 8kun user a day before the siege. 'As many Patriots as can be. We will storm the government buildings, kill cops, kill security guards, kill federal employees and agents, and demand a recount'" (Collins and Zadrozny, 2021).

Contrast this with the largely peaceful protests by Black Lives Matter (BLM). In the four-day period between May 30 and June 2, 2020, 427 "unrest-related" arrests were made in Washington, DC, including 24 juveniles (Hart, 2021). On the afternoon of June 1, peaceful protesters were chased, without warning and before curfew, out of Lafayette Park by US Park Police and National Guard troops using teargas, simply so that President Trump could get a photo opportunity at a nearby church. On the evening of June 1, 2020, riot police pushed back protesters from all sides, boxing in many, in DC's Chinatown, where two Blackhawk military helicopters paced the protesters, one eventually hovering just 45 feet above the protesters, between buildings and low enough to cause large branches to break off of trees from the helicopter downdraft (Horton, 2020).

This blazing example of differential treatment by law enforcement alone should be enough for any rational person to reject differential involvement as the starting point for understanding the cause of non-White overrepresentation in the justice system. There is a well-documented example of a violent, largely White group who publicly advertised their intentions to murder public officials, bureaucrats and police and planned to kidnap members of Congress, only to be treated with deference and respect, even as they were finally removed from congressional offices. Just a few months earlier, in the same city, there was a group of largely non-White folks protesting yet another death of an unarmed Black man at the hands of the police. Yet those Black protesters and supporters of equal police treatment of Blacks and other minorities were treated more harshly, in the immediate aftermath, than were the Trump supporters attempting a coup and causing deaths.

It is not only in the extreme actions that one sees differential treatment, however. Most differential treatment of non-Whites is more subtle and less severe. Most of these are micro-aggressions involving individual instances of differential treatment due to racism that is hard to prove until a larger pattern is observed. This "death by a thousand cuts" form of differential treatment is seen in lesser justice actions as well as other, non-judicial aspects of everyday life. Most readers are likely familiar with the term "driving while Black," but we hope to show the overwhelming extent of racial bias utilizing numerous studies, often commissioned by local authorities, all of which have strikingly similar findings. Non-Whites, especially Blacks, are pulled over much more often in traffic stops than are Whites. Black and other non-White drivers are searched more often than are White drivers. Perhaps most importantly, Black drivers are much *less* likely to be found with contraband or to have broken any laws. While the studies are overwhelming and quite redundant, we feel it is important to include this small slice of available evidence to drive home the extent and consistent nature of differential treatment, especially as it illustrates the "garbage in–garbage out" aspect of race and crime rates. Black drivers are pulled over more often because of the incorrect assumption that they are more criminalistic. Each of these mostly small jurisdictional findings (though national studies are also included) draws the same conclusion: that Black drivers are actually less likely to be breaking the law.

Driving while Black

- A national study of 100 million-plus traffic stops, nationwide, found that Black drivers were pulled over most often, including in nighttime stops, and that Black and Latinx drivers were most likely to be searched during a stop (Pierson et al, 2020).
- A study commissioned by the city of Charlottesville, Virginia, found significant racial disparities in (a) seriousness of charges, (b) number of companion charges (stacking charges), (c) bail-bond release decision, (d) length of time to trial and (e) outcomes of guilt. Black men make up 8.5 percent of the city population and 4.4 percent of the county population but made up more than 50 percent and 37 percent of the arrests for those areas, respectively (The Daily Progress, 2020).

- A study of California traffic stops, conducted by Public Policy Institute of California, found that Black drivers were stopped by police 2.5 times as often as White drivers and that the percent of Blacks pulled over was larger at night. Black drivers were three times more likely than any other group to be searched (Thompson, 2020).
- The Burlington, Vermont, police department conducted a study that found that Black drivers made up less than 7 percent of the driving population but 8 percent of drivers pulled over. However, Black drivers were six times more likely than White drivers to be searched (Quigley, 2019).
- An analysis of 20 million-plus traffic stops showed Black drivers to be almost twice as likely as White drivers to be pulled over and that Black drivers are almost four times as likely to be searched. Among those searched, Black drivers were less likely to have any illegal items compared with Whites (Baumgartner, 2018).
- An analysis of Washington, DC, police stops found Blacks made up 70 percent of traffic stops and 86 percent of non-traffic enforcement stops despite being 46 percent of the city's population (Duggan, 2019).
- A study utilizing traffic stop data from the 100 largest police departments in North Carolina found that Blacks and Latinx were more likely than Whites to be searched as a result of a traffic stop, despite Whites being the most likely to have contraband (Simoiu et al, 2017).
- A study of Cincinnati traffic stops found Black drivers were 30 percent more likely than White drivers to be pulled over and made up 76 percent of arrests after a traffic stop despite being 43 percent of Cincinnati's population (Enquirer editorial board, 2019).
- An analysis of vehicle stops in Los Angeles found that Blacks were four times as likely as Whites to be searched and Latinx were three times as likely to be searched as Whites, despite Whites being more likely (20 percent of searches) to have contraband than were Blacks (17 percent) or Latinx (26 percent) (Poston and Chang, 2019).
- An Oregon study found that Black and Latinx motorists and pedestrians were much more likely to be stopped, receive a citation and be arrested for drug possession than were White pedestrians and motorists (Oregon Criminal Justice Commission, 2019).
- Despite similar rates of finding contraband, police in Austin, Texas, stopped, searched and arrested Blacks and Latinx at a significantly higher rate than Whites (Austin Office of Police Oversite, Office of Innovation and Equity Office, 2020).
- The City of Charleston's Black population constitutes 25 percent of the city's population, while in North Charleston Blacks make up 47 percent of the population. For those areas, 40 percent of Charleston police stops and 65 percent of the stops in North Charleston were of Black drivers (CNA, 2019).

- Kansas City traffic stops that did not result in a citation were 2.7 times more likely to involve Black drivers, and Black drivers were five times more likely to be searched (Epp et al, 2014).
- Between 2012 and 2014, Blacks in Ferguson, Missouri, accounted for 85 percent of vehicle stops, 90 percent of citations and 93 percent of arrests, despite comprising only 67 percent of the population. Blacks were more than twice as likely as Whites to be searched after traffic stops, even though they proved to be 26 percent less likely to be in possession of illegal drugs or weapons. Blacks also received 95 percent of jaywalking tickets and 94 percent of tickets for "failure to comply." The US Justice Department further found that the racial discrepancy for speeding tickets increased dramatically when researchers looked at tickets based only on an officer's word vs. tickets based on objective evidence such as radar. Black people facing similar low-level charges as White people were 68 percent less likely to see those charges dismissed in court. More than 90 percent of the arrest warrants stemming from failure to pay/failure to appear were issued for Black people (US Department of Justice Civil Rights Division, 2015).
- The city of Carmel, Indiana, just outside Indianapolis, cites Black drivers 18 times more often than White drivers (WISH TV 8, 2019).
- A 2016 Rhode Island study found that 11 percent of stops were of Black drivers, although Blacks only constitute 6.5 percent of the population. Blacks were also significantly more likely to pulled over during daylight hours (Ross et al, 2018).
- Some of the towns in St. Louis County derive 40 percent or more of their annual revenue from the petty fines and fees collected by their municipal courts. A majority of these fines are for traffic offenses, but they can also include fines for fare-hopping on Metrolink (St. Louis's light rail system), loud music and other noise ordinance violations, zoning violations for uncut grass or unkempt property, violations of occupancy permit restrictions, trespassing, wearing "saggy pants," business license violations and vague infractions such as "disturbing the peace" or "resisting" that give police officers a great deal of discretion to look for other violations. Of those impacted by these policies, Blacks made up 27 percent of the population at the time of the study, but they constituted 71 percent of drivers stopped (Balko, 2014).
- An Oregon study found that Black and Latinx motorists and pedestrians were much more likely to be stopped, receive a citation and be arrested for drug possession than were White pedestrians and motorists (Oregon Criminal Justice Commission, 2019).
- A Connecticut study found that 29 percent of White drivers searched had contraband compared with only 19 percent of Black drivers. Black drivers were also more likely to be searched than were White drivers after stops for registration, license, seatbelt and cellphone violations (Lyons, 2019).

- A survey of citizen complaints found that complaints from White citizens against North Charleston were 1.7 times more likely to be sustained than were complaints from Black citizens. That number jumps significantly for the subgroup of excessive force complaints, where complaints filed by Whites were seven times more likely to be sustained than were Black complaints of excessive force (NAACP, 2017).
- A study of police data from 2012–16 showed Springfield, Missouri, police were significantly more likely to stop Black drivers, more likely to search stopped Black drivers, and more likely to arrest Black drivers despite no evidence of Blacks being any more likely than Whites to possess contraband (Stout, 2017).
- Black drivers are pulled over at a much higher rate than are White drivers in Charleston (CNA, 2019).
- A study of Bloomfield, New Jersey, traffic stops found that in a city that is 70 percent White, 78 percent of ticketed motorists were Black or Latinx. The study also found a disproportionate number of stops of non-White drivers occurred at the southern end of the city, where it meets areas with large non-White populations (Denbeaux et al, 2016).

Use of force

A nationwide study published by the National Academy of Sciences utilizing data on police shootings between 2013 and 2018 found that Black males were 2.5 times as likely as White males to be shot by police, and Latinx males were 1.35 times as likely. Black females were 1.4 times more likely than White females, and Latina females were significantly *less* likely than White women, to be shot by police (Edwards et al, 2019). 53 percent of police use of force incidents in Columbus, Ohio, in 2017 were against Black residents, who make up 28 percent of the population (Bush, 2019).

Blacks constitute 22 percent of Charleston's population but were the focus of 61 percent of use of force incidents, and White officers were more likely than Black officers to be involved in a use of force incident (CNA, 2019). In a now viral video, a Boston Police Department officer admits to purposefully running over Blacks protesting for Black Lives Matter while being video and audio recorded by a fellow officer's bodycam (Villarreal, 2020).

Despite Blacks making up just under 12 percent of the population of Texas, according to a database kept by the Texas Justice Initiative, they comprise 29 percent of deaths in police custody since 2005 and 27 percent of civilians shot by police officers. Hispanics were underrepresented in both categories (Texas Justice Initiative Home Page, 2020).

Misdemeanors and lesser drug arrests

Nationally, Blacks are three times as likely as Whites to be arrested for possession of marijuana. In South Bend, Indiana, that number was 4.3 times as likely as Whites (Grim et al, 2019). A Travis County, Texas, study found that Blacks make up 9 percent of the county's population but 30 percent of the county's arrests for possession of less than a gram of an illicit drug, despite studies showing similar levels of drug use between Blacks and Whites (Texas Criminal Justice Coalition, 2020).

General differential treatment in the justice system

Black women make up 5.8 percent of San Francisco's population but, in 2015, they constituted 45.5 percent of all female arrests, 53 percent of all drug arrests among females and 51 percent of all traffic violations by females (Males, 2015). Body cam footage analysis found that "officers speak with consistently less respect toward black versus white community members, even after controlling for the race of the officer, the severity of the infraction, the location of the stop, and the outcome of the stop" (Voit et al, 2017).

Not a single one of the 1,356 complaints filed by non-Whites against Los Angeles Police Department (LAPD) officers in a two-year period resulted in a finding of bias from the LAPD (Mather, 2015). An analysis of three years of stop-and-frisk incidents not resulting in arrest in Boston found that Blacks, who make up 24 percent of the city's population, constituted 63 percent of the incidents, and only 2.5 percent of the stop-and-frisks of Blacks resulted in arrest or discovery of contraband (ACLU, 2014). A 2014 study found that, among urban men, more police contacts corresponded to more trauma and anxiety and these impacted men of color more than Whites (Geller et al, 2014).

There are millions of non-Whites represented in this list of studies—more than a million non-Whites who were either innocent or guilty of only minor criminal actions yet were treated differently because of their race/ethnicity. These individuals must endure being treated as guilty and are required to prove their innocence. Their differential treatment by the justice system is due, without any question, to the color of their skin. If criminological theories could explain all but small parts of minority overrepresentation, one would have to assume that both BLM protesters and Black motorists are more criminalistic, and then we would look for an explanation for that greater level of criminal behavior. However, as the studies mentioned previously show, Blacks and other non-Whites, who were policed more often and more severely, were less likely to be guilty. This is not a criminological issue. It is a society-wide racial issue. Furthermore, it cannot be simply a criminological issue if the data show the same racialized patterns in other aspects of daily life.

In the following sections we explore some areas of society where criminality is unlikely to play much of a role—missing children, healthcare, education, travel and shopping—to further illustrate the full range of systemic racism.

Missing children

Data show that missing White children receive far more media coverage than missing Black and Brown children, despite higher rates of missing children among communities of color (Kaur, 2019). The FBI's National Crime Information Center (NCIC) database lists 424,066 missing children under 18 in 2018, the most recent year for which data is available. About 37 percent of those children are Black, even though Black children only make up about 14 percent of all children in the United States (Federal Interagency Forum on Child and Family Statistics, 2019). According to Robert Lowery, vice president of the missing child division at the National Center for Missing and Exploited Children (NCMEC), proportionally, non-White children are more likely to be missing. He adds that the high number of Black girls reported missing is particularly concerning (Federal Interagency Forum on Child and Family Statistics, 2019).

News media organizations have often been criticized for not giving missing Black children the amount of attention they give missing White kids. A 2010 study found that missing Black children were significantly underrepresented in TV news. Even though about a third of all missing children in the FBI's database were Black, they only made up about 20 percent of the missing children cases covered in the news (Federal Bureau of Investigation, 2019). A 2015 study was bleaker: though Black children accounted for about 35 percent of missing children cases in the FBI's database, they amounted to only 7 percent of media references (Federal Bureau of Investigation, 2019).

"There's a sense of distrust between law enforcement and the minority community," said Natalie Wilson, co-founder of the Black and Missing Foundation. According to Wilson, law enforcement often classifies children of color as runaways without having all the details (Kaur, 2019). Because those kids are considered to have voluntarily left home, Amber alerts aren't sent out about them and they typically aren't covered in the news. Families do not always have the financial resources to respond appropriately when their child is missing. They may not be able to afford a private investigator or to take time off work to help look for their child and follow up with law enforcement and the media, and many non-White families are hesitant to contact law enforcement, even if they think their child is missing. In fact, a significant number of non-White children who go missing are either homeless or in foster care, said Wilson, and many are at risk for sex trafficking. Data show that Black children are overrepresented in foster care and are at a much higher risk for homelessness.

Death by police shooting

Black children were six times more likely to be shot to death by the police, and Latinx children were three times more likely to suffer the same fate, as their White peers over a 16-year period, according to a study published in the journal *Pediatrics*. These findings are likely an underestimate of the true toll. This rate did not include children who were shot but did not die (Badolato et al, 2020).

Health: COVID-19

Black and Hispanic children are impacted more severely by COVID-19, with higher case rates, hospitalizations and virus-related complications than White children. The Centers for Disease Control and Prevention (CDC) examined hospitalization records from 14 states and found 576 COVID-19 cases among children who needed hospitalization from March through July 25, 2020. The report found Hispanic children were hospitalized for COVID-19 at the highest rate, 16.4 per 100,000 people, followed by Black children at 10.5 per 100,000. In contrast, White children were hospitalized at a rate of 2.1 per 100,000 (Lindsay et al, 2020).

Racial health disparities have existed for years, and the COVID-19 pandemic has exacerbated them. Experts say that social determinants of health have led to increased rates of underlying health conditions such as diabetes, heart disease and hypertension in minority communities, placing many at greater risk for COVID-19 complications.

Structural conditions also play a role. Rashawn Ray, a David M. Rubenstein Fellow with the Brookings Institution, recently noted that social distancing is a privilege that people of color, who often live in densely populated areas, are not afforded. He said discrimination is "baked into" our society. People of color are also less likely to have access to healthy food options, recreational spaces and healthcare (Ross et al, 2018).

Healthcare

On February 23, 2021, the *Journal of the American Medical Association* (JAMA), one of the most prestigious medical journals in the world, released a new podcast entitled "Structural racism for doctors—what is it?" in which a journal editor named Edward Livingston publicly dismissed the idea that systemic racism in medicine exists when he stated: "Personally, I think taking 'racism' out of the conversation would help." He went on to claim that "many people like myself are offended by the implication that we are somehow racist." JAMA even promoted the podcast online, with a tweet stating: "No physician is racist, so how can there be structural racism in health care?" It should be noted that Livingston's superior, editor-in-chief for JAMA Howard Bauchner, will be stepping down from his position at JAMA due to the backlash from this absurd statement. It is striking how similar this view, that medicine and its practitioners are somehow above the structural racism fray, is to views about the justice system.

Racial inequality is a determinant of racial/ethnic inequalities in health (Paradies et al, 2015; Bravemen, Egerter and Williams, 2011; Phelan and Link, 2015), even for educated middle-class Black women (Sacks, 2019), including racial differences in gestation length and low birthweight (Collins et al, 2004; Mustillo et al, 2004), and non-Whites receive lower dosages of medicine than Whites with similar diagnoses, including pain medication (Goyal et al, 2015). A disproportionate number of Asian Americans and Asian immigrants are affected by Hepatitis B virus (HBV), many of whom are a unaware that they are affected and therefore do not receive treatment (Strong et al, 2012).

Racial and ethnic minorities living in the United States have worse healthcare and more adverse health outcomes compared with non-Hispanic White people (Son et al, 2017). For example, Blacks are less likely to quit smoking than Whites (Piper et al, 2010) and twice as likely to be blind or visually impaired than White Americans. (Wilson et al, 2005). Blacks are the most likely to suffer vision impairment, and Whites are the least likely. Latinx fall about midway between the two (Wilson et al, 2005). Diabetes, a major contributor to loss of sight as well as multiple other medical issues, is 1.6 times more common in Blacks than Whites (Wilson et al, 2005).

Between 1992 and 2009, the proportion of late-stage breast cancer diagnoses increased among White women but was statistically unchanged among Black women, and the breast cancer mortality rate declined among Whites but remained statistically unchanged among Blacks (Akinyemiju et al, 2013). Furthermore, Blacks represent over half of all HIV/AIDS cases, despite being just 13 percent of the population (Earl et al, 2013). Weak patient–provider relationships also disproportionately affect Black HIV/AIDS patients and they bear a disproportionate burden of HIV morbidity and mortality (Earl et al, 2013). Black patients with HIV/AIDS face communication and care challenges associated with seeing providers of a racial and ethnic background that is different from their own (Earl et al, 2013).

Latinx and Blacks are more likely to delay healthcare because of organizational barriers (King et al, 2015). Even with higher education, Black women are more likely to experience preterm births, low birthweight babies and other complications than poor or lower educated White women (Dekker, 2018).

The Affordable Care Act was necessary to reduce multiple barriers for Native Americans to gain insurance coverage and access to healthcare (Carden et al, 2016). Native Americans were found to have higher body mass index, prevalence of smoking, diabetes and hypertension compared with Whites. This remained constant for both males and females (Raizada et al, 2014). Calcium scores were statistically higher in Native American males and females compared with their White counterparts (Raizada et al, 2014). A calcium score or more specifically, a coronary artery calcium score, is a measure of the accumulation of fats, cholesterol and other substances on the artery walls. The score provides a reliable assessment of risk for major cardiovascular outcomes such as stroke or heart attack, heart failure and stroke.

Blacks, Hispanics and Native Americans were 3.5–8.1 percentage points less likely than Whites to complete treatment for alcohol and drugs, with only Asians faring better than Whites for both types of treatment (Saloner and LeCook, 2013). Racial/ethnic minorities who report being socially assigned as White are more likely to receive preventive vaccinations and are less likely to report healthcare discrimination compared with those who are socially assigned as non-White (Macintosh et al, 2013).

Blacks have worse outcomes than Whites with thyroid cancer, due to unequal access to healthcare (Brown et al, 2010). Non-White cancer survivors ages 18 to 64 are more likely to delay or forgo care than their White counterparts (King et al, 2015). Finally, Black newborns have a higher mortality rate than do White newborns. That difference is halved when Black newborns are cared for by Black physicians (Greenwood et al, 2019).

Racialized healthcare differences give multiple meanings to the term "differential treatment," as non-Whites simply do not have the same access to nor the same quality of healthcare as do Whites.

Health: mortality rates and surgical complications

Black newborn babies in the United States are more likely to survive childbirth if they are cared for by Black doctors, but they are three times more likely than White babies to die when looked after by White doctors. The mortality rate of Black newborns in hospital shrunk by between 39 percent and 58 percent when Black physicians took charge of the birth, according to the research, which laid bare how shocking racial disparities in human health can affect even the first hours of a person's life. By contrast, the mortality rate for White babies was largely unaffected by the doctor's race.

The findings support previous research showing that while infant mortality rates have fallen in recent decades, Black children remain significantly more likely to die early than their White counterparts. Researchers from George Mason University analyzed data capturing 1.8 million hospital births in Florida between 1992 and 2015 for the study (Greenwood et al, 2020).

Within 30 days of surgery, Black children had a greater risk of suffering complications and death than White children and were nearly 3.5 times more likely to die within that time period. The prevailing cause of such disparity may be that, before surgery, Black children have higher rates of chronic diseases—in addition to other potential factors such as implicit bias and structural racism. According to the lead author of the study, "the expectation should be that complication rates and/or mortality among healthy children won't vary based on racial category—what we found is that they do" (Nafiu et al, 2020).

In addition to their higher risk of death within 30 days of surgery, Black children had an 18 percent greater chance of developing complications. These kids also had a 7 percent higher likelihood of developing "serious adverse events," especially bleeding that required blood transfusions, and sepsis—the malfunctioning of organs, shock and death as a result of the body's response to harmful bacteria or viruses in the blood or tissues. Black children, moreover, were at greater risk for undergoing surgeries and intubations for a second time that weren't part of the plan (Rogers, 2020). "Racism, not race, is a critical determinant of health," in the words of California pediatrician Dr. Rhea Boyd, who teaches nationally on the relationship between structural racism, inequity and health. Boyd also states: "Racism makes people sick and contributes to premature death, even for our kids." Note that she wasn't involved in the study (Rogers, 2020).

Travel

A study of New York City's predominantly Black neighborhoods found that White hosts consistently earned a dramatically larger share of revenue on Airbnb than their share of the population (Wachsmuth and Weiser, 2018). Asian and Latinx hosts charge 8–10 percent lower prices relative to their White counterparts on equivalent rental properties in an attempt to compete with customer-preferred White property owners (Kakar et al, 2018). In 2016, a white paper found that Airbnb hosts are prone to reject Black guests even if it means a loss in possible income (Wachsmuth and Weiser, 2018). Usage of Airbnb short-term rentals had risen more than 50 percent faster in Black neighborhoods than in New York City, as a whole, which is a form of gentrification (Wachsmuth and Weiser, 2018).

Hilton Properties has been the target of numerous lawsuits filed by Black travelers, registered in their hotels, who were accused by staff of not belonging in the hotel (Woodyard and Oliver, 2020). In air travel, the National Association for the Advancement of Colored People (NAACP) issued a nation travel advisory to Black travelers due to repeated racist incidents on American Airlines (BBC News, 2017). Transportation Security Administration (TSA) supervisors were put under investigation after numerous employees told investigators they were told, by supervisors, to search Black and Latinx travelers with "baggy clothes or gaudy jewelry" (Schneider, 2019).

Shopping

A detailed case study on the topic of "shopping while Black" documents a Black couple who suffered racial discrimination (e.g., forced to wait for service longer than White customers, harassed by a White server) while patronizing a national chain restaurant (Harris et al, 2005). Stereotypes of Blacks as more criminalistic and living in poverty results in Black consumers being judged by store employees as not legitimate customers worthy of service (Pittman, 2020). Retailers justify discriminating against Black customers as necessary to fight shoplifting (Williams et al, 2001). High-status products, such as quality, mainstream clothing, does not confer status or respect to Blacks from store employees as it tends to for Whites (Pittman, 2020). Instead, Gabbidon's (2003) analysis of false arrest cases in retail stores found numerous cases of racial profiling by store representatives.

Education

It has long been known that much of the racial achievement gap could be reduced by the hiring of highly qualified teachers for low-income minority students, yet few programs have attempted to address this on a large scale (Darling-Hammond, 2013). Poor non-White students are least likely to have highly qualified teachers, and Black, Hispanic and Native American students have less access to honors and advanced placement programs (Nittle, 2019).

There is a stark difference between the treatment of White and non-White children in K–12. Black third graders are less likely to be part of gifted and talented programs than their White peers (Nittle, 2019), and White teachers overlook gifted and talented Black students (Nittle, 2019). Non-White teachers, however, are more likely to identify non-White students as gifted and talented, which is positive, except that there is a shortage of qualified non-White teachers in Title I schools (schools with subsidized meal programs for students living in poverty) (Nittle, 2019). Racial segregation within the school curriculum (advanced vs. less advanced courses) has been found to play a significant role in health behaviors and decreased educational aspirations among Black males (Walsemann and Bell, 2010).

The result of the failure to identify and academically nurture non-White students is that they are pushed into the school-to-prison pipeline. Non-White, lower-income children continue to participate in early education at much lower rates than children in higher-income homes, and the unequal allocation of resources leads to the very real resegregation of schools

(Darling-Hammond, 2013). In an all-too-common double whammy, non-White children are disciplined more harshly in K–12 and are less likely to be identified as gifted (Nittle, 2019). In fact, according to the US Department of Education, Black children are suspended three times more often than their White peers. Regionally, this can be much worse. Black students make up just 18 percent of children in preschool, but they represent nearly 50 percent of students suspended. In 2015, 13 Southern states were responsible for 55 percent of suspensions of 1.2 million Black students suspended. In 84 Southern K–12 schools, there was a 100 percent suspension rate among Black students. That is not a typo. All Black kids in 84 Southern schools were suspended at one time or another (Nittle, 2019).

Race operates in a similar fashion in higher education. Black and Latinx Americans increase their likelihood of obtaining and maintaining a good job by going to college, but their White peers still disproportionately hold better jobs compared with their overall education levels (Inside Higher Ed, 2019). As we look toward a growing economy once COVID-19 is under control, it will likely remain true that jobs created after a recession tend to require college degrees. However, as college costs rise, more low-wealth Blacks are borrowing to attend college, yet Blacks are less likely than Whites to complete college and more likely to default on student loans, adding to the Black–White wealth gap (Lee, 2020).

After controlling for high school grades and family income, White students are 20 percent more likely than Black students to receive a two-year associates degree (Barshay, 2020), and Black and Latinx students are overrepresented at less selective public and private colleges and drastically underrepresented at more selective institutions (Washington, 2020).

Much of this can be explained by the way in which Americans show more concern for ending wealth-based school achievement gaps than they do for Black–White and Latinx–White academic achievement gaps (Valant, 2020). Most American believe they live in a color-blind society where non-Whites often are not disadvantaged and are even suspected of actually being advantaged, despite all evidence to the contrary. When Americans were asked "how much of the difference in test scores between white students and Black students can be explained by discrimination against Blacks or injustices in society?" 44 percent of respondents chose "none" and only 10 percent chose "a great deal" (Valant, 2020).

This myopic vision of the impact of race goes much deeper. The authors, after completing this study, met with the superintendent of one of the urban schools that took part in the study. We were telling him about our early findings and mentioned that much of what he heard in the interviews, especially with police officers, was strikingly similar to what we heard from the high school teachers. As noted earlier, Ketchum is a former high school teacher, and the three began talking about how they would improve K–12 education, if given the chance. One thing led to another, and six years later, the authors are still both teaching concurrent enrollment students, on site, at the high school.

In this role, we have had some specific experiences that demonstrate frequently unintended color-blind racism. For example, there is a regional credit union that both authors can and do recommend to people as fair, honest and very well intentioned. This credit union has opened mini-branches at a few area Title I high schools. The branches handle some school banking matters, and many teachers utilize the on-campus branch for their personal banking. The school branch is run by two students per class period, all school day, every school day. Students in the program are required to commit to a full semester at that time period, and the school and credit union are very selective in choosing the students. The stated purpose of the position is to give urban students the job application and work skills necessary for entry-level jobs after they graduate from high school. Oddly, 98 percent of the students in the program come into it already having a part-time job, after school and on weekends. This would still make sense for students if the credit union also offered college scholarships, or jobs in one of their branches, yet they do neither. As each participating school has a branch manager, the credit union appears to have invested fairly heavily in this well-meaning but ineffective program designed to help poor, non-White kids. The value of the entire program collapses, however, because the folks who put it together never bothered to check if their assumption that these kids needed entry-level job application and job skills was correct.

The authors teach concurrent enrollment/dual credit offered by the University of Oklahoma, at no cost to students. The state has a program to pay tuition for high school seniors enrolling in concurrent enrollment courses, and the University of Oklahoma College of Arts and Sciences has a donor who covers the fees for the courses. Before this program was set up, no students from this school had applied to the University of Oklahoma in the prior seven years, and fewer than a dozen had been accepted in the previous two decades. Few students attended any four-year schools. Obviously, there is no difference between the academic potential of students from poor, non-White, urban schools and largely White, more affluent students in wealthier suburban schools. There is no difference in the percentage of academically talented students in suburban schools versus those from urban schools. In fact, universities are overlooking an incredibly large number of very talented students who should have the option of attending a top university. The University of Oklahoma basically recruits from the top 1–2 percent of students in the poorer Oklahoma City schools, compared with the top 30–50 percent of students from the more affluent suburban schools.

This is how systemic racism works. This is how color-blind racism operates. Title I high schools encourage more students to pursue vocational and technical training than four-year college degrees. Parents, teachers and even the students subscribe to the notion that the top few should attend a local directional college and the rest should train for blue-collar jobs. During our first year working with the school, we witnessed a high school senior with an ACT score of 24 (the average score for those admitted to the University of Oklahoma that year), who is Native American with tribal membership, being pushed by the school counselor toward a vocational/technical program despite his dream of attending college. The volunteers from the University of Oklahoma did not have enough time to work with him, and he never attended college. He is not a one-off story, though. Time after time, we heard well-meaning, mostly but not exclusively White teachers and administrators explain that vocational/technical training was best for these kids. One non-White administrator, who is no longer employed as an administrator, often stated publicly that "someone needs to be the apple-pickers in society, and these kids are the apple-pickers."

Since starting the concurrent enrollment program, this urban Title I high school has had 8–18 percent of each year's senior class accepted to the University of Oklahoma, with an even larger number going to other area universities. For the 2018–19 senior class, 54 percent of the senior class had been accepted to one or more four-year colleges or universities. We do not mention this to talk about our program, because it is not terribly unique. It is also not terribly expensive. Simply by taking non-credit college courses as high school juniors and then retaking the same classes as seniors, students have developed the skills necessary for success at major research colleges/universities (R-1 institutions).

Compare this with the city's incredibly well-funded science, technology, engineering and math (STEM) program, which takes students from all area high schools for half-days. This program has well-trained, talented STEM teachers and all the resources they could ever need. However, the entire program is funded by local industry, and their focus is on vocational and technological training. Top students from the very selective STEM program are less likely to attend a four-year college than the senior class at the school we work with. We would love to say that the authors are just that talented, but the difference is one of racism, classism and sexism in the form of setting the bar much lower for even the best students at Title I schools. At a wealthy suburban school, most kids will be expected to go to college. At urban Title I schools, almost no students are expected to attend college. Of course, some urban schools are much better at this than the average, but the difference in expectations is broad. On top of the typically less experienced teachers at urban schools, students also face low expectations. One could argue that this has to do with the costs of college, but our state has a program for low-income families that covers tuition and fees at state institutions, and the University of Oklahoma, like other large R1 institutions, has many scholarships available for other costs, including a work study program that offers room and board for 20 hours of work on campus.

Our overarching point in this chapter is that differential treatment is easily observable in all areas of society. It can be seen in traffic stops, healthcare, education and every other aspect of our daily lives. Given the overwhelming evidence of differential treatment of non-Whites, it is unclear why researchers and policymakers are still awaiting evidence of differential treatment for policy ideas, and why so many assume differential involvement, despite so much evidence to the contrary.

3

Law Enforcement Contact with Juveniles: Arrests and Citations

> Our job is to respond to the crimes that we're dispatched to and to stop and detain and arrest, if warranted, the person that committed the crime. ... We don't pick and choose that by race.
> Bob Kroll, Minneapolis
> Police Officers Federation President

Introduction

As outlined in more detail in previous chapters, disproportionate minority contact (DMC) is defined as the overrepresentation of minorities throughout the juvenile justice system. By definition, overrepresentation implies a comparison of the racial and ethnic characteristics of those in the juvenile justice system to racial and ethnic characteristics of a general geographic location. In addition, DMC refers not to a single comparison but to comparisons of the racial and ethnic makeup at multiple points—contact or decision points—in the juvenile justice system. As such, we examine race and ethnicity differences at three key points in the juvenile justice system to assess the extent of DMC. These points roughly correspond to the typical progression through the system: police contact, intake and detention, and the legal outcome or status of the referral. These decision points have also been described as "front-end" and "back-end" decision points (Charish et al, 2004). Front-end decisions refer to decisions made by police to arrest or detain. Back-end decisions refer to decisions made by the juvenile courts. These decisions include all adjudicatory and dispositional decisions. Between the front- and back-end decisions are those decisions made by court officials such as district attorneys whether to refer juveniles to the courts.

Figure 3.1: Typical progression through the juvenile justice system

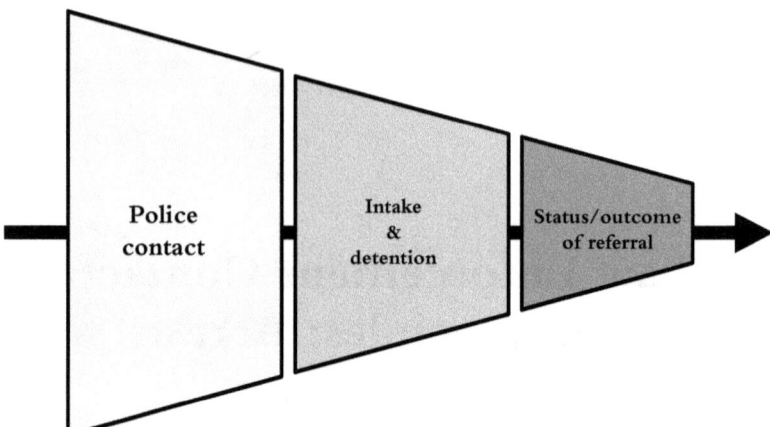

Figure 3.1 is a graphical depiction of the typical progression through the juvenile justice system. The figure illustrates several important features of the juvenile justice system. First, the simple progression through the system typically begins with police contact, followed by intake and detention, followed by the legal status or outcome of a case. Second, the figure illustrates the decreasing number of youths in the system as they progress through the system. More juveniles have contact with law enforcement than are detained; fewer juveniles have a legal outcome than have an intake or detention decision or contact with law enforcement. Finally, the figure is representative of the discretion employed by authorities at the various points in the system. Police have more discretion when they come into contact with a juvenile compared with judges at sentencing, simply because any interaction before the contact becomes official is limited to good judgment and existing laws. Similarly, the decision to walk away, verbally warn, give a written warning, cite or arrest is, within parameters, left to the judgment of the officer. We will return to this issue of discretion in the process at the end of this chapter when discussing the findings.

For most juveniles, their first encounter with the juvenile justice system involves police contact. In this chapter, we examine differences in the outcomes of police encounters. Specifically, we examine differences in arrests and citations from police report data. Before diving too deeply into an examination of the data, we need to describe briefly the juvenile justice process at the front-end decision points.

When coming into contact with juveniles, law enforcement officers have several options from which to choose. Said another way, law enforcement officers have discretion in terms of how to deal with the juvenile. First, the officer can take no formal action. In this case, the officer releases the juvenile to a parent or guardian or simply sends the juvenile to his or her home. No formal action or record is made. Second, the officer can issue a ticket or citation. In this case, the juvenile is formally cited and typically released to a parent or guardian or sent home. Finally, the officer can make an arrest. If a juvenile is arrested, the officer may release the juvenile to a guardian, request placement in a secure detention facility or place the juvenile in a Community Intervention Center (CIC). CICs are non-secure holding facilities for juveniles arrested for minor offenses who are not deemed in need of secure detention. Juveniles are typically held in CICs for up to 24 hours, until a parent or guardian can be located.

In this chapter, we present data about the initial decision point that potentially starts a juvenile's journey in the justice system: what the officer does when encountering a juvenile. We examine racial differences in officers' decisions to issue a citation and release or to arrest and detain the juvenile.

Police report data

We use data from police reports from the Oklahoma City metropolitan area. The data are from alternating years between 2006 and 2014. We included data for multiple years to determine if there were differences over time, that is, if the relationship between race and ethnicity and interactions with police changed over a six- to eight-year period. We used data from alternating years because of the extensive amount of data cleaning, coding and matching that was required. Using data from every other year permitted us to assess any changes but also reduced the amount of data cleaning and data management by half. We found no differences over time. Therefore, we do not stratify the data by year of police encounter.

The data contain a total of 44,126 police reports across the study period. Of those, 1,074 reports did not identify the juvenile's race or ethnicity. Our baseline dataset, then, contains information on 43,052 police reports. In fact, the police records have missing data on other variables as well. We note those in the results when we discuss specific analyses with variables with missing data.

Our primary focus is on racial and ethnic differences. The data provided the following race and ethnicity categories: White, Black, Native American,[1] Asian and Hispanic/Latinx. We present the findings using these categories. In addition, we present the data using the collapsed categories White, Asian and non-White. At first glance, it may seem excessive to present results using both sets of categories, especially since social scientists often overuse simplified race categories such as White and non-White (Kahn, 2017). Researchers typically rely on simplified categories of race and ethnicity for two general reasons. The first reason is empirical. That is, datasets often do not have enough observations that fall into various race or ethnicity categories. For empirical reasons, analysts simply combine non-White respondents in a catch-all "other" or "non-White" category. The second reason is more theoretical, or more accurately non-theoretical. That is, researchers often do not have a good theoretical explanation for how or why there might be differences between races, say between Native American and Latinx, as many Latinx have tribal ancestry no different from Native Americans, with the category being based on which side of the US border a tribe is from. We will discuss this a bit more in the final chapter. Neither of these reasons is particularly convincing. More than 100 years ago, the American sociologist W. E. B. Du Bois argued against the notion that race is a simple construct consisting of discrete groups such as "White" and "Black" (Du Bois, 1968, 2007).

We present findings using both the full list of race and ethnicity categories from the police reports (White, Black, Native American, Asian, Hispanic/Latinx) and the simplified categories of White, Asian and non-White. The non-White category is a combination of categories that represent Black and Brown people (Black, Native American and Hispanic). The reason for our choice is mostly theoretical. It is certainly not empirical, at least not in terms of the relative number of juveniles in the different categories of race and ethnicity. Our dataset is sufficiently large that we have enough observations within each racial and ethnic category (described in more detail in a later discussion). Our reason for presenting collapsed categories of race and ethnicity is mostly theoretical in that we believe that while differences between non-White juveniles exist and are important, it is also important to view the differences of non-White Black and Brown (Latinx, Native American) youth relative to the White majority. We do not categorize Asian juveniles in the non-White category because the outcomes for Asian juveniles are so different from juveniles who are Black or Brown. This is a somewhat empirical issue. In general, Black, Native American and Hispanic/Latinx juveniles have similar outcomes relative to White juveniles. Those similarities are generally to the disadvantage of non-White juveniles. Asian juveniles, however, tend to have outcomes very different than the other non-White juveniles. Asians generally have more positive outcomes. In fact, as the data show, Asian juveniles typically have advantageous outcomes even compared with White juveniles.[2]

The juveniles

Table 3.1 shows the summary descriptions of the characteristics of the juveniles listed in the police reports. In terms of race and ethnicity, there are more police encounters involving White juveniles (38.2 percent) than any other specific race and ethnic group, followed by encounters with Black juveniles (33.6 percent). Encounters with Hispanic/Latinx juveniles comprise almost a quarter (24.4 percent) of the cases.[3] Encounters with Native Americans and

Table 3.1: Summary descriptions of the study group characteristics (N = 43,052)

Characteristic	Frequency	Percentage
Race		
White	16,462	38.2
Black	14,450	33.6
Native American	1091	2.5
Asian	544	1.3
Hispanic/Latinx	10,505	24.4
Gender[a]		
Female	14,617	34.0
Male	28,426	66.0
Age		
Under 12	353	0.8
12–15	7,642	17.8
16–18	35,057	81.4

[a] There were nine cases where gender was not recorded on the police report.

Asian juveniles comprise less than 5 percent of the study group (2.5 percent and 1.3 percent, respectively). As noted previously, we present findings using the individual race and ethnicity categories (White, Black, Native American, Asian and Hispanic/Latinx) as well as the collapsed race and ethnicity categories (White, Asian and non-White). Table 3.1 shows that the combined non-White group of juveniles comprises well over half (60.5 percent) of all the encounters.[4] The encounters are overwhelmingly with male juveniles. Just under two thirds (66 percent) of all the police reports involve a male, while about one third (34 percent) of the encounters were with a female. In nine instances, the police report did not include the gender of the juvenile. Thus, in our statistical models that use gender, the number of observations is reduced by nine. The age of the juveniles ranges from as young as eight to as old as 18. Less than 1 percent of the juveniles were under the age of 12 (0.8 percent). Just under one fifth were between 12 and 15 years old (17.8 percent). The majority of the police encounters were with juveniles between the ages of 16 and 18 (81.4 percent). The mean and median ages of the juveniles in the police encounters are 16.4 and 17, respectively.

Contact with police

It is important to note that the number of observations (N = 43,052) presented in Table 3.1 does not represent 43,052 youths, rather the cases represent the number of formal police reports filed. Some of the juveniles are included in the dataset more than once. That is, there may be more than one report in which a given juvenile is cited or arrested. In fact, we are not certain precisely how many individuals are represented in the dataset. The police data are from different locations (precincts and districts) within the same metropolitan area. Data from some of the districts did not include a unique identifier for individual juveniles. In addition, some years of data from the districts included a unique identifier, while other years did not. As such, we do not know exactly how many individual youths are represented in the data. We can, however, estimate the number of individuals based on the data from districts and years that do contain unique identifiers for individual juveniles. Of the 43,052 police reports, 10,083 have a unique identifier for each juvenile. Using those data, we estimated the number of individuals in the dataset. In the police reports with unique juvenile identifiers ($N = 10,083$), there are 6,663 unique individuals. The ratio of unique cases to the total number of cases is 0.6608 ($6,663 \div 10,083 = 0.6608$). Based on the records with unique identifiers, we estimate that about two thirds (66.1 percent) of all the cases are unique individuals. An alternative way to think about the number of juveniles in the dataset is to consider the inverse of the previous ratio. There are 10,083 total observations with identifiers; 6,663 are unique. That ratio is 1.51 ($10,083 \div 6,663 = 1.51$). Based on the records with unique identifiers, we estimate that each individual is represented in the dataset, on average, about one and a half times (1.51). Using data with identifying information, we estimate that the 43,052 observations represent approximately 28,449 youths ($43,052 \times 0.6608 = 28,449$).

Estimating the number of unique individuals in the dataset of juvenile arrests and citations is more than an academic exercise. It is, in fact, an estimate of DMC. It is a crude measure, but it is a measure nonetheless. A recent United Nations report drew harsh conclusions about the state of the US criminal justice system based on aggregate percentages in the justice system versus in the general population: "Roughly 12 percent of the United States population is black. Yet in 2011, Black Americans constituted 30 percent of persons arrested for a property offense and 38 percent of persons arrested for a violent offense. Black youths account for 16 percent of all children in America yet make up 28 percent of juvenile arrests" (The Sentencing Project, 2013). Recall that the very definition of DMC is the overrepresentation of minorities throughout the juvenile justice system compared with the representation of minorities in the general population for the same geographical location. We calculate the estimated number of youths in the juvenile justice system at this front-end point of entry into the justice system to determine if there are differences between the racial makeup of the geographical location and those in the juvenile justice system.

Table 3.2: Distribution of individual youths in the dataset

Race	Observed distribution of the 6,663 unique individuals		Estimated distribution of unique individuals for the entire study group	
	Frequency	Percentage	Frequency	Percentage
White	2,881	43.2	18,598	43.2
Black	1,983	29.8	12,830	29.8
Native American	169	2.5	1,076	2.5
Asian	72	1.1	474	1.1
Hispanic/Latinx	1,558	23.4	10,074	23.4
Total	6,663	100.0	43,052	100.0

Table 3.2 shows the frequency and percentages of race and ethnicity for the 6,663 unique juveniles identified in the dataset.[5] The breakdown by race shows that White juveniles are the largest category (43.2 percent), followed by Black (29.8 percent) and Hispanic/Latinx (23.4 percent) juveniles. Using those percentages, we calculated the estimated count of unique juveniles in the full dataset (N = 43,052). The specific counts by race are of less interest than the percentages, but we estimate that our dataset contains just under 20,000 White juveniles (N = 18,598). The estimated counts for each race and ethnic group are listed in Table 3.2.

The estimated counts and percentages of the race and ethnic groups are most interesting and useful compared with the counts and percentages from the general population. The race and ethnicity comparisons are presented in Table 3.3. We do not have specific estimates for the number of juveniles by race in the Oklahoma City metropolitan area. We do, however, have good estimates from the US Census for the number of juveniles by race in the entire state (column 1 in Table 3.3) and the number of adults by race in the Oklahoma City metropolitan area (column 2 in Table 3.3). Inspection of the race and ethnicity percentages shows a clear pattern. Whites are underrepresented in the arrest and citation data compared with their numbers in the general population. By contrast, juveniles of color (especially Black and Hispanic/Latinx juveniles) are overrepresented. According to the US Census Bureau (2010), the 2010 juvenile population in Oklahoma was 72.3 percent White. Yet White juveniles comprise only 43.2 percent of the youths who were issued a citation or arrested and detained. Similar to White juveniles, Asian juveniles are underrepresented in the police data compared with their representation in the general population. Asian youths account for 1.1 percent of the law enforcement encounters but comprise double that in the general population for the state (2.2 percent).

Table 3.3: Comparison of percentages by race in Oklahoma and in the study group

Race	2010 Oklahoma juvenile census[a]	2010 Oklahoma City adult census[b]	2006–2014 police data
White	72.3	67.7	43.2
Black	11.0	14.5	29.8
Native American	14.6	2.8	2.5
Asian	2.2	4.5	1.1
Hispanic/Latinx[c]	16.4	19.1	23.4
Total Number	510,256	579,999	43,052

Note: The numbers are percentages.
[a] Source: Office of Juvenile Justice and Delinquency Prevention, 2010. The data are state-level data of individuals aged 8–17.
[b] Source: US Census Bureau, 2010. The data are for adults age 18 and over in the Oklahoma City census metropolitan area.
[c] The total for Hispanic/Latinx may include individuals of various racial groups.

The story is very different for juveniles of color. Juveniles who are Black, for example, make up approximately 11 percent of the statewide youth population, yet Black juveniles make up almost a third (29.8 percent) of those arrested or issued a citation. Hispanic/Latinx youths are also overrepresented in the police report data; Hispanic/Latinx youths comprise almost a quarter (23.4 percent) of the arrest and citation data but account for only about 16 percent of the youth in the state.

The case of Native American juveniles is interesting. Native youth account for about 2.5 percent of the arrest and citation police data. They make up about 14.6 percent of the statewide youth. Note the large difference in the percentage of Native American youth in the state (14.6 percent) versus the number of Native American adults in the Oklahoma City metropolitan area. This is consistent with demographic patterns. Generally, there are higher concentrations of minorities in the urban areas of Oklahoma City. The opposite is true for Native Americans. Many of the tribal lands are located well outside the Oklahoma City area.

Race and arrest

With a clear picture of the police encounter contact data in hand, we turn to examining the relationship between race and ethnicity and the outcome of the police encounter. Specifically, we will examine in detail differences in receiving a citation or a ticket versus being arrested. As noted in more detail in previous discussions, encounters with the police typically are the entry point for juveniles to move into the justice system. Police often have a high level of discretion in terms of how to proceed in each situation with a youth (Bishop and Leiber, 2011; Peck and Jennings, 2016). We examine racial differences in whether police officers issue a simple citation or ticket versus arresting and detaining the juvenile.

A final note about data-related issues. Recall these data are from all formal police reports from the Oklahoma City metropolitan area that involved a juvenile. As such, the data represent the population of all observations in the time period of the study. The data are not a sample. Therefore, we do not present inferential statistics such as p-values or confidence intervals. The values presented are not estimates of the population values derived from a sample. The values presented are the values in the population.

Figure 3.2 shows the percentages of police encounters with youth that ended in either a ticket or citation and arrest. Most encounters end with a ticket or citation. In fact, almost three quarters of the encounters (72.2 percent) resulted in a citation. A little more than one quarter (27.8 percent) resulted in arrest. Figure 3.3 presents the citation and arrest results by race and ethnicity categories. The figures show a clear and distinct pattern: encounters involving White and Asian youth have a higher percentage of tickets and citations compared with encounters involving youth of color. The percentages for White and Asian youth are very similar (80.3 and 82.9 percent, respectively). By contrast, the percentages of tickets and citations for the Black, Native American and Hispanic/Latinx youth range from 62.2 percent (Native American) to 70.4 percent

Figure 3.2: Summary of arrests and tickets/citations (N = 43,052)

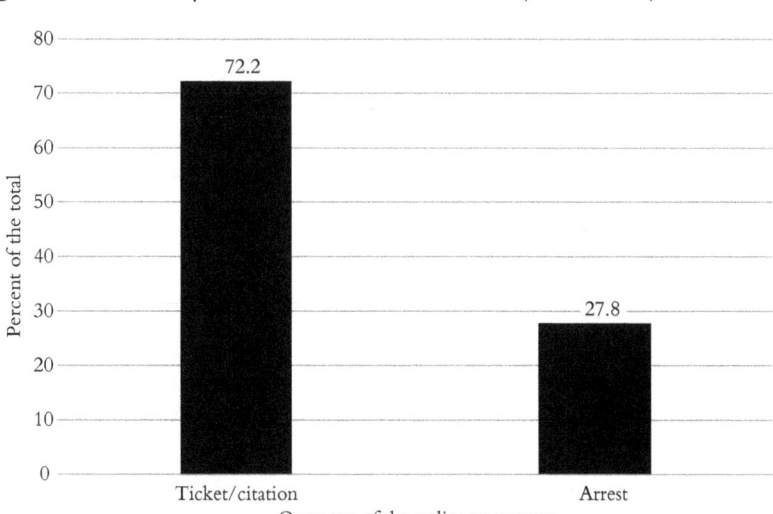

Figure 3.3: Arrests and tickets/citations by race/ethnicity (N = 43,052)

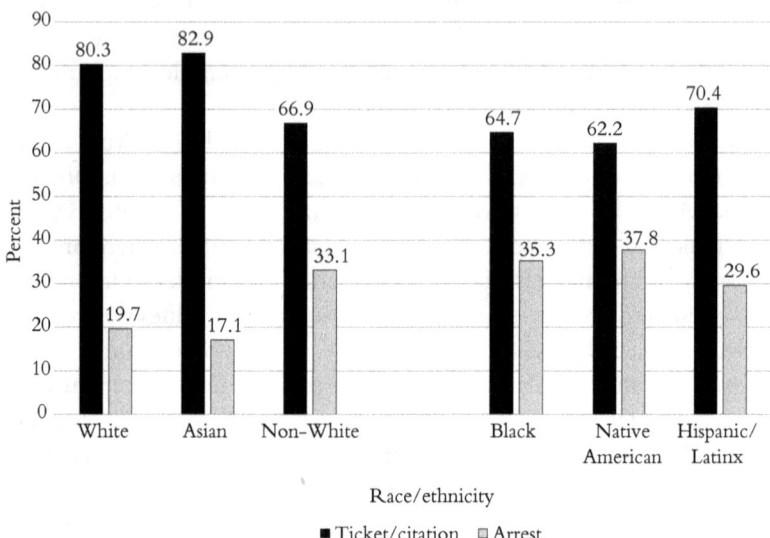

(Hispanic/Latinx). Interestingly, but similar to previous studies (Johnson and Betsinger, 2009), we find that not only are Asian youth similar to White youth compared with Black, Latinx and Native American youth, but Asian youth have a slight advantage compared with White youth. Asian youth are more likely to receive a citation or ticket compared with White juveniles. We analyzed data from other counties and found that in counties such as the one used in this study, Asian juveniles were treated significantly better than Whites. This was true in other counties with small Asian populations. In one county with a small city but a large military base and a much larger Asian population, Asian juveniles were no longer much less likely than Whites to have official contact but were now arrested and charged at levels almost identical to Whites. That is to say that the Asian advantage, in terms of coming under the scrutiny of the juvenile justice system, seems to disappear as the Asian population comes to represent a greater share of the area population. Though not specific to juveniles, studies show that Asians are expected by society to commit crimes both by type and frequency at a rate similar to Whites (Chai, 2014).

The inverse is true as well. Encounters involving White and Asian youth have a lower percentage of arrests compared with encounters with juveniles of color. Encounters with White (19.7 percent) and Asian (17.1 percent) youth result in arrest less than 20 percent of the time. For non-White and non-Asian youth, however, the percentages are significantly higher. The percentage of encounters ending in arrest for Native American youth (37.8 percent) is almost double that of White and Asian youth. Encounters with Black and Hispanic/Latinx youth result in arrest 30 percent or more of the time.

The figures and tables presented to this point are generally descriptive in nature. They show the percentages of observations that fall into one category or another, for example, the percentage of encounters that end in arrest or that same percentage by race categories. In later analyses, we present more complex (multivariate), predictive analyses using log binomial regression models.[6] These statistical models show the relative risk of an event (e.g., being arrested) for the different racial and ethnic groups while controlling for other factors. These other factors are described in more detail in a later section. We present risk ratios (RR), also referred to as relative risk, from these log binomial regression models. Risk ratios indicate the relative probability of some occurrence or event (such as being arrested) for two (or more) groups (such as non-White and White juveniles). A risk ratio of 1.0 indicates that the event is equally likely in the two groups. A risk ratio greater than 1.0 indicates that the event is more likely in the first group. A risk ratio less than 1.0 indicates that the event is less likely in the first group.[7]

Before presenting the multivariate statistical models, we present the results of unadjusted log binomial regression analyses that estimate the risk (probability) of arrest by racial and ethnicity categories. These unadjusted models have no other variables in the analysis. Figure 3.4 shows the results from the unadjusted models. The unadjusted analyses produce results that are identical to the percentages shown in the previous figures. We are presenting

Figure 3.4: Unadjusted risk ratios of arrest by race/ethnicity (N = 43,052)

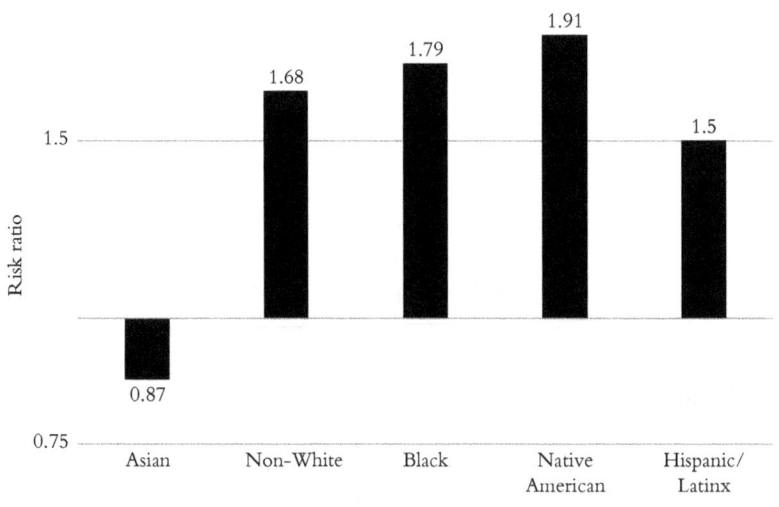

the data using the risk ratios as a baseline for the multivariate models we present later in the chapter. In addition, the results in Figure 3.4 (and the other figures that present risk ratios) show the risk ratios for the juveniles in the race and ethnicity groups listed in the figure compared with White juveniles. In other words, White juveniles are the reference group, and the categories presented in the figures are all relative to the reference group.

One final note about the figures showing the risk ratios: the figures are presented on a log scale. The reason for this is simple. The adjusted risk ratios are calculated by exponentiating the generalized linear regression coefficients. Because the coefficients are exponentiated, they are no longer symmetric on a linear (arithmetic) scale. If the exponentiated ratios were presented on a linear scale, they would visually misrepresent the values of the risk ratios.[8]

Figure 3.4 shows that non-White juveniles collectively have a risk more than one and a half times that of White juveniles (RR = 1.68). Native American youth have the highest risk of arrest: they are almost twice as likely to be arrested than White youth (RR = 1.91). Hispanic/Latinx juveniles have the lowest risk of the non-White juveniles, though their risk of arrest is 50 percent higher (RR = 1.50) than that of White juveniles.[9] Like the percentage differences shown previously, the risk ratios show that Asian juveniles are less likely to be arrested than White juveniles (RR = 0.87). Asian youth have 0.87 times the risk of arrest compared with White youth. To illustrate the point that risk ratios produce the same results as the percentage differences presented in previous tables and figures but are merely a different way of expressing those differences, consider the percentages for White youth (19.7 percent) and Asian youth (17.1). The percentage difference is calculated as $(17.1 - 19.7)/19.7 = -13.1$. The same percentage difference is expressed by the risk ratio of 0.87 ($0.87 - 1.0 = -13$).

Types of offenses and arrest

The data—both the percentages and the risk ratios—show a clear difference in arrest rates by race and ethnicity. These differential arrest rates, however, are not necessarily indicative of differential treatment, bias or other problems in the juvenile justice system. The simple version of the argument that the differences are not necessarily indicative of differential police treatment or bias is that juveniles of color (Black, Hispanic/Latinx and Native American) are committing more offenses or more severe offenses. In fact, some research has suggested that non-White youth tend to have more legal issues compared with White youth, such as a prior record and more serious offenses (Feld, 1999a; Mitchell, 2009). The factors tend to combine with race to create disadvantages for non-White juveniles (Leiber and Fox, 2005), such as higher arrest rates. We will take up the issue of whether non-White youth are committing more offenses in Chapter 5. In this section, we will address

Figure 3.5: Summary of types of offense (N = 32,966)

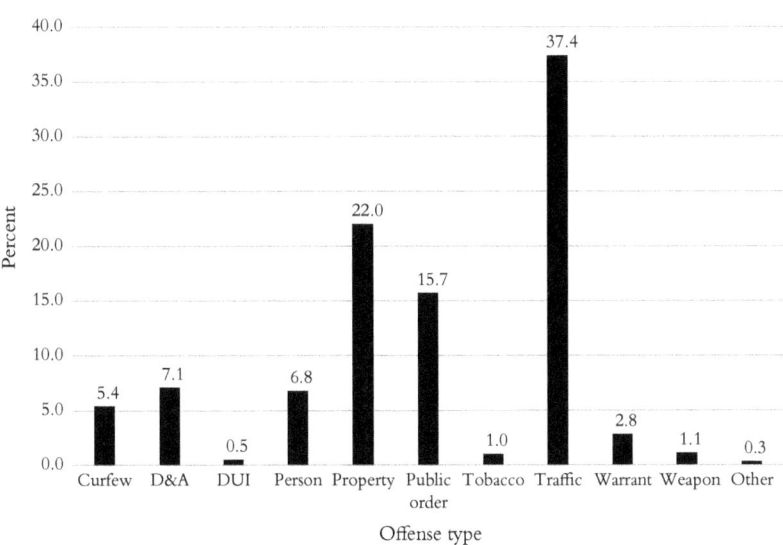

the issue of more severe offenses as a reason for the differential arrest rates. Specifically, in this section we present data that show the types of crimes for which the youth are cited or arrested.

Figures 3.5 and 3.6 show the types of offenses recorded in the police data. There are a couple of important notes about the figures. First, the number of observations in the figures is lower than in the previous analyses. There are 32,966 observations represented in Figures 3.5 and 3.6. There are fewer observations than in the previous analyses because 10,086 of the police records did not have an offense listed on the report. Second, all offenses were categorized into the 11 different offense types presented. Most are straightforward, though several need explanations. Curfew offenses are violations for youth being outside or loitering without adult supervision typically at night or other specified hours. D&A offenses are drug- and alcohol-related offenses other than driving while impaired. DUI (driving under the influence) is the offense of driving, operating or being in control of a motor vehicle while impaired by alcohol or other drugs. Person offenses are those in which an individual is the victim of some action; these are typically some form of assault or intimidation. Property offenses, by contrast, are those offenses in which property is the object of the action; these are typically some form of action to take or damage property. Public order offenses refer to those violations that are generally prohibited by society; these offenses are generally "victimless" crimes such as prostitution, gambling or playing loud music. Tobacco offenses relate to minors buying, selling and using tobacco. In Oklahoma for the years included in the analysis, state law prohibited juveniles

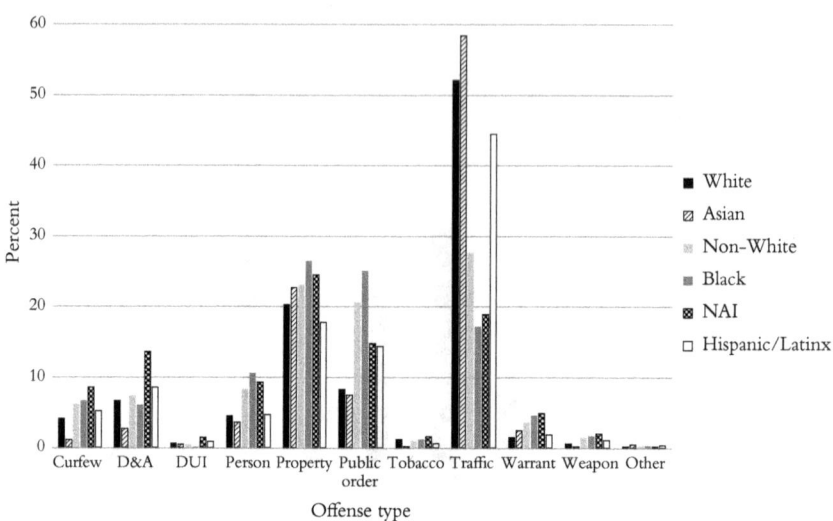

Figure 3.6: Types of offense by race/ethnicity (N = 32,966)

under the age of 18 from buying, selling and using tobacco products. As of May 2020, the minimum age is 21. Traffic offenses are violations related to operating a motor vehicle. Infractions labeled as Warrant offenses refer to situations when a court has issued a warrant for an individual's arrest for a separate offense. Weapons offenses are violations of regulations that control deadly weapons, such as firearms, ammunition, knives and explosives. The Other offense category is a residual category for infractions that do not fit into any of the other ten categories.

Traffic violations are the most common type of offense. Over one third (37.4 percent) of the police reports were for traffic violations. The next most common types of offenses were property crimes (22.0 percent) and crimes against the public order (15.7 percent). The least common offenses were for warrants, weapons, tobacco and DUIs, each representing less than 5 percent of the total. The offenses listed by race (Figure 3.6) show some interesting trends. Traffic offenses are the most frequently occurring charge overall as well as for Whites, Asians and Hispanics. Traffic offenses are not, however, the most frequent charge for Black (17.2 percent) or Native American (18.9 percent) juveniles. In fact, for Blacks, two categories of charges are more frequent than traffic offenses: property crimes (26.5 percent) and crimes against the public (25.1 percent). In addition to lower rates of traffic offenses for Black and Native American youths, other noticeable differences are the significantly lower percentages of curfew, drug and alcohol, tobacco and weapons charges against Asian youths, with each percentage being at or less than 1 percent. Drug and alcohol charges against Native American youths is also significantly higher than for the other race and ethnicity categories.

Figure 3.7: Offenses that ended in arrest by race/ethnicity (N = 10,275)

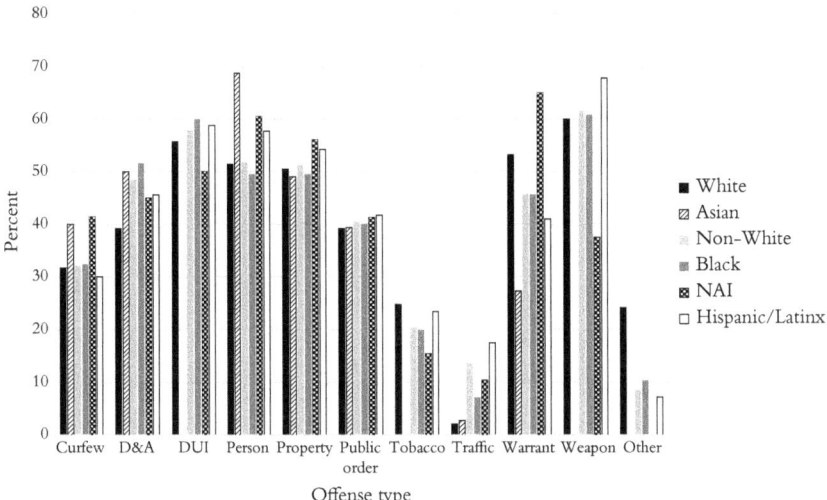

The previous figures show the overall percentages of the offense categories. Most of the police encounters end with a citation or ticket being issued to the juvenile (72.2 percent, see Figure 3.2). Figure 3.7, however, presents the encounters that resulted in arrest by the offense type and race and ethnicity. The number of observations in Figure 3.7 is 10,275. This represents the number of arrests out of the 32,966 police reports that included an offense category or charge category. The most obvious finding is that while traffic violations are the most common offense overall, traffic violations have the lowest percentage of encounters that end in arrest. Interestingly, Hispanic/Latinx youth are almost twice as likely to be arrested on a traffic charge compared with the next highest group. Almost a fifth of Hispanic/Latinx youth (17.5 percent) were arrested for a traffic violation. The next highest group, Native American youth, had a percentage of 10.4 percent. By contrast, White and Asian youths were arrested for traffic offenses at significantly lower rates, 2.0 percent and 2.7 percent, respectively.

We now turn to the multivariate statistical models calculating risk of arrest (versus being issued a citation). Recall from Figure 3.4 that the unadjusted (bivariate) models showed that Asian youth were less likely to be arrested than White youth and that Black, Latinx and Native American non-White youth were roughly 1.5 to 2.0 times more likely than White youth to be arrested. Those models did not control for or take account of any other factors. The multivariate models include control variables for the offense type as just outlined. In addition, the multivariate models control for the age and gender of the juvenile.

Figure 3.8: Adjusted risk ratios of arrest by race/ethnicity (N = 32,966)

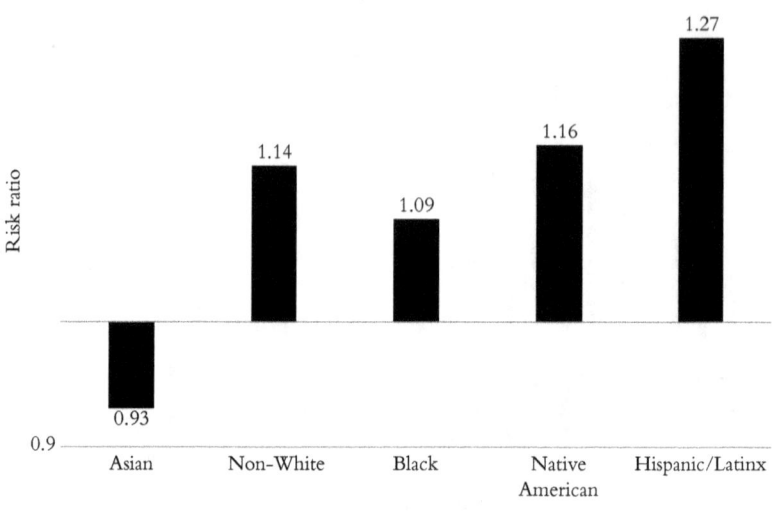

The results from the multivariate regression models are presented in Figure 3.8. The findings are clear: after controlling for offense type, gender and age, race and ethnic group maintains a strong relationship with arrest. As a group, non-White (Black, Native American and Hispanic/Latinx) juveniles are 14 percent more likely to be arrested than are White juveniles, after controlling for type of offense and gender and age. Examining the specific race and ethnicity category differences compared with White youth shows that Hispanic/Latinx juveniles have the highest risk of arrest (RR = 1.27), about 27 percent higher than White juveniles. Black youth have the lowest disadvantage among the non-White juveniles with a 10 percent higher risk of arrest compared with White juveniles (RR = 1.09). As in the previous unadjusted (bivariate) analyses, Asian juveniles have a lower probability of arrest (RR = 0.93) compared with White juveniles. Asian youth have a 7 percent lower probability of arrest than do White youth.[10]

Conclusion

Entry into the justice system typically begins with an encounter with the police. This chapter examined differences in contact with police and police officers' decisions to arrest versus issuing a citation or ticket. As in many previous studies (see, e.g., Piliavin and Briar, 1964; Sealock and Simpson, 1998; Charish et al, 2004; Piquero, 2008; Donnelly, 2017), we found substantial racial and ethnic group differences in police contact and arrest.

Though the findings are consistent with previous studies, these findings are important for a number of reasons. First, the findings indicate these data are similar to other data. The implication is that police officers in our dataset interact with juveniles similarly to police officers in other areas. Moreover, the juveniles in our dataset behave similarly to juveniles in other areas. This is no trivial point. Our argument is largely empirically based; we rely on the data to tell the story of DMC. The findings show that non-White youth, especially Black, Latinx and Native American youth, are more likely to have a formal interaction with police that results in a citation or arrest. Black youth are represented in the police report data between two and three times their representation in the population. Similarly, Hispanic/Latinx youth are overrepresented in the police report data, though not to the same extent as Black youth. Native American youth are represented in the police data approximately proportionate to their numbers in the population.[11] White and Asian youth are underrepresented in the police data. The data also show that once a juvenile has had contact with a police officer, non-White youth are more likely to be arrested as opposed to cited or ticketed. Furthermore, after controlling for other legal (offense type) and extralegal (gender and age) factors, the racial and ethnic group differences remain: Asian youth are less likely than White youth to be arrested, while Black, Native American and Hispanic/Latinx youth are more likely than White youth to be arrested.

Second, the findings cast doubt on the argument that DMC is simply the product of non-White juveniles committing more severe criminal or deviant acts. This line of argument typically suggests that non-White youth commit more offenses and/or more severe offenses. We address the issue of criminality in more detail in Chapter 5. The findings presented here suggest that even after controlling for types of offenses, the outcomes of police encounters differ by racial and ethnic categories.

It is important to note that the data presented here represent only those police encounters with juveniles for which there is a formal record. Our data do not include encounters in which an officer addressed the juvenile in an informal manner and did not submit a formal report. As such, it is possible the data overestimate or underestimate the extent of contact non-White youth have with police. It is well established that police officers have a high degree of discretion when they address an issue with a member of the public (Young, 2011). It may be the case that officers tend to release non-White and White juveniles without making a report at roughly the same rates. If this were the case, the formal report data would accurately capture the total amount of police contact and the degree of non-White contact.

Alternatively, it could be the case that police tend to release non-White youth with no formal report at a higher rate than they release White youth. This scenario seems highly unlikely given the distribution of White and non-White youth in the general population and in the police report data.

White youth comprise roughly 70 percent of the general population in Oklahoma. Non-White youth comprise about 30 percent of the general population. By contrast, White youth make up about 40 percent of the police data, while non-White youth comprise about 60 percent of the police data. These numbers are almost the inverse of one another. If the police data are representative of the amount of deviance and criminality in the population, it would mean that White youth commit offenses at about half the rate of non-White youth, or that non-White youth commit offenses at about double the rate of White youth. On its face, this seems unlikely. The more plausible explanation is that police encounters are more likely to result in no formal report for White youth compared with non-White youth (Pryor et al, 2020). As such, our use of formal police report data likely underestimates the problem of disproportionate minority contact.

Notes

[1] The police reports use the term 'Native American Indian' but we use the term 'Native American' throughout the book.

[2] Our intention is not to contribute to the so-called model minority myth related to Asians. The myth of the model minority is founded largely on stereotypes that characterize Asian Americans as polite, law-abiding and high achieving. Asian children are often viewed as math or music geniuses with high levels of drive and ambition. The negative and divisive social and psychological consequences of the model minority stereotype are well documented (Kiang et al, 2017). Our purpose is not to further the model minority myth. It may be the case that the differences between Asian, non-White and White juveniles are a manifestation of the myth.

[3] We recognize the complexity and issues surrounding usage of the terms Latino/Latina and Hispanic. The terms "Hispanic" and "Latino" generally have been used in the United States to refer collectively and interchangeably to individuals of Latin American or Spanish origin (Oquendo, 1995; National Advisory Committee on Racial, Ethnic and Other Populations, 2014). More accurately, Hispanic refers to persons who speak Spanish natively (or who have Spanish-speaking ancestry) and Latino refers more generally to persons of Latin American origin and ancestry (Oquendo, 1995). Nevertheless, we use the combined label of Hispanic/Latinx. As part of the label, we use the term Latinx, which is a gender-neutral alternative to Latino. The term more fully includes people who are gender fluid and addresses the issues around using inherently masculine terms to describe all genders of Latin origin (Cashman, 2018).

[4] The percentages represent the race and ethnicity of juveniles in the encounters with police. The unit of analysis is the encounter. These percentages are not based on the number of unique individuals in the dataset in a particular race and ethnicity category. The issue of the unit of analysis and how it reflects disproportionate minority contact is discussed in more detail in this chapter.

[5] Of course, it is not necessary to calculate the estimated number of unique individuals in the dataset to establish disproportionate representation of minorities in the juvenile justice system. The important point from the table is the percentages. However, calculating the number of unique individuals allows us to compare the number of individuals in our dataset with the number of individuals in the population. The data in Table 3.1 show a similar pattern to findings from other studies of DMC, both in Oklahoma and in other states.

6. The log binomial model is a binomial generalized linear model (GLM) with a log link function. The model is an alternative to logistic regression (Long and Freese, 2001). It is becoming increasingly popular as an alternative to logistic regression because the model estimates adjusted relative risk (risk ratios) rather than adjusted odds ratios (McNutt et al, 2003).

7. Often, logistic regression has been the analytic method of choice for modeling a binary outcome. The logistic regression model estimates adjusted odds ratios. Odds ratios are hard to comprehend directly and are usually interpreted as relative risk, the probability of the event occurring in one group versus another. Using odds ratios as an estimate of relative risk is fraught with problems, namely because odds ratios overestimate relative risk (McNutt et al, 2003). This is especially the case when the modeled event is relatively common, generally anything greater than 10 percent (Davies et al, 1998). Because we are interested in estimating risk of an event (e.g., arrest), not the ratio of the logged odds of the event, we present risk ratios from the log binomial regression models.

8. Displaying these values on a linear scale would be very misleading because changes in the ratio of the risk cannot be lower than zero, and a change from a risk ratio between 0.5 and 0.4 is the same relative change as that between 2.0 and 2.5. On a linear scale, however, the difference between 0.5 and 0.4 is only 0.1. The difference between 2.0 and 2.5 is 0.5. On a linear scale, 0.5 is 5 times larger than 0.1. Such visual discrepancies get larger and larger the closer the coefficients get to zero (Szklo and Nieto, 2018).

9. Another way to express the risk ratio is in terms of the percentage difference between the group of interest and the reference group. The percent difference is calculated by $((RR - 1.0) \times 100)$. Thus, a risk ratio of 1.50 represents a 50 percent higher risk $((1.50 - 1.0) \times 100) = 50$.

10. These risk ratios may appear somewhat less dramatically different from other studies. The reason is because we are presenting risk ratios rather than odds ratios. Previously, we noted that odds ratios always overestimate the probability or risk of an event. Sometimes the overestimation is extreme, especially as the probability of an event exceeds 0.10. For example, a previous study assessing arrest rates in Oklahoma showed that Black youth were 1.2 times (OR = 1.20 or 20 percent) more likely than White youth to be arrested (Charish et al, 2004). The risk we report is that Black youth have about a 10 percent higher risk of arrest (RR = 1.09). That difference is certainly attributable to the use of risk ratios versus odds ratios. In fact, we ran logistic regression analyses on our data to estimate the odds ratios. Those analyses showed, for example, that Black youth have an odds ratio of 1.16.

11. The distribution of Native American Indians in Oklahoma is significantly different than that of other racial and ethnic groups. In the greater Oklahoma City area, where the data were collected, Native American Indians comprise less than 3 percent. Yet Native American Indian youth comprise almost 15 percent of juveniles statewide. Native American Indian youth are represented in the police data at 2.5 percent, very near the numbers in the Oklahoma City area. The other racial and ethnic minority groups have higher percentages in the Oklahoma City area compared with their number statewide.

4

The Juvenile Justice System: Intake Decisions and Outcomes

> We've got to make sure that the young, violent, serious juvenile offender is punished, that it's fair punishment, that it's punishment that fits the crime and that is understood and that is anticipated and expected.
>
> Janet Reno, Attorney General of the United States

Introduction

In this chapter, we focus on the disproportionate contact and outcomes within the juvenile justice system. The justice system has so-called front-end decision points and back-end decision points. The front-end points refer to decisions about intake of the juvenile. These are decisions about what to do with the referred juvenile, for example, whether to file a petition (charge) or decline to file a charge. The back-end points refer to decisions about how to handle a juvenile's case once a charge has been filed. These are the outcomes or disposition of the case, such as referring the juvenile to custody, dismissing the case or probation, to name a few.

Researchers, justice-reform advocates and policymakers have focused a great deal on disproportionate contact and outcomes within the juvenile justice system since Congress passed the Juvenile Justice and Delinquency Prevention Act (JJDP Act) in 1974. This has resulted in a significant amount of research beginning with when a juvenile enters the system. However, the court system is much better documented than is the police part of the system. Once a juvenile enters the juvenile justice system, a record of every decision, action and outcome is recorded. By contrast, juveniles' interactions with police are not necessarily documented. Many police interactions have no formal report or data recorded (see the discussion in the previous chapter).

A voluminous amount of available data shows a consistent pattern: non-White adults and non-White juveniles tend to have less favorable outcomes in both the front-end and back-end decision points compared with White juveniles (Piquero, 2008; Peck and Jennings, 2016). In fact, a comprehensive review of differential treatment in the juvenile justice system found that juveniles of color are overrepresented at every point in the juvenile justice system from arrest to sentencing (National Council on Crime and Delinquency, 2007; Leiber and Peck, 2015). Research suggests that race differences tend to be lowest at the front-end decision points (detention and intake) compared with back-end points (adjudication and judicial disposition) (Bishop and Leiber, 2011), though many studies show a "correction effect" where judges or district attorneys (DAs) charge fewer non-Whites than Whites, though this "correction effect" does little to change the total rate of disproportionate minority contact (DMC) (Secret and Johnson, 1997; Bishop and Frazier, 1988; Lieber and Jamieson, 1995; Bishop et al, 2010).

Finally, what happens in the justice system has significant consequences. Whether due to labeling, differential association or other mechanisms, once a juvenile is in the system, the likelihood that he or she will stay in the system or return to the system increases. In fact, some literature suggests that what has the most substantial effect on juvenile court outcomes is prior experience in the system, especially prior record and prior disposition (Rodriguez, 2010; Bishop and Leiber, 2011).

In the pages to follow, we examine differences by race and ethnicity within the juvenile justice system. We examine these differences at both the front-end intake decision point and the back-end point. At the front-end intake point, we examine whether referred cases are declined, diverted, placed on informal probation or have a petition filed. At the back-end disposition point, we analyze the disposition of how those cases are resolved. Specifically, we examine the likelihood of the juvenile cases being dismissed, placed on probation, transferred to adult court, placed in Oklahoma Office of Juvenile Affairs (OJA) custody, or convicted and sentenced as an adult.

Area police

Before turning to an analysis of the data, it is important to have a basic understanding of the way the juvenile justice system works in the area studied, that is, the basic components of the system and its processes. Juvenile courts, even within a state, may work very differently (Feld, 1999b). For this reason, we will give the broad parameters of the system relevant to this study.

Multiple entities comprise the juvenile justice system in Oklahoma. The system consists of agencies and organizations at the state and county levels, as well as local and municipal levels. These agencies and organizations include district juvenile courts, DAs, county judges and commissioners, and state, county and city law enforcement agencies. OJA is the state agency charged with coordinating and integrating these components of the system.

In addition, OJA is responsible for developing juvenile justice programs, coordinating out-of-home residential placement and operating three secure juvenile detention centers. OJA has district offices throughout the state. The various agencies and organizations are subject to the provisions of the state juvenile code in Title 10 of the Oklahoma Statutes.

As described previously, law enforcement officers have considerable discretion when encountering a juvenile. Officers have several options for dealing with a juvenile: do nothing/give a verbal warning, issue a ticket or citation, or make an arrest. Without documentation of a police–civilian interaction there are typically no data on these informal events. By definition, no written warning, citation or arrest occurs, so there is no formal interaction. If the officer issues a ticket or citation, the juvenile is formally charged and typically released, depending on the circumstances, to a parent or guardian. If a juvenile is arrested, the officer may release the juvenile to his/her guardian, place the juvenile in a Community Intervention Center (CIC) or request placement in a secure detention facility.

Area court system

If the juvenile is charged with an offense, the charge sheet prepared by the officer may be sent to the city attorney or to the county's DA for an intake disposition. The intake disposition typically involves an intake assessment and preparation of intake recommendations by OJA staff. Juveniles placed in a non-secure CIC may be charged in municipal court or county district court depending on the specific terms of any existing interlocal agreement. Interlocal agreements between tribes and local police are common, with most juvenile tribal members moved to a tribal-run juvenile facility. This facility is run by a single local tribe, however this tribe has agreements with others, so that most area juveniles with tribal membership are sent to this facility.

Regardless of an existing interlocal agreement, by state law, juveniles placed in a secure detention facility cannot be charged in municipal court. If law enforcement officers have submitted the charges to the local city attorney, the city attorney may refer the case to the county's DA, dismiss the case or process the case through the municipal court, with outcomes ranging from dismissal to the imposition of fines and/or terms and conditions involving receipt of services and/or participation in community service.

As is common in many jurisdictions, the county juvenile court works very differently from the criminal courts. Full trials are rare as almost all cases proceed by agreement between the DA and the public defender's office, with the judge having the final say. The DA decides which cases to proceed with and will then typically meet with the public defender. The two will typically agree to some sort of treatment or punishment, with the expressed desire to do what is in the best interest of the child. It is extremely rare to see a public defender argue for innocence; rather, like many courts, the county juvenile court has a McDonaldized pattern of plea agreements with fairly standard treatment for different offenses as well as for repeat offenders. Judges tend to have preferred programs to which they send juveniles they deem in need of further treatment. The system is surprisingly informal (Ketchum, 2008).

Officially, when a juvenile case is assigned to the juvenile division of the DA's office, the DA in that division receives the intake information and accompanying recommendation by OJA or juvenile bureau staff and makes a final decision on how to proceed from the following options.[1] The DA can (a) decline or dismiss the case from prosecution; (b) divert the juvenile to voluntary services available from community-based providers; (c) initiate a deferred prosecution or deferred filing agreement with specific terms and conditions for completion by the juvenile in order to avoid prosecution—this is commonly referred to as "informal probation;"[2] or (d) file a petition to charge the juvenile in court either as an adult, as a delinquent or as a youthful offender.

If detained in a secure detention center as a result of an arrest, a juvenile is entitled to a detention hearing within two judicial days. Detention hearings are presided over by the local juvenile court judge; the DA represents the state's interest. The juvenile may have legal counsel to represent her or his interest. At the detention hearing, the judge may order the juvenile released or may hold the juvenile in detention for up to five days pending the filing of a petition by the DA. Once a petition is filed, a juvenile may be held in detention pending an adjudicatory hearing, although a detention hearing must be held every ten days thereafter. If juveniles are adjudicated as delinquents by the juvenile court, they may be placed in detention periodically to ensure their appearance in court or if they have been charged with contempt of court. Juveniles charged as youthful offenders may be treated as adults and placed in adult jails pending the decision by the DA to file the charges in adult criminal court or juvenile court.

Juveniles charged with status offenses may not be placed in detention and if petitions are filed, they can only be adjudicated as status offenders (child in need of supervision), and the juvenile court's dispositional finding after adjudication is limited to ordering their supervision by a responsible party.

When the intake decision of a DA is to decline or dismiss the case or to divert the juvenile to a community-based volunteer program, no further action by the juvenile justice system is taken. The juvenile is released from the system. In the case of a deferred prosecution or deferred filing decision (informal probation) by the DA, the juvenile is subject to case-related terms and conditions as well supervision by OJA or juvenile bureau staff. Pending progress on completion of the terms and conditions by the juvenile, the DA may revoke the agreement to defer prosecution and file a petition for court involvement. If the DA files a petition with a motion to certify the juvenile as an adult, the case is transferred to adult criminal court if the juvenile court grants the motion. Cases with petitions filed in the juvenile court charging the juvenile as a delinquent are processed by the juvenile court. For these cases, the juvenile court may decide any of three options: (a) dismissal, in which case the juvenile returns to her or his legal guardian and no further action is taken by the juvenile justice system; (b) deferred adjudication, in which case the juvenile court defers a decision to adjudicate and may or may not impose conditions contingent on that deferral; ultimately, the case may be dismissed, or the juvenile court may proceed to adjudicate the juvenile as a delinquent; or (c) adjudication as a delinquent.

Following adjudication of juveniles as delinquents, the juvenile court makes a dispositional decision. That dispositional decision is generally what the court believes to be in the best interest of the juvenile. There are three possible decisions. The first is court supervision, in which case the court directly supervises the juvenile or assigns that responsibility to another responsible party other than the juvenile bureau or OJA. The party responsible for the juvenile is obligated to report back to the court at periodic court review hearings until the court is satisfied that the case can be dismissed. The second option is court-ordered probation, in which case the court assigns supervisory responsibility to either the juvenile bureau or to OJA until such time as the juvenile completes her or his probationary treatment. The third possibility is court-ordered custody, in which case the court assigns the juvenile to the custody of a responsible party (generally OJA) until such time as the court is satisfied that the case can be dismissed.

Delinquent juveniles on court-ordered probationary status may live with their legal guardian (parent or relative or another individual) and are under supervision by the juvenile bureau or OJA. During the probation period, the juvenile and guardian are obligated to follow a court-approved treatment plan and to attend periodic court review hearings until the case is dismissed.

Delinquent juveniles in custody of OJA are assessed with respect to risk and needs. The juvenile may or may not be placed in out-of-home custody arrangements. The juvenile is required to complete a court-approved treatment plan and to attend periodic court review hearings until the case is dismissed. The out-of-home custody facilities vary in the level of restrictiveness. The least restrictive out-of-home custody arrangement is a foster home; the most restrictive is a physically secure detention institution. Between these two extremes are the Level E staff secure group homes. Juveniles stay in these custody placements until they have completed their treatment plans or are released by court order. Out-of-home custody placements are for indeterminate lengths of stay, but delinquent juveniles cannot remain in them after age 18, while youthful offenders cannot remain in out-of-home custody after age 21.

The juvenile justice data

The data we use to examine the racial and ethnic differences in the juvenile justice system come from two separate sources. The first dataset is the Juvenile On-Line Tracking System (JOLTS). Maintained and operated by OJA, the JOLTS database is an extensive statewide juvenile justice information system. The JOLTS system houses information on every transaction with every juvenile in the database. JOLTS contains data that uniquely identify each juvenile in the system, as well as the referrals from the state- and county-based juvenile justice system components, reflecting reports from a variety of individuals and agencies including law enforcement.[3] Representatives from the various agencies and organizations described previously that comprise the juvenile justice system enter data into the JOLTS database. These entities include county juvenile bureaus, the statewide network of statutorily designated nonprofit youth services agencies, the secure detention centers and the CICs.

As noted, the database includes all transactions for a referred juvenile. In other words, each offense associated with each referral for each juvenile is recorded in the JOLTS system. Additionally, each related intake decision by OJA, a member of the juvenile bureau staff or a DA's office is part of the system. Likewise, every associated court petition, adjudication and disposition, every in-home and out-of-home placement, and all related referrals for programs and services are stored in the JOLTS system. Clearly, the data housed in the JOLTS system are comprehensive for juveniles referred to the state juvenile agency or to a county juvenile bureau.

What is not included in the JOLTS system is information from municipal courts. Not all juveniles are referred to the state or county level. Because there is no mechanism for sharing data between OJA and municipalities, the JOLTS system does not contain information on juveniles arrested or cited and processed in municipal courts. As noted in an earlier discussion, Oklahoma City has an interlocal agreement with the county agencies and does process juveniles in municipal court. To capture information on those juveniles, we included a second data source: records from juvenile proceedings in Oklahoma City municipal court. The municipal court data contain similar information to the JOLTS system as described previously. The primary difference in the two data sources is that the JOLTS system is a statewide database, while the municipal data are for a single city (Oklahoma City).

To examine differences by race and ethnicity within the juvenile justice system, we use a dataset merged from the two data sources previously described: the JOLTS database and records from the Oklahoma City municipal courts. The data are from alternating years between 2006 and 2014. Like the data from the police encounters with juveniles, we included multiple years of juvenile justice system data to determine if there were differences over time, that is, to determine if the effect of race and ethnicity within the justice system changed over time. We used data from alternating years because of the extensive amount of data cleaning, coding and merging that was required. Using data from every other year permitted us to assess potential change but also reduced by half the required amount of data cleaning and data management. Like the results from the police encounters with juveniles, we found no significant differences over time. Consequently, we do not stratify the data by the different years.

We began with data for 6,863 juveniles. This included the juveniles for the study years who were in the statewide system and referred from Oklahoma City, Oklahoma County or OJA District 3.[4] The 6,863 juveniles also included the juveniles in the Oklahoma City municipal courts system. We removed juveniles from our dataset whose race was not known (less than 1 percent), as well as the small number of juveniles whose race was recorded as "Other" (less than 2 percent) and "Asian" (less than 1 percent). We excluded the juveniles with an unknown or other race designation because the focus of the study is race. We excluded Asian juveniles because their numbers were so small: only 33 of the juveniles in the dataset were identified as Asian, and these numbers were too small to perform analyses. Similar studies using Oklahoma juvenile justice system data have used a similar approach (Charish et al, 2004). In addition, we excluded 16 cases because they were missing the variable age. We excluded these observations because we wanted to know for certain that all data were for juveniles. Since we could not verify the age for these small number of cases, we excluded them. After excluding observations, the final dataset contained information for 6,612 juveniles in the justice system.

Our primary focus is on racial and ethnic differences. The data contain the following race and ethnicity categories: White, Black, Native American and Hispanic/Latinx. We present the findings using these categories. In addition, we present the data using the collapsed categories White and non-White. Recall that in the chapter on police encounters we used the collapsed categories of White, non-White and Asian. Because we exclude the few observations identified as Asian in this chapter, the collapsed categories in this chapter are White and non-White. See the discussion in the chapter on police encounters for a detailed discussion of why we present the data using both sets of race and ethnicity categories.

The juveniles in the system

Demographic characteristics of the juveniles

Table 4.1 shows the summary descriptions of the characteristics of the juveniles in the dataset. The largest specific race category of youth is Black

Table 4.1: Summary descriptions of the study group characteristics (N = 6,612)

Characteristic	Frequency	Percentage
Race		
White	2,201	33.3
Non-White	4,411	66.7
Black	3,171	48.0
Native American	307	4.6
Hispanic/Latinx	933	14.1
Gender		
Male	5,132	77.6
Female	1,480	22.4
Age		
Under 12	319	4.8
12–15	2,784	42.1
16–18	3,509	53.1

(48.0 percent), followed by White (33.3 percent) and Hispanic/Latinx (14.1 percent). Native American youth are the smallest category, making up 4.6 percent of the total. Non-White youth comprise exactly two thirds (66.7 percent) of the juveniles in the juvenile justice system in Oklahoma City. The percentages are striking, especially for Black and Native American youth. Black youth make up almost half of the juveniles in the system, despite making up significantly less than 20 percent of the general population in Oklahoma. The concentration of non-White (especially Black) youth is a common finding in DMC studies (Bishop and Frazier, 1988; Lieber and Jamieson, 1995; Secret and Johnson, 1997; Bishop et al, 2010) and illustrates another common finding: that the effects of DMC are compounded as the focus moves further along the process (Bishop and Frazier, 1988; Lieber and Jamieson, 1995; Secret and Johnson, 1997; Bishop et al, 2010). Said another way, because minorities are overrepresented in police encounters, they are even more overrepresented in the juvenile court system. As we will show later, overrepresentation in the court system leads to increasing overrepresentation in incarceration and detention.

A large majority of the youth are male (77.6 percent). Less than a quarter (22.4 percent) of the juveniles in the court system are female. Similar to the case for race and ethnicity, the overrepresentation of males in police encounters results in a concentration of males in the court system. The age of the juveniles ranges from as young as eight to as old as 18. The median age is 16; the mean age is 15.1. Less than 5 percent of the juveniles are under the age of 12. A little less than half (42.1 percent) are between 12 and 15 years old. The majority (53.1 percent) of the juveniles in the court system are between the ages of 16 and 18.

Nature of the referred offenses

All the juveniles are in the justice system because they have been referred for an offense. The referral does not mean the juvenile is guilty of the offense; it is merely the crime or violation that resulted in the referral. Some of the referrals are for felony offenses; some are for misdemeanor offenses; while others are for non-felony and non-misdemeanor violations, such as status offenses and technical violations. A status offense is a non-criminal act that is considered a law violation only because of a youth's status as a minor. Technical violations occur when a juvenile who has already been placed on probation does not complete the terms and conditions of the probation.[5] Table 4.2 shows the overall distribution of the referred charges. The original data included the specific charge or code violation. There were nearly 250 specific charges represented in the data. We coded the specific charges into categories. We coded whether the referred charge was a felony or a misdemeanor. Within the felony category, we grouped the specific crimes into six different categories: sex crimes, crimes against persons, drug crimes, weapons-related crimes, property crimes and crimes against the public order.[6] Within the misdemeanor category, we grouped the specific charges into five different categories. The misdemeanor group includes the same categories as the felony group, but without sex crimes. There were no misdemeanor sex crime charges in the data.

The top panel of the table shows the felony referred charges. More than half (60.2 percent) of all the referrals include a felony charge. The most frequent felony charges are those classified as property crimes (33.3 percent).[7] The next most frequent group of offenses are crimes against persons (11.9 percent).[8] The remainder of the felony crimes constitute less than 10 percent of the total. It is worth noting that the percentages listed in the table do not sum to 100 percent because there are juveniles with multiple charges per referral. To illustrate, there are 3,981 juveniles (60.2 percent) with at least one felony charge. However, the six categories of felony charges (sex crimes, crimes against persons, drugs, weapons, property crimes and crimes against the public order) add up to more than 3,981 because some juveniles have more than one felony charge. Similarly, a juvenile can have more than one misdemeanor charge. In fact, a referred case could have both felony and misdemeanor charges.

The middle panel of Table 4.2 shows the misdemeanor referred charges. The table shows that the various misdemeanor charges are distributed fairly evenly. Four of the five misdemeanor charge categories—person, drug and

Table 4.2: Summary of referred offenses (N = 6,612)

	Frequency	Percent
Felonies	**3,981**	**60.2**
Sex crimes	168	2.5
Against persons	784	11.9
Drug crimes	650	9.8
Weapons crimes	305	4.6
Property crimes	2,200	33.3
Public order	156	2.4
Misdemeanors	**2,792**	**42.3**
Against persons	708	10.7
Drug crimes	818	12.4
Weapons crimes	197	3.0
Property crimes	716	10.8
Public order	733	11.1
All others	**549**	**8.3**
Status offenses	518	7.8
Technical violations	32	0.5

property crimes, and crimes against the public order—each represent about 10 percent of the total. The most frequent misdemeanor charge is for drug- and alcohol-related offenses (12.4 percent). The category with the fewest misdemeanor charges is for weapons crimes (3.0 percent). The bottom panel of Table 4.2 shows the distribution of status offenses and technical violations in the referrals. These non-criminal offenses are described in a previous section in more detail. These offenses comprise less than 10 percent (8.3 percent) of the total referrals.

Tables 4.3 and 4.4 show the distribution of the referred charges by race. Table 4.3 shows the distribution by all the race categories (White, Black, Native American and Hispanic/Latinx); Table 4.4 shows the distribution for the collapsed race categories (White and non-White). The data show a familiar pattern. Non-White juveniles have a higher percentage of felony criminal referrals (62.6 percent) compared with White juveniles (55.3 percent). There are a few crime-specific differences by race. For example, the percentage of White youth with a felony sex crime charge (3.8 percent) is double that of non-White youth (1.9 percent). For felony weapons charges, non-White youth (5.3 percent) are referred at almost double the rate for White youth (3.2 percent). It is worth noting, however, that these two offenses are among the lowest overall percentages of the

Table 4.3: Summary of referred offenses by race (N = 6,612)

	White N = 2,201	Black N = 3,171	Native American N = 307	Hispanic/ Latinx N = 933	Total N = 6,612
Felonies	55.0	61.0	59.3	69.2	60.2
Sex crimes	3.8	1.9	1.6	1.9	2.5
Against persons	8.4	13.8	13.0	12.9	11.9
Drug crimes	9.2	9.8	6.5	12.5	9.8
Weapons crimes	3.2	4.9	4.2	7.2	4.6
Property crimes	31.7	33.0	35.8	37.0	33.3
Public order	2.2	2.5	3.6	1.7	2.4
Misdemeanors	47.0	41.2	37.1	36.8	42.3
Against persons	11.3	11.6	8.5	7.1	10.7
Drug crimes	16.4	9.1	13.7	13.6	12.4
Weapons crimes	2.2	3.1	1.6	4.9	3.0
Property crimes	11.9	11.1	10.7	7.5	10.8
Public order	11.6	11.2	13.7	8.7	11.1
All Others	10.0	7.9	17.3	2.7	8.3
Status offenses	9.8	7.3	16.3	2.3	7.8
Technical violations	0.2	0.6	1.0	0.4	0.5

Note: The numbers are percentages.

felony charges. There are race-specific differences as well. Table 4.3 shows that Hispanic/Latinx youth have a significantly higher percentage of felony charges (69.2 percent) compared with White youth (55.3 percent). The other obvious race-specific difference in the type of charge in the referrals is for the non-felony and non-misdemeanor charges. Native American youth have an extremely high percentage of status offenses and technical violations (17.3 percent) compared with Whites (10.0 percent) and the other non-White categories. The percentage for Hispanic/Latinx youth, for example, is 2.7 percent. It is worth noting that the rate of commission of crimes, by type, is fairly consistent by race and ethnicity. This suggests that non-Whites follow the same pattern by rate and type of crime as Whites, but by a multiplier. For example, referring to Table 4.4, 9.2 percent of White felonies are drug crimes. For non-Whites, the rate is 10.1 percent. About 10 percent of each group's felonies are drug crimes. This pattern is pretty consistent throughout. However, non-Whites are charged for these crimes much more often, meaning that either the ratio of types of crimes is the same for Whites and non-Whites at the same time the volume of

Table 4.4: Summary of referred offenses by White/non-White race categories (N = 6,612)

	White N = 2,201	Non-White N = 4,411	Total N = 6,612
Felonies	55.3	62.6	60.2
Sex crimes	3.8	1.9	2.5
Against persons	8.4	13.6	11.9
Drug crimes	9.2	10.1	9.8
Weapons crimes	3.2	5.3	4.6
Property crimes	31.7	34.1	33.3
Public order	2.2	2.4	2.4
Misdemeanors	47.0	39.9	42.3
Against persons	11.3	10.4	10.7
Drug crimes	16.4	10.3	12.4
Weapons crimes	2.2	3.4	3.0
Property crimes	11.9	10.3	10.8
Public order	11.6	10.8	11.1
All others	10.0	7.4	8.3
Status offenses	9.8	6.8	7.8
Technical violations	0.2	0.6	0.5

Note: The numbers are percentages.

crimes for non-Whites is more than twice that of Whites, or non-Whites are committing the same crimes at pretty much the same rates but are being caught and prosecuted more than twice as often.

Results: race and intake decisions

In the previous sections, we described the basic demographic characteristics of the juveniles who were referred into the juvenile justice system. We also described the types of charges that precipitated the juveniles' referral into the justice system. We now turn to the primary task at hand: to describe the differences in the processes and outcomes in the juvenile justice system. We begin with an examination of the intake decisions.

Recall from the previous section describing the Oklahoma juvenile justice system that once a juvenile's case is referred to the system, one of four decisions is made about the referral. Two of the decisions essentially move the case out of the juvenile system (i.e., cases declined or diverted). The other two decisions at intake move the case through

Figure 4.1: Summary of intake decisions (N = 6,433)

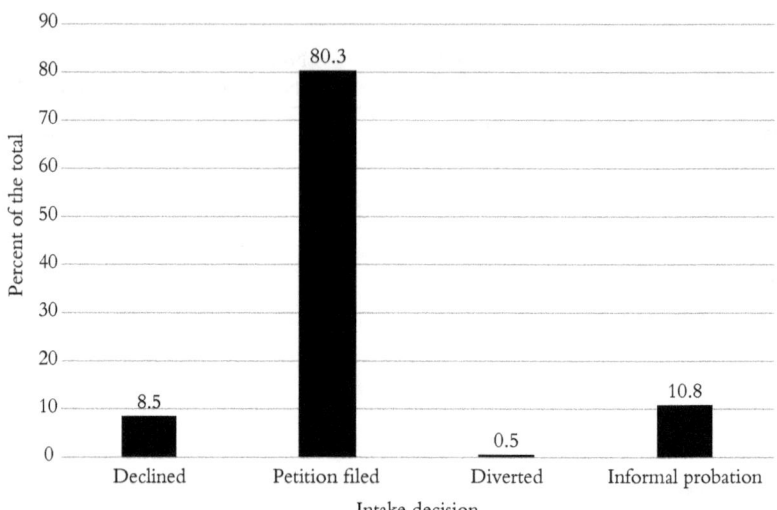

the juvenile justice system (i.e., filing a petition or informal probation). Figure 4.1 shows the distribution of the referred cases. Note that the data for the intake decisions are based on 6,433 cases, not 6,612 as in the previous analyses. There were 179 cases for which no intake decision was reported. These cases were pending the intake decision at the time the data were compiled.

The juvenile justice authorities filed a petition for a large majority of the referred cases (80.3 percent). The second most common decision was to recommend informal probation (10.8 percent). Taken together, over 90 percent of the referred cases were moved into the juvenile justice system. A little under a tenth of the cases were declined (8.5 percent) or diverted. The number of cases diverted is extremely small, less than 1 percent. As such, we exclude those cases in the analyses modeling the different intake decisions. Figure 4.2 shows the distributions of the same intake decisions by race and ethnicity. A slightly higher percentage of cases involving non-White youth have a petition filed (80.9 percent) compared with White youth (79.1 percent). This difference between cases with White and non-White juveniles is true for each specific non-White racial and ethnic group. That is, cases for Black, Native American and Hispanic/Latinx juveniles all show higher percentages of having a petition filed compared with White juveniles. The decision regarding informal probation shows the inverse relationship. Compared with non-White juveniles, White juveniles have a higher percentage of their cases placed on informal probation (13.8 versus 9.3 percent). Again, this is true for each specific non-White racial and ethnic group. They all have lower percentages of their cases put on informal probation compared with White juveniles.

Figure 4.2: Intake decisions by race/ethnicity (N = 6,433)

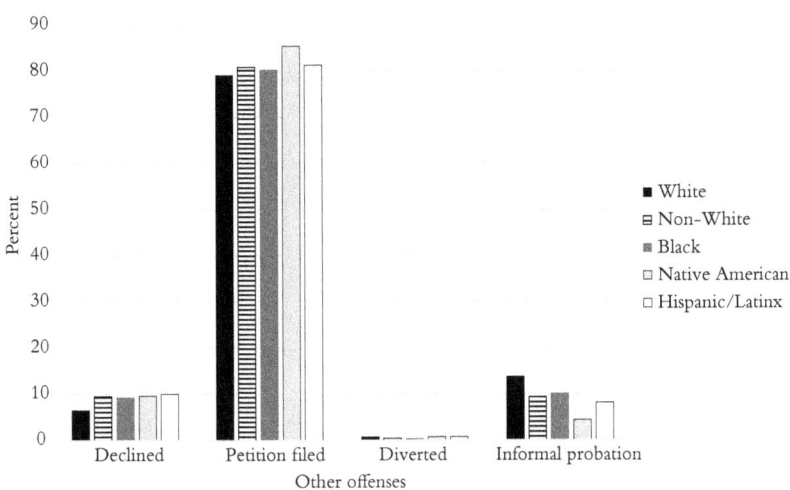

Interestingly, non-White youth are slightly more likely to have their cases declined for adjudication. Almost 10 percent of non-White cases (9.5 percent) were declined, versus 6.5 percent of cases involving a White juvenile. Cases with Black, Native American and Hispanic/Latinx juveniles all had higher percentages of declined cases compared with White juveniles. Cases with Hispanic/Latinx juveniles had the highest percentage of cases declined (10.0 percent). Black juveniles had the lowest percentage of the non-White cases declined (9.3 percent).

The finding that non-White juveniles are more likely than White juveniles to have their case declined at intake is not altogether surprising. Previous research has been somewhat mixed. Many studies have found a "White advantage" at all stages of the juvenile justice process (Peck and Jennings, 2016). Other studies, however, suggest that non-White minority youth may receive leniency in some instances (Dannefer and Schutt, 1982; Rodriguez, 2007, 2010; Bishop et al, 2010). This so-called correction effect is thought to be an attempt by judges and justice administrators to attenuate the effect of racial biases that occurred at earlier points in the process, such as the initial referral or prior court proceedings.

Figures 4.3 to 4.5 show the results of statistical models that calculate the risk (or probability) of a specific intake decision. As noted previously, there are four possible intake decisions. Because the number of cases that were diverted was so low, we present models showing the probability of an intake decision of having the case declined, a petition filed and informal probation. We present risk ratios (RR) from log binomial regression models. These are the same statistical models described and presented in the previous chapter on police encounters. See that chapter for a more detailed discussion of the log binomial model and risk ratios. The figures show both the unadjusted and adjusted models. The unadjusted (bivariate) relationships between race and the intake decisions do not control for any other factors. It is the crude relationship between race and the intake decision. The adjusted models show these same relationships between race and the intake decisions while controlling for other factors. These other factors are gender, age and the severity of the referral charge.

There are a number of legal factors pertinent to the processing of juveniles by the juvenile justice system. The most relevant of these is the severity of the charge. We include two measures of severity in the statistical models: the *number* of offenses and the *severity score* of the offense(s). Each referral may contain a single alleged offense or multiple counts of offenses. As noted previously, many of the juveniles had multiple offense counts. We also include the severity score for each offense. The severity score used by OJA is a cumulative index score based on the statutory class of each offense and severity rankings from juvenile justice decision-makers.[9] The statutory class refers to whether the offense is a felony, misdemeanor, technical violation of probation or parole, status offense, or traffic or municipal violation. We coded each juvenile data record to reflect the total number of counts in the current referral and the severity score for each count in the referral. If a juvenile record had multiple offenses in the charge, we used the average severity score of all the offenses in the referral.

Figure 4.3 shows the unadjusted and adjusted risk ratios of having the referral declined for prosecution by race and ethnicity.[10] The figure shows the combined category of non-White and each specific race and ethnicity category (Black, Native American and Hispanic/Latinx). The risk ratios for each of the race and ethnicity groups are in relation to Whites. The unadjusted risk ratios show the effect of only race on the risk of the referral being declined. The adjusted risk ratios show the effect of race after controlling for or taking account of the other variables in the model (i.e., gender, age, number of counts and severity of the counts). When the adjusted and unadjusted odds ratios are similar to each other, it indicates that the other variables, the control variables, do not mitigate or change the relationship between race and the predicted outcome (in this case, a declined referral). We will focus most of the discussion on the adjusted risk ratios. Figure 4.3 shows that all the non-White racial and ethnic groups have a higher probability of their referral being declined compared with Whites. Native American and Hispanic/Latinx juveniles, for example, both have a 49 percent higher probability of having their referrals dismissed (RR = 1.49). Taken as a whole, the non-White juveniles are 41 percent more likely (RR = 1.41) to have their referrals declined for prosecution.

The findings for the effects of race on informal probation show a different story (Figure 4.4). Juveniles from all the non-White racial and ethnic

Figure 4.3: Risk ratios of declined referral by race/ethnicity (N = 6,433)

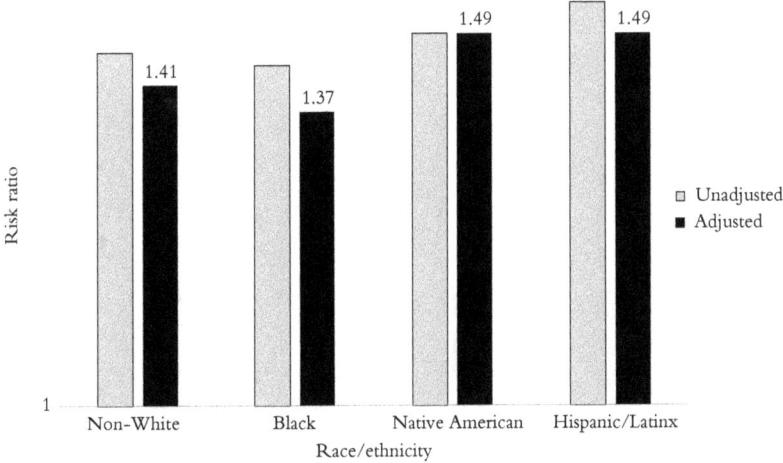

Figure 4.4: Risk ratios of referral to informal probation by race/ethnicity (N = 6,433)

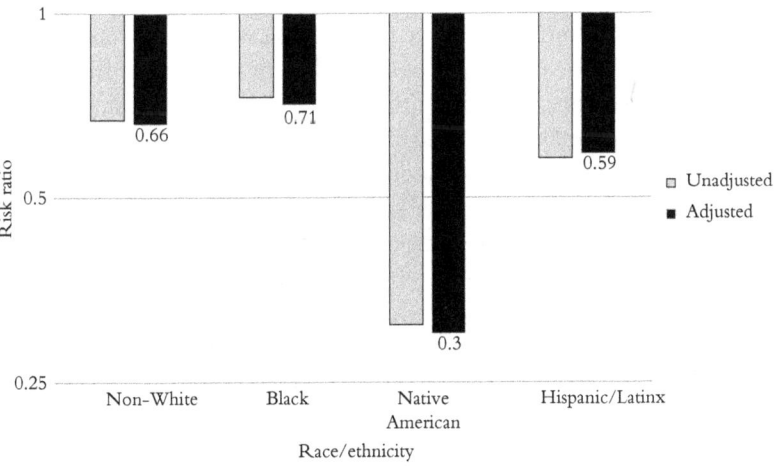

groups have a lower probability compared with White juveniles of their referral resulting in informal probation. The difference for Native American youth is especially pronounced. Native American juveniles have a 70 percent lower probability (RR = 0.30) than White juveniles of receiving informal probation. As a group, non-White youth are substantially less likely (34 percent) to receive informal probation than White youth (RR = 0.66). As in the previous analyses, adjusting for the effects of race on probation makes very little difference. The differences

Figure 4.5: Risk ratios of referral petition filed by race/ethnicity (N = 6,433)

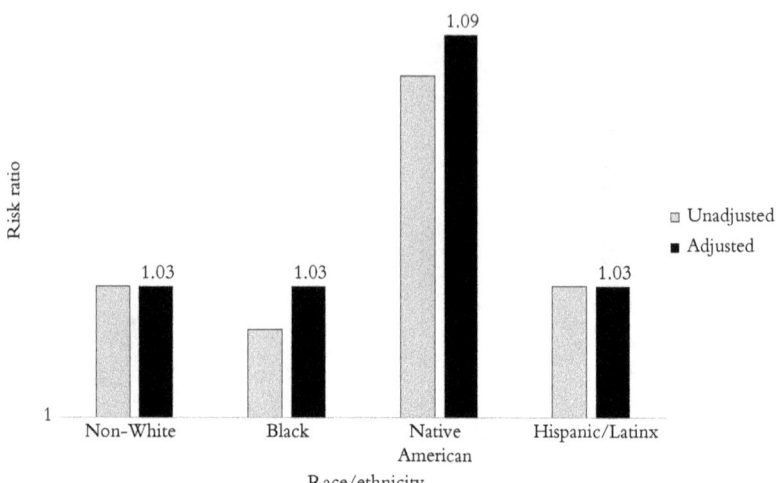

between race and the intake decision for informal probation are not mitigated by the other legal and extralegal factors. Race is a strong predictor of intake decision.

The most serious intake outcome for juveniles is the decision by a district attorney (or city attorney if the case is handled by the city) to file a petition for court involvement. The potential outcomes from a court hearing can be severe, including being placed in secure detention. Figure 4.5 shows the analyses examining the association between a juvenile's race and having a petition filed in the case. Juveniles from all non-White racial and ethnic groups have a higher risk or probability of having a petition filed compared with White juveniles. The biggest difference is that between Native American and White juveniles. Native American juveniles are about 10 percent more likely (RR = 1.09) to have a petition filed in their case than White juveniles. The risk ratio for Black (RR = 1.03) and Hispanic/Latinx (RR = 1.03) youth are not as high but are still higher than for White youth. Black and Hispanic/Latinx youth both have an increased probability compared with White youth of about 3 percent even after accounting for the demographic and severity variables.

The analyses of the intake decision outcomes are very consistent (see Figure 4.6). Non-White youth are less likely to have their cases placed on informal probation compared with White youth. This is true for all non-White racial and ethnic groups. Non-White youth are more likely to have a petition filed on their cases. Finally, youth from all non-White groups are more likely than Whites to have their cases declined for further adjudication. These data are from all referred cases in the Oklahoma City juvenile justice system. As such, the data represent the population of all observations in the

Figure 4.6: Summary of intake decisions by race/ethnicity (from the multivariate log binomial regression models)

Race and ethnicity	Intake decision on referral		
	Declined	Informal probation	Petition filed
Black	↑	↓	↑
Native American	↑	↓	↑
Hispanic/Latinx	↑	↓	↑

Note: The arrows represent the direction of difference for each race and ethnic group compared to Whites for each intake decision outcome.

time period. These differences represent the differences in the population, not estimated differences based on a sample.[11] As such, we have not presented inferential statistics such as *p*-values or confidence intervals.

Results: race and court process outcomes

If a petition is filed in a case, that case then moves into the court system. The processes of the juvenile court system are relatively complex (see the overview discussed previously), with several decision points and outcomes. The first decision point is whether to keep the case in the juvenile system or transfer the case to the adult criminal court system.[12] For those juveniles who remain in the juvenile court system, the second decision point involves the court determining the facts alleged in the petition. There are three potential outcomes. The court may (a) dismiss the case, (b) defer adjudication pending completion of court-ordered terms and conditions, or (c) adjudicate the juvenile as a delinquent or as a youthful offender.[13] Finally, for juveniles who have been referred for adjudication as a delinquent or youthful offender, the third and last decision point is the court disposition of the case. There are three possible outcomes at this stage.[14] The court may (a) dismiss the case, (b) place the juvenile on court-ordered probation or (c) place the juvenile in OJA custody. In this section, we describe these outcomes at the various points in the juvenile court process with a focus on differences by racial and ethnic group.

The analyses of the court dispositions are based on a subset of the referred cases. Of the 6,433 cases referred to the juvenile justice system, 5,163 had a petition filed (see Figure 4.1). The analyses are based on 3,698 cases—rather than all 5,163 of the cases on which a petition was filed—because a sizeable

Figure 4.7: Summary of disposition of referrals (N = 3,698)

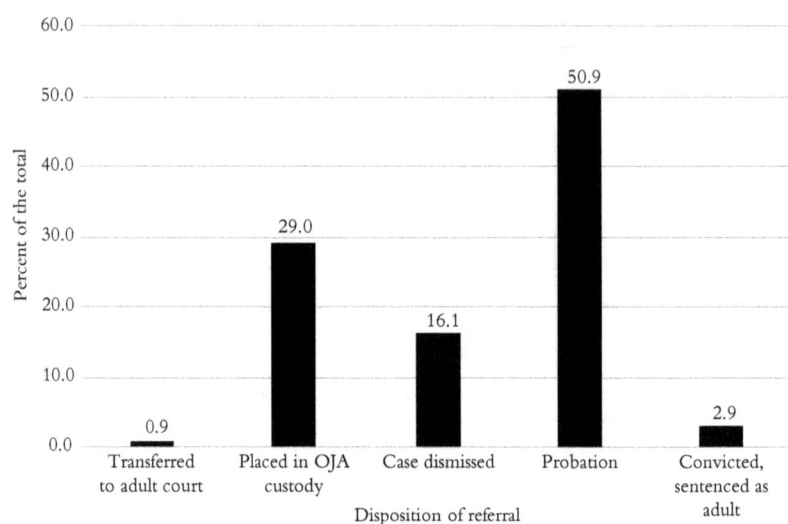

number of cases were still pending a court outcome. There were 1,465 cases with a decision pending at the time of the data compilation.

The distribution of the dispositions of the cases is presented in Figure 4.7. The majority of cases are placed on court-ordered probation (50.9 percent). A little less than a third of the cases result in the juvenile being placed in OJA custody (29.0 percent). Less than a fifth of the cases are dismissed by the court (16.1 percent). About 3 percent of the cases (2.9 percent) were transferred to the adult criminal court and ended with a conviction with the juvenile sentenced as an adult. An additional number of cases (0.9 percent) were transferred to the adult criminal court but were still pending.

Figure 4.8 presents the same case dispositions by race and ethnicity. Again, we present the data by racial and ethnic group categories and by the collapsed categories of White and non-White. Several of the differences by race and ethnicity are striking. The absolute number of juveniles transferred to adult court and awaiting adjudication is quite low. Even so, the racial differences stand out. Very few White juveniles are transferred to adult court (0.1 percent). The number of non-White juveniles in this category is quite high by comparison (1.3 percent). The percentage is 12 times higher than for non-White youth. The difference is even higher for Black juveniles (1.4 percent). For those juveniles who were transferred to adult court and convicted—these are transferred cases with a known disposition—the pattern is similar. Non-White youth are substantially more likely than White youths to be transferred and convicted, 3.7 percent versus 1.4 percent. The group with the highest percentage of youth tried and convicted in adult criminal

Figure 4.8: Disposition of referred cases by race/ethnicity (N = 3,698)

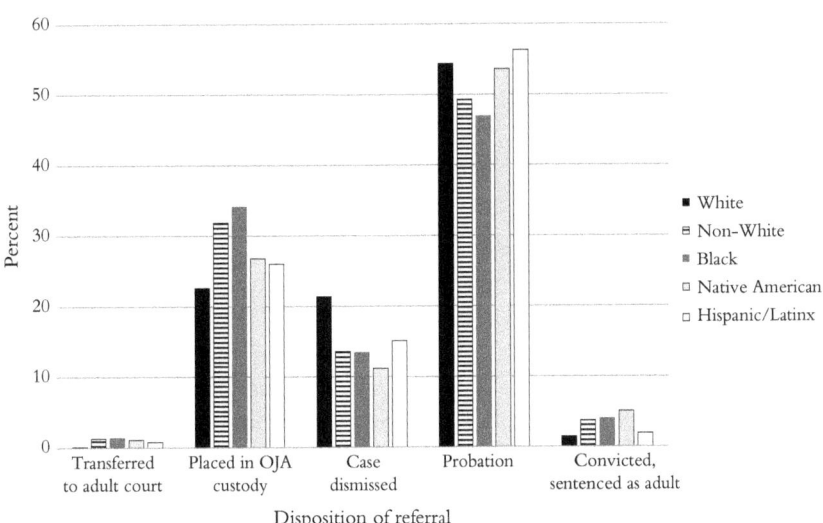

court is Native Americans (5.0 percent), followed by Black (4.0 percent) and Hispanic/Latinx youth (1.9 percent).

The findings related to juveniles placed in OJA custody and having the case against them dismissed show a similar pattern: non-White youth are disadvantaged compared with White youth. Slightly less than a quarter of White youth (22.6 percent) are remanded to custody in an OJA facility. By contrast, almost one third of the non-White youth (31.9 percent) are placed in OJA custody. Furthermore, juveniles from each of the racial and ethnic non-White groups have higher percentages compared with White juveniles. Black youth have the highest percentage remanded to OJA custody (34.2 percent). Similarly, non-White youth are disadvantaged when it comes to their cases being dismissed. Cases involving White youth are dismissed at higher rates (21.4 percent) than those of non-White youth (13.6 percent). Again, all non-White youth have lower percentages of cases dismissed compared with White youth. Native American youth have the lowest percentage (11.2 percent) and Hispanic/Latinx youth have the highest percentage (15.1 percent) of the cases involving non-White youth.

The cases involving court-ordered probation are interesting and slightly different than the other dispositions. Taken together, non-White youth are disadvantaged compared with White youth. Just under half of the non-White juveniles (49.3 percent) are given court-ordered probation compared with just over half of the White juveniles (54.4 percent). The differences, however, are not uniform for all non-White groups. Hispanic/Latinx juveniles (56.3 percent) are more likely to receive probation than Whites. Native

American youth receive probation (53.6 percent) at almost the same rate as White youth. Black youth, however, have a substantially lower percentage of cases that receive probation (46.9 percent).

Like previous studies that focused on representation of racial groups at various points in the juvenile justice process, we find that juveniles from racial and ethnic minority groups are generally disadvantaged compared with White juveniles. We now turn to a presentation of the statistical models that examine several of the judicial dispositions. We present separate models that analyze four of the judicial process outcomes: (a) case dismissed, (b) court-ordered probation, (c) detained in OJA custody and (d) transferred, tried and convicted in adult criminal court. We do not present the analyses for the juvenile cases that were transferred to adult criminal court but were still pending. That decision outcome is both interesting and important. However, there were too few cases in this category to run statistical models. Fewer than 1 percent of the cases fall in this category. We present both unadjusted (bivariate) and adjusted models. Like the previous statistical models presented, these models calculate the probability or risk of a specific court process outcome. The adjusted models calculate the risk ratios controlling for several demographic factors (gender and age) and offense severity (the number of current counts and the severity of the counts). In all the statistical models, youth in the non-White minority racial and ethnic groups are compared with White youth.

Figure 4.9 presents the results of the models predicting having the referral dismissed. The unadjusted models mirror the descriptive analyses (percentages) already shown but present the results in terms of risk ratios. The results in Figure 4.9 show, for example, that Black youth have a probability of their case being dismissed that is 33 percent lower than for White youth (RR = 0.67). After controlling for gender, age, number of referrals and the severity of those referrals, Black youth are still 33 percent less likely than White youth to have their case dismissed by the court. The relationship between race (being Black in this instance) and having a case dismissed is hardly attenuated by the control variables. Said another way, Black and White youth of the same gender and age and with the same offense severity have different case dismissal outcomes. Black juveniles with the same characteristics as White youth are 33 percent less likely to have their case dismissed.

The results for Native American and Hispanic/Latinx youth show the same pattern. Both groups have a lower probability of having their case dismissed compared with White juveniles. Native American youth are especially disadvantaged, with a probability that is 51 percent lower (RR = 0.49) than for White youth of their case being dismissed. Interestingly, for Native American youth, the probability of dismissal actually goes down after controlling for the other factors. The adjusted

Figure 4.9: Risk ratios of referral dismissed by race/ethnicity (N = 3,698)

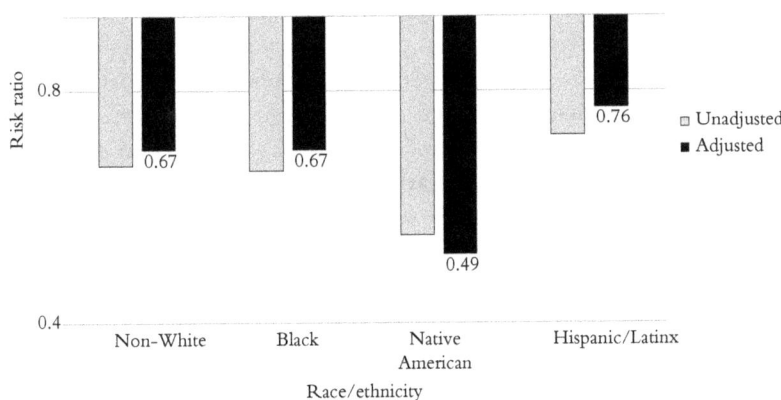

Figure 4.10: Risk ratios of referral placed on court-ordered probation by race/ethnicity (N = 3,698)

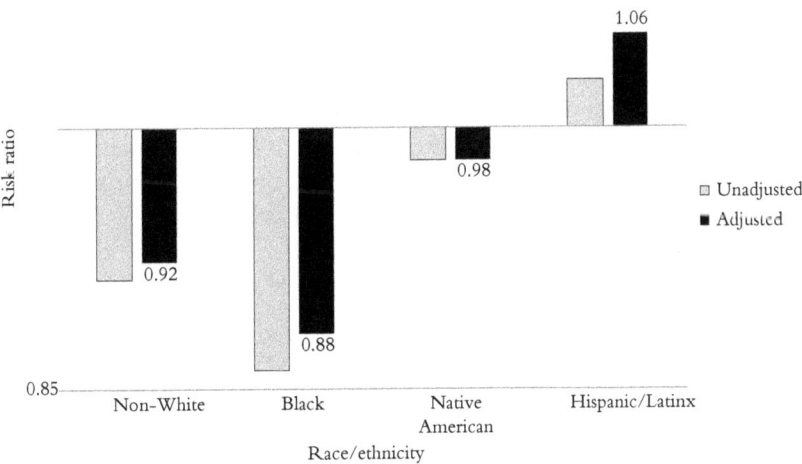

risk ratio is lower than the unadjusted risk ratio. As a group, non-White juveniles are 33 percent less likely (RR = 0.67) than White juveniles to have their cases dismissed.

The results of the models calculating the risk of being placed on court-ordered probation are presented in Figure 4.10. As a group, the non-White youth have a lower probability (RR = 0.92) of being placed on probation compared with White youth. The interesting differences within the non-White racial and ethnic groups shown in the descriptive analyses are evident in the multivariate adjusted models. Black juveniles are much less likely to be placed on probation (RR = 0.88) compared with White juveniles. Native American youth are slightly less likely than White youth to be placed on probation (RR = 0.98). Hispanic/Latinx youth, by contrast, are more likely (RR = 1.06) to be placed on probation than White youth.

The previous analyses show that non-White youth are disadvantaged in terms of having their case dismissed or being placed on court probation. Having a case dismissed or placed on probation are favorable outcomes, especially dismissal. The previous analysis has shown that non-White juveniles do not receive those favorable outcomes at the same rate as White juveniles. We now turn to outcomes that are not favorable. They are, in fact, the most consequential outcomes—being detained in custody. We examine being detained in juvenile custody (in an OJA facility) and in adult custody.

The analyses showing outcomes for being detained in OJA custody are presented in Figure 4.11. The racial and ethnic group differences are evident in the figure. As in many of the previous analyses, non-White youth are shown to be disadvantaged compared with White youth, especially Black youth. Black juveniles are almost 50 percent more likely (RR = 1.46) to be remanded to OJA custody compared with White juveniles. Juveniles from the other race groups fare better than Black juveniles but are detained in OJA custody at higher rates than White juveniles. The rate for Native American youth is 25 percent higher (RR = 1.25) than for White youth. Hispanic/Latinx youth are the most similar to White youth, though they are still almost 10 percent more likely (RR = 1.08) to be detained in OJA custody. As a group, non-White youth have a much higher risk of being sentenced to detention in an OJA facility than White youth (RR = 1.37).

Figure 4.11: Risk ratios of referral placed in OJA custody by race/ethnicity (N = 3,698)

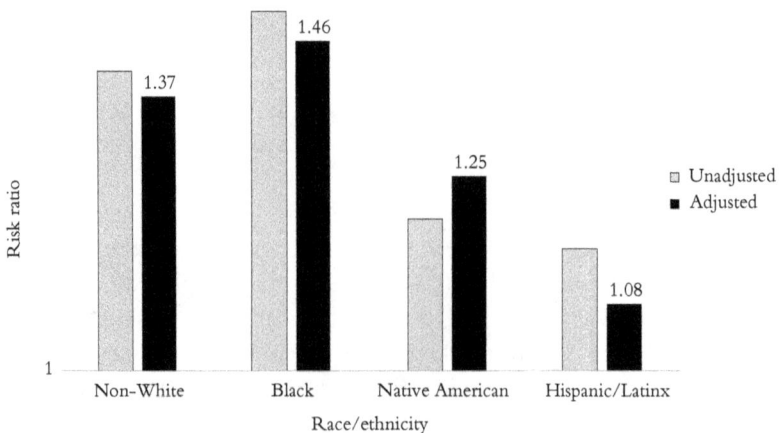

Figure 4.12: Risk ratios of referral convicted and sentenced as adults by race/ethnicity (N = 3,698)

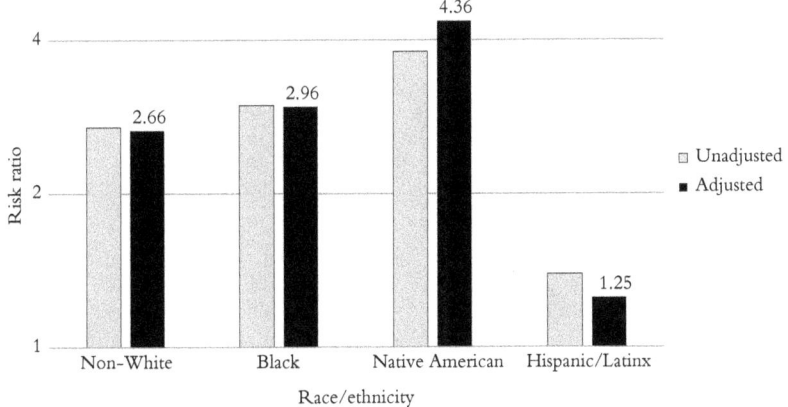

As striking as the racial and ethnic differences are for being detained in juvenile custody, they pale in comparison with the differences for adult criminal conviction and detention. Figure 4.12 shows those differences. Non-white youth have an almost 2.7 times (RR = 2.66) higher risk than White youth of being convicted and sentenced as an adult. The difference can be expressed in another way: non-White youth have a probability 167 percent higher than White youth of being convicted and sentenced as an adult. Both Native American and Black juveniles have risk ratios very near or over 3.0. Black youth have a probability three times higher (RR = 2.96) and Native American youth have a probability almost 4.5 times higher (RR = 4.36) of being convicted and sentenced in adult criminal court than White youth. Hispanic/Latinx juveniles have outcomes most similar to White juveniles but their probability is still 25 percent higher (RR = 1.25).[15]

Conclusion

The data presented in this chapter show that non-White youth are disadvantaged at nearly every point in the juvenile justice system, from the front-end intake decisions to the back-end disposition decisions. In fact, data in the previous chapter about police interactions suggest that non-White youth are disadvantaged at that point as well. These points are cumulative. Because non-White juveniles are overrepresented in police encounters, they are overrepresented at the front-end decision points in the justice system. Because non-White juveniles are overrepresented in intake decisions, they are overrepresented in court processes. Cumulatively, the overrepresentation leads to the large race and ethnicity differences in detention.

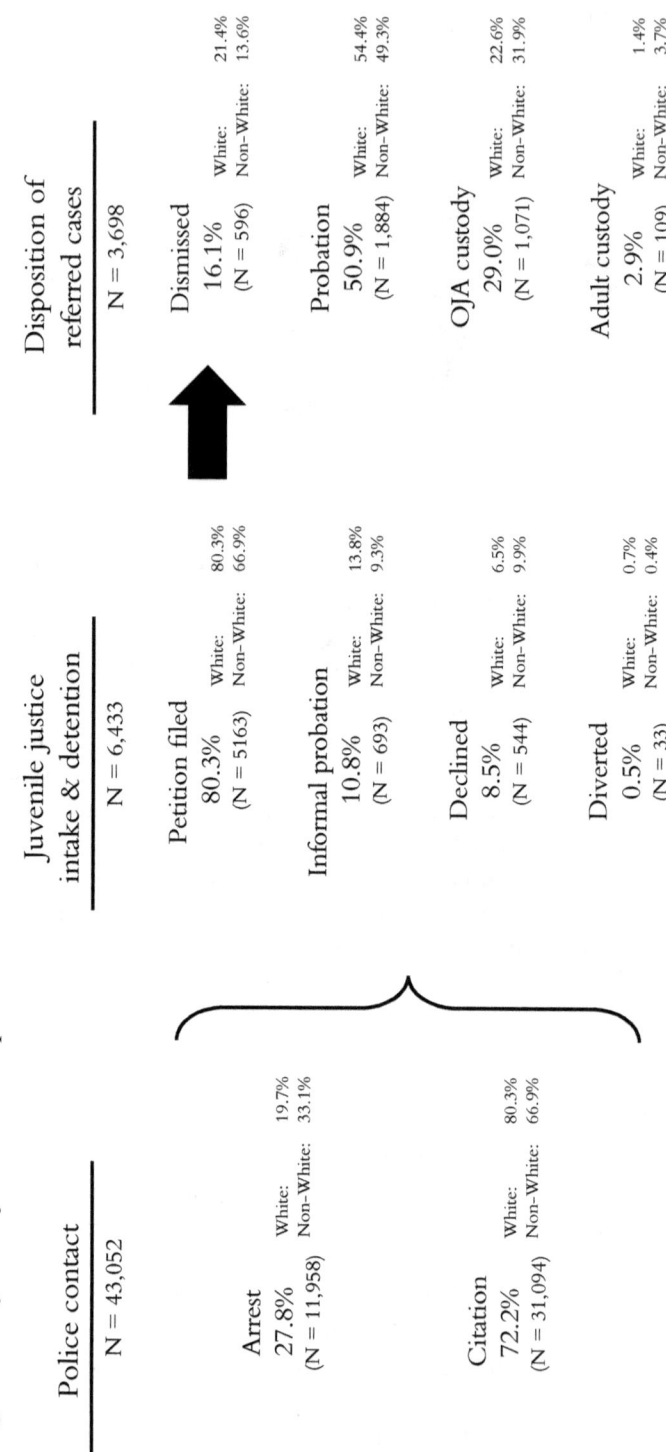

Figure 4.13: Juvenile justice decision points

Figure 4.13 summarizes the major decision points from police interactions to the disposition of court cases. Non-White juveniles are disadvantaged or have worse outcomes compared with White juveniles in all decision points, except one. Non-White juveniles (of all racial and ethnic groups) are more likely than White juveniles to have their referral declined for adjudication. The consistency and robustness of the racial and ethnic group differences are striking. They are also hard to rationalize or explain. The most common approach to explaining these differences revolves around the "differential behavior" argument. That is, non-White youth, especially Black youth, are presumed to behave differently. They are presumed to behave more criminally. The implication is that the system is not biased, nor are the people in the system biased. Rather, the non-White youth are different.

The adjusted models presented in this chapter largely refute the argument that non-White overrepresentation is not a race issue and that non-White youth are treated similarly to White youth in the juvenile justice system. Statistical comparisons of similarly situated juveniles—those with similar demographic and criminal profiles—show that non-White youth are treated differently in the system. Even if non-White juveniles are more criminal or more deviant, on average, than White juveniles, the system is treating all non-White juveniles as if they are more criminal. In Chapter 5, we examine if, in fact, non-White juveniles are more deviant or criminal than White juveniles.

Notes

[1] At any time, district attorneys may elect to revise the charges against a juvenile and may elect to revise their intake decision.

[2] Under the terms of informal probation, the DA may later file a petition in the case for a juvenile not meeting the terms and conditions of the deferment.

[3] Law enforcement agencies account for the overwhelming majority (about 90 percent) of all juveniles referred to the juvenile justice system. While there is some variability by counties, law enforcement is the agency that most often refers juveniles into the system.

[4] The Oklahoma Office of Juvenile Affairs (OJA) has district offices geographically dispersed throughout the state. Oklahoma City is in District 3.

[5] Typical status offenses include acts such as violating curfew, school truancy and running away from home. Typical technical violations include similar acts that are prohibited due to conditions of probation.

[6] There were 238 specific charges represented in the referred cases. We coded related charges into the six categories (five categories for the misdemeanors). For example, the "drug crime" category includes all specific charges related to drug or alcohol violations, such as possession of drug paraphernalia, hypodermic syringe violations, minor in possession, public drunkenness, possession of a controlled substance and so forth.

[7] Violations categorized as property crimes are those in which a victim's property is stolen or destroyed, without the use or threat of force against the victim. Property crimes include burglary and theft, as well as vandalism and arson.

[8] Offenses considered crimes against persons are those offenses with an element of the use, attempted use or threatened use of physical force or other abuse of a person. These offenses include assaults, robbery and homicide, to name a few.

9   The OJA severity score is similar to the crime severity index developed in 1977 by the US Department of Justice, Bureau of Justice Statistics (BJS). The BJS severity index was created from a large survey (N = 60,000) of persons 18 years of age or older from the general population as part of the National Crime Survey. The OJA severity score was created using similar rankings but relied on experts in the field of juvenile justice rather than the general population.
10 Like the risk ratios presented in the previous chapter on police encounters, the graphs are presented on the logarithmic scale. The baseline horizontal access is 1.0 representing equal risk between juveniles in the group specified in the graph and White juveniles. For a more detailed discussion of the arithmetic (linear) scale versus the logarithmic scale, see the previous chapter on police encounters.
11 The size of the effect of race on the intake decisions may appear small. The risk ratios for having a petition filed, for example, ranged from 1.03 to 1.09, indicating a 3–9 percent higher probability for non-White juveniles compared with White juveniles. As noted previously, risk ratios are always lower than odds ratios. Odds ratios overestimate the risk or probability of an event. This is especially true the more common the event being modeled. The decision to file a petition is the most common intake decision, 80.3 percent, for the referred cases. As a comparison, we ran logistic regression analyses on our data to estimate the odds ratios for having a petition filed. The odds ratios ranged from 1.41 to 1.57, compared with the risk ratios of 1.03 to 1.09. The risk ratios provide a more accurate estimation of the risk or probability of the event occurring.
12 The decision to transfer a juvenile to the adult criminal court system is typically based on the DA or the city attorney filing a motion to certify the juvenile as an adult. The court rules on that motion. If the motion is granted, the juvenile is transferred to adult criminal court. If the motion is not granted, the juvenile remains in the juvenile justice system.
13 The courts can classify a juvenile as a youthful offender even if the DA or other justice officer did not. The youthful offender designation is for juveniles who have committed certain serious offenses at defined ages (see previous discussion). Youthful offenders can be bridged to the adult corrections system under certain conditions.
14 There are several other possible outcomes. For example, the judge may designate the juvenile as a child in need of supervision and order the juvenile to a protective, out-of-home placement. The judge may also order the juvenile to be placed in an inpatient psychiatric care facility. These outcomes are relatively uncommon. In our data, less than 0.1 percent of the cases were disposed in this manner.
15 Again, to illustrate the relationship of odds ratios as an estimate of relative risk and how those estimates are dependent on how common or uncommon the event is, consider the case of being transferred, tried and convicted as an adult. This is the least common of the outcomes we examined using multivariate models. Just under 3 percent of the cases (2.9 percent) were disposed in this manner. The adjusted risk ratios are 2.96, 4.36 and 1.25 for Black, Native American and Hispanic/Latinx youth, respectively. The adjusted odds ratios are 3.01, 4.49 and 1.25 for the same race and ethnicity groups, respectively. The odds ratios are a close approximation of the relative risk when the event is relatively uncommon.

5

Juvenile Self-Reports of Deviant and Criminal Behavior

> The two main groups are Blacks and Hispanics that commit the crimes. ... Both groups do drive-by [shootings]. Both groups do armed robberies.
> Anonymous Police Officer, Interviewee

Introduction

The previous chapters focusing on police encounters and court processes show a familiar pattern: non-White youth are overrepresented in the system and generally have worse outcomes compared with White youth. This overrepresentation and the disadvantage in outcomes are often attributed to the notion that non-White youth, especially Black youth, are different and behave differently. In other words, non-White youth behave in ways that are more deviant and more criminal. Proponents of this "differential behavior" argument point to police and court data as evidence that non-White youth are different. Those data show that non-White youth are arrested and detained at higher rates than White youth (see, e.g., Figure 3.6). Similarly, non-White youth are charged in juvenile court with more offenses and more serious offenses (see, e.g., Tables 4.2 and 4.3). Non-White youth would not be arrested or charged with more crimes if they were not committing more crimes, so the argument goes.

In this chapter, we examine this major tenet of the differential behavior argument. We assess whether non-White youth are, in fact, more deviant and criminal than White youth. We make this assessment using self-report data from juveniles. Elsewhere we make the case for using self-report data (see Chapter 6). Kaba (2020) points out that police officers spend most of their time dealing with non-criminal issues. Issues such as parking and traffic citations and noise complaints make up most of their day. Most officers make only one felony arrest per year (Kaba, 2020). This is very different than the

TV version, which often shows police moving from one major felony to another. Instead, as poor non-White juveniles tend to conduct their daily activities in public spaces more than do suburban and rural juveniles, they may be more likely to catch the eye of an officer fishing for a felony.

Juvenile self-report data

The data come from a series of surveys of juveniles conducted in the same study area—the Oklahoma City metropolitan area—where the other data (police interaction data, juvenile court data and interviews with juvenile justice officials) were collected. The complete survey is presented in Appendix A. The surveys were conducted within the same general time frame as the other data were collected. We collected the survey data in 2015 and 2016. We collected data from 520 juveniles from three different schools in the Oklahoma City metropolitan area.[1] We selected the schools purposively to collect data from schools with different demographic and academic profiles, but within the same police and juvenile justice system jurisdictions.

The schools generally represent an inner-city urban school, a suburban school and a rural school on the outskirts of the metropolitan area. The urban school is a typical inner-city school. The school is located in a relatively poor neighborhood and district. The school is comprised mostly of non-White students. Relatively few of the students who graduate from the school attend college. We collected data from 366 juveniles from the urban school (about 70 percent of the total surveys). The suburban school, by contrast, is in a more affluent community within the metropolitan area. A slight majority of the students at the suburban school are White. A high number of students from the school attend college. We collected surveys from 109 students from the suburban school (21 percent of the total). The rural school is on the outskirts of the metropolitan area. Like the inner-city urban school, the rural school is located in a relatively poor community in the metropolitan area. Unlike in the urban school, students from the rural school are largely White. Relatively few students from the rural school attend college. We collected surveys from 45 students at the rural school (9 percent of the total). Table 5.1 shows several demographic and academic characteristics of the schools. The information in Table 5.1 come from official data reported from the Oklahoma State Department of Education (OSDE). The "letter grades" shown in the table are from the OSDE School Report Card evaluation and reporting system.[2] The letter grades indicate the performance of each school on the reported indicator.

The report card grades in Table 5.1 are a small selection from many other characteristics reported in the OSDE performance evaluation. "Academic Achievement" is an assessment of how well the school prepares students for the next grade, the next course or the next level of education. "Postsecondary

Table 5.1: Summary of characteristics of the schools in the study

Characteristics	Urban school	Suburban school	Rural school
Eligible free/reduced lunch[a]	>95%	34%	46%
Racial/ethnic minority[a]	92%	37%	42%
Average ACT score[a]	16	23	21
Academic achievement[b]	D	B	C
Postsecondary opportunities[b]	C	B	B
Overall performance[b]	D	B	C

[a] From the Oklahoma State Department of Education.

[b] The letter grade (A, B, C, D or F) is based on the Oklahoma State Department of Education's School Report Card performance evaluation using federal and state performance accountability criteria.

Opportunities" measures how well a school provides information about college and career opportunities. The "Overall Performance" is just that, how well the school performed cumulatively across all the performance and evaluation criteria.

Data collection process

We collected the self-report data from the juveniles in classrooms in the schools described in the previous section. We used cluster-type sampling within a school. First, with the aid of officials at each school, we identified required courses at each grade level. We randomly selected a required course from each grade level to administer the survey. Before collecting data from the students, we had to obtain informed consent from each school,[3] a parent or guardian of each student, and each student.[4] The consent process proceeded in order, from schools, to parents and guardians, to students. That is, after receiving consent from a school, we consented parents and guardians. After receiving consent from parents and guardians, we consented students.[5]

Consent from a parent or guardian is required, obviously, because most of the students in the schools are minors. We opted to get parent or guardian consent for all the students regardless of their age. Getting informed consent from the students' parent or guardian was the most challenging component of the consent process. We used two methods to obtain informed consent. First, we solicited parental informed consent to participate from parents and guardians at school registration confirmation events at each school. Each of the schools holds a registration confirmation and "back-to-school" night several days before the start of the school year. We attended that event and set up a table with information about the study at each of the selected schools. Parents and guardians could provide consent for their student(s). As anticipated, many parents provided consent, but their student(s) ended up not being in a class that was selected for participation. Conversely and more importantly, there were many students in a class that was selected for participation whose parent or guardian had not submitted informed consent at the back-to-school event. The second method of obtaining consent was aimed at those parents and guardians who did not submit informed consent at the back-to-school event. For the specific students in a classroom selected for participation, we sent letters home with the students asking for parental consent.[6] We made two requests by letter. If a student did not return a consent form, the student was excluded from completing the questionnaire.

On the days the survey was administered, we attended the selected classes. Students who did not have a parent or guardian consent form on file were sent to the school library. The remaining students were given the opportunity to opt out of the survey if they did not want to participate.[7] The remaining students completed the survey in the classroom. When a student completed the survey, he or she placed the survey in a secure, locked file box. The surveys were anonymous. The students were asked to not write their names or other identifying information on the survey.

Variables

Our focus in this chapter is on self-reported race and ethnicity and self-reported deviant and criminal behaviors, as well as juveniles' reports of interactions with police. We note that juveniles' race and ethnicity are self-reported because that was not necessarily the case in the datasets used to analyze the police interactions (Chapter 3) or the court processes and outcomes (Chapter 4). Interviews with police officers and juvenile justice authorities suggest that in some instances those data are self-reported. In other instances, however, the police officer or justice official makes the determination of race and records it. The data are self-reported, and the survey instrument permitted the juveniles to select more than one category to describe their race and/or ethnicity. The survey included the following categories: Asian, Black, Hispanic/Latinx, Native American/American Indian, White and Other. For the "Other" category, the juveniles were asked to specify the race and ethnicity with which they identified.[8] It is also worth noting that we collected a total of 530 surveys from juveniles. However, five of the surveys did not have a response for race recorded. Those surveys were excluded from the analyses. There were also only five responses of "Asian" to the race question. There were too few responses in this category to perform analyses. We excluded those surveys from the analyses as well, leaving a total of 520 surveys. There were a few surveys with missing data on a few of the other questions. Most of those variables were not as central to the analyses. We note in the analyses if cases are missing on these other variables. Some of the other variables we collected were gender, age, grade level and whether the student was eligible for free or reduced-price lunches.

To assess self-reported deviant and criminal activity, we asked the students a battery of questions about different types of activities and behaviors. Students were asked to indicate if they had engaged in the following activities (yes or no) in the previous six months:

- Use any tobacco product (cigarette, cigar, chewing tobacco, dip)?
- Drink any alcoholic beverage?
- Smoke/use marijuana or hash/hashish?
- Use meth, cocaine, heroin, LSD or mushrooms?
- Vandalize and/or spray-paint any property?
- Steal or shoplift any items where the total value is less than $50?
- Steal or shoplift any items where the total value is over $50?
- Break into a home or business and take things from it?
- Use a weapon or threat of force to obtain property from someone?
- Illegally possess a firearm not used for hunting?
- Get in a fight or argument which led to physical violence?
- Use a weapon to injure another person?
- Injure someone critically/seriously or kill another person?
- Are you a member of a gang?

In addition to these 14 items, we created additional variables using the responses to the 14 items. First, we created a summed index of the number of behaviors the juvenile reported from the 14 items. The variable could theoretically range from 0 to 14. The variable actually ranged from 0 to 11. No juvenile reported having been involved in all 14 behaviors. Second, we created a series of binary variables that indicated if a juvenile had committed any crimes that were similar in nature. For example, three of the 14 questions deal with alcohol and drug use. We created a new binary variable that indicated if the juvenile reported engaging in any of the three drug/alcohol behaviors. We created a total of five composite index variables that indicated if the juvenile engaged in behaviors related to (a) drug or alcohol use, (b) crimes against persons, (c) weapons-related crimes, (d) property crimes and (e) crimes against the public order. Some of the individual items fall into more than one composite index. For example, if a juvenile indicated he or she used a weapon to obtain property from someone, that juvenile would be coded as having committed a weapons-related crime and also coded as having committed a crime against persons.

We also collected data from juveniles about their interactions with law enforcement. The students were asked to indicate if they had had any of the following interactions (yes or no) in the previous six months:

- Any interaction or communication with a police or law enforcement officer?
- Asked any law enforcement officer for help or assistance?
- Has a police or law enforcement officer provided help or assistance to you?
- Any interaction with a police officer where the officer was rude or disrespectful to you?
- Has a police officer given you a verbal warning?
- Has a police officer given you a written warning?
- Has a police officer given you a ticket or citation?
- Been detained, questioned, or handcuffed by the police?
- Been transported by police to a detention facility, juvenile hall, jail, etc.?
- Been physically struck or injured by a police officer?

The schools

Before we present the data describing the juveniles in the sample, we show how the samples from each of the schools compares with the actual population data from the schools. Tables 5.2–5.4 show basic demographic characteristics of the sample data from each school alongside the actual distribution (i.e., the population distribution) of those demographic characteristics from the entire school for the year the survey was conducted. The population information for each school is based on data reported from each school to the OSDE. The comparison of sample and population variables in each school provides some assurance that the sample is reasonably representative of the school.[9] Table 5.2 shows the comparison for the inner-city urban school. Inspection of the percentages suggests the sample is similar to the population on many of the characteristics. The largest absolute percentage difference is for the race category Hispanic/Latinx. The percentage of Hispanic/Latinx in the sample is slightly (7 percentage points) lower than the percentage in the school. The differences between the other variables are between three and five percentage points.

Table 5.3 shows the same comparisons for the suburban school. The biggest differences between the sample and population are the grade level percentages. These differences were expected because we collected data only from junior–senior level courses at the suburban school. We had consent to collect data from upper division courses only. There are a handful of freshmen (9th graders) and sophomores (10th graders) in the dataset because a small number of students take advanced placement courses or take required courses at an earlier age. The other fairly significant difference between the sample and population data is the estimated percentage of students eligible

Table 5.2: Comparison of the sample and population data from the urban school

Variable	Population[a]	Sample
Race		
White	8	13
Non-White	92	87
Black	11	14
Hispanic/Latinx	73	66
Gender		
Male	56	53
Female	44	47
Grade		
Freshman	26	22
Sophomore	29	29
Junior	23	23
Senior	22	26
Eligible free/reduced lunch	> 95	95

Note: The numbers are percentages.

[a] The population information for the school is based on data reported from the school.

for free or reduced-price lunch. The sample estimate is 25 percent, while the actual number at the school is 34 percent. This difference, too, is somewhat expected and likely related to the sampling frame from the suburban school. In essence, we over-sampled juniors and seniors. It is well established that SES is related to dropping out of high school (Bradley and Lenton, 2007; Archambault et al, 2009; Henry et al, 2011; Lundetra, 2011). In fact, a recent study suggests that students from families with low socioeconomic standing had a risk of not completing a secondary education three times that of students from high SES families (Winding and Andersen, 2015). It is likely that students from lower socioeconomic families have dropped out before their junior or senior year. Juniors and seniors are likely from a higher SES family than the school as a whole.

The other characteristics are fairly similar between the sample and the population. The percentage differences for the race and ethnic groups, for example, are generally around four to five percentage points. Interestingly, the largest race and ethnicity difference is for Hispanic/Latinx group. As in the urban school, the sample underestimates the number of Hispanic/Latinx students (seven percentage points). The sample and population values for gender are very similar, with only a two percentage point difference.

Table 5.3: Comparison of the sample and population data from the suburban school

Variable	Population[a]	Sample
Race		
White	63	57
Non-White	37	43
Black	5	5
Hispanic/Latinx	11	4
Gender		
Male	52	54
Female	48	46
Grade[b]		
Freshman	27	6
Sophomore	26	11
Junior	25	32
Senior	22	51
Eligible free/reduced lunch	34	25

Note: The numbers are percentages.
[a] The population information for the school is based on data reported from the school.
[b] We collected data from junior and senior level courses only at this school.

The final comparison is for the rural school. The rural school is the smallest school by enrollment. It is also the smallest within-school sample (N = 45). The differences between the sample estimates and the population values are the largest of the three comparisons. The sample estimates of race and ethnicity group are fairly accurate. The largest difference is (again) for the Hispanic/Latinx group. The sample (again) underestimates the number of Hispanic/Latinx students. The grade-level estimates are also relatively close to the population values. The other comparisons, however, are relatively large in their differences. For example, the actual distribution of gender shows a slight majority of males in the school (56 percent). The sample, however, is only about one third (34 percent) male. Similarly, the sample underestimates the percentage of students eligible for free or reduced-price lunch. The rural school included in this study is a bit of a "mixed bag" economically. The area has a large Latinx and Native American population but is mostly White. There is a very wealthy area with large, mostly horse ranches, though the median income in the area is fairly low. The one notable difference is the very small Black population, which is only about 40 percent the size of the small Black population in the suburban schools.

Table 5.4: Comparison of the sample and population data from the rural school

Variable	Population[a]	Sample
Race		
White	58	64
Non-White	42	36
Black	2	0
Hispanic/Latinx	12	4
Gender		
Male	56	34
Female	44	66
Grade		
Freshman	28	22
Sophomore	28	20
Junior	21	25
Senior	23	33
Eligible free/reduced lunch	46	22

Note: The numbers are percentages.

[a] The population information for the school is based on data reported from the school.

Academically, this school falls between the urban and suburban schools in this study.

The juveniles

In the previous section, we presented selected demographic data by school as a way to illustrate the representativeness of the samples to the schools. We now turn to describing the data more generally. Table 5.5 presents the summary descriptions of the characteristics of the juveniles surveyed. There are considerably more non-White juveniles (73.1 percent) in the study group than White juveniles (26.9 percent). Hispanic/Latinx juveniles make up most of the non-White students. As noted previously, one of the schools in the study is predominantly Hispanic/Latinx. Black juveniles comprise just over 10 percent of the study group (11.0 percent), followed closely by juveniles who indicated they had a multi-heritage background. These juveniles selected multiple categories when asked to identify their race and ethnicity. Multi-heritage juveniles comprise 9.6 percent of the total. Native American juveniles make up the smallest percentage (5.2 percent) of the sample. Unlike the other data sources used in the previous analyses—the police reports and juvenile court data—which were predominantly male,

Table 5.5: Summary descriptions of the characteristics of the study group

Characteristic	Frequency	Percentage
Race		
White	140	26.9
Non-White	380	73.1
Black	57	11.0
Hispanic/Latinx	246	47.3
Native American	27	5.2
Multi Heritage	50	9.6
Gender		
Female	254	48.8
Male	266	51.2
Age[a]		
13–14	130	27.1
15–16	159	33.2
17–18	190	39.6
Eligible free/reduced lunch		
Yes	384	73.8
No	136	26.2
School location		
Urban	366	70.4
Suburban	109	21.0
Rural	45	8.7

[a] 41 observations do not have a reported age.

Table 5.5 shows that the distribution of gender is fairly even. There are slightly more males (51.2 percent) in the study than females (49.8 percent). In terms of age of the juveniles, there were 41 surveys from students who did not report their age. As such, there are 479 observations for the variable age. The median age is 16 and the mean age is 15.8. The largest age category is 17–18 years old (39.6 percent), followed by ages 15–16 (33.2 percent) and 13–14 (27.1 percent). There is a sizeable number of 13-year-olds in the dataset. One of the schools divided grade levels differently than the other two schools. Two of the schools were comprised of students in the 9th through 12th grades (freshmen through seniors). One of the schools, however, included only 10th through 12th graders (sophomores through seniors) in the high school. We surveyed 9th graders (freshmen) in that school system separately. There were some 8th grade students in the predominantly freshman classroom.

Table 5.5 also shows the distribution of juveniles from the different school locations, that is, urban, suburban and rural. A considerable majority of the surveys are from the inner-city urban school (70.4 percent). About one fifth (21.0 percent) of the juvenile surveys are from the suburban school. Just under one tenth are from the rural school (8.7 percent). As described in more detail previously, all the schools are from the same metropolitan area. As such, they are within the police and juvenile court jurisdiction described in the previous chapters.

Race and juvenile deviant and criminal behavior

As described in detail previously, we asked the juveniles about 14 specific deviant and criminal behaviors. Table 5.6 shows the frequencies and percentages for the responses to those questions. The most common behaviors are those involving alcohol and drugs. More than a quarter of the juveniles reported using alcohol (29.6 percent) and marijuana (21.9 percent). Aside from substance use, the most frequently reported activity was using physical violence in a fight or argument (18.8 percent). The least frequently reported behaviors were breaking into a home or business (1.3 percent) and using a weapon or threat of force to obtain property (1.5 percent).

Table 5.6 also shows the composite indices that measure if a juvenile reported any of several related deviant/criminal behaviors. As expected from the frequencies of the individual items, the most commonly reported types of behaviors were drug crimes: 38.8 percent of the juveniles reported one or more of the drug- and alcohol-related behaviors. The least frequently reported types of behaviors were weapons-related crimes. Only 5.6 percent of the juveniles reported weapons-related crimes. More than half of the juveniles (51.2 percent) reported having engaged in at least one of the 14 behaviors.

Table 5.7 shows the same deviant and criminal behaviors by the full set of race categories. The table shows several behavioral differences by race. Note that we present an indicator of statistical significance—a p-value—in the table. The juvenile self-report data are from a sample. As such, we make inferences from the sample data about the population using p-values. In technical terms, the p-value is the probability under a specified statistical model that a statistical summary of the data (e.g., percentage differences between two groups) would be equal to or more extreme than its observed value (Wasserstein and Lazar, 2016). As such, the p-value can indicate how incompatible the data are with a specified statistical model. The most common application is a model, with a given set of assumptions, together with a null hypothesis that postulates the absence of an effect (e.g., no difference between the two groups). The smaller the p-value, the greater the statistical incompatibility of the data with the null hypothesis. This incompatibility is interpreted as providing evidence against the null hypothesis (Wasserstein and Lazar, 2016).[10]

Table 5.6: Summary of self-reported deviant and criminal behaviors

Behavior/activity	Frequency	Percentage
Tobacco	76	14.6
Alcohol	154	29.6
Marijuana	114	21.9
Hard drugs	17	3.3
Vandalism	34	6.5
Steal < $50	53	10.2
Steal > $50	19	3.7
Break & enter	7	1.3
Weapon–property	8	1.5
Illegal firearm	13	2.5
Physical violence	98	18.8
Weapon to injure	16	3.1
Killed or injured	15	2.9
Gang	40	7.7
Composite indices		
Crime–persons	106	20.4
Crime–drugs	202	38.8
Crime–weapons	29	5.6
Crime–property	81	15.6
Crime–public order	196	37.7
Crime–any	266	51.2

Several of the behavioral differences by race are statistically significant at the $p \leq 0.05$ level: tobacco use, stealing items worth less than $50, using physical violence in a fight or argument, and using a weapon to injure someone. The composite indices also show several statistically significant racial and ethnic group differences: crimes against persons, drug-related behavior, crimes against property and having committed any crime. None of the other differences are statistically significant.[11] It is important to note that the statistical tests reported in Table 5.7 (and Table 5.8 shown later) are the significance level from the chi-square (χ^2) test of independence. The χ^2 tests whether one categorical variable (e.g., race) is associated with another categorical variable (e.g., engaging in a specific behavior). The χ^2 test does not indicate which categories of the independent variable are different from one another. There is not a straightforward statistical procedure to make individual comparisons of percentage differences.[12] Rather, we present the

Table 5.7: Self-reported deviant and criminal behaviors by race

Behavior/activity	Black	Latino	NA/AI	Multi	White	p-value
Tobacco	8.8	8.9	11.1	22.0	25.0	.000
Alcohol	26.3	26.0	29.6	32.0	36.4	.279
Marijuana	26.3	19.1	22.2	20.0	25.7	.546
Hard drugs	5.3	2.0	3.7	2.0	5.0	.477
Vandalism	7.0	6.5	18.5	6.0	4.3	.110
Steal < $50	15.8	4.9	11.1	12.0	16.4	.003
Steal > $50	7.0	2.0	0.0	2.0	6.4	.086
Break & enter	1.8	1.6	0.0	2.0	0.7	.884
Weapon–property	1.8	1.2	3.7	0.0	2.1	.711
Illegal firearm	5.3	1.6	3.7	0.0	3.6	.324
Physical violence	31.6	10.2	37.0	22.0	24.3	.000
Weapon to injure	8.8	1.6	7.4	2.0	2.9	.043
Killed or injured	5.3	1.6	3.7	4.0	3.6	.547
Gang	14.0	8.9	7.4	8.0	2.9	.078
Composite indices						
Crime–persons	35.1	10.6	40.7	24.0	26.4	.000
Crime–drugs	40.4	32.5	37.0	42.0	48.6	.040
Crime–weapons	10.5	3.7	7.4	2.0	7.9	.129
Crime–property	21.1	10.2	22.2	18.0	20.7	.030
Crime–public order	36.8	32.5	37.0	40.0	46.4	.112
Crime–any	52.6	42.7	59.3	68.0	57.9	.003

Note: The numbers are percentages.

deviant and criminal behaviors by the collapsed White and non-White race categories.

The White and non-White differences in the deviant and criminal behaviors are shown in Table 5.8. The data show interesting trends. Of the 14 behaviors, eight are not statistically different. Six of the behaviors show statistical differences by race category. All but one of the six differences show that White juveniles engage in the behavior or activity at higher rates than non-White juveniles. White youth report higher percentages for using tobacco and alcohol, stealing (both less than and more than $50) and using physical violence. The one behavior that non-White youth report at a statistically higher rate is belonging to a gang. About 10 percent (9.5 percent) of the non-White juveniles report being a member of a gang, compared with 2.9 percent of the White juveniles ($p = .012$). The composite indices

Table 5.8: Self-reported deviant and criminal behaviors by race (non-White/White)

Behavior/activity	Non-White	White	p-value
Tobacco	10.8	25.0	.000
Alcohol	27.1	36.4	.039
Marijuana	20.5	25.7	.205
Hard drugs	2.6	5.0	.178
Vandalism	7.4	4.3	.207
Steal < $50	7.9	16.4	.004
Steal > $50	2.6	6.4	.041
Break & enter	1.6	0.7	.448
Weapon–property	1.3	2.1	.497
Illegal firearm	2.1	3.6	.342
Physical violence	16.8	24.3	.050
Weapon to injure	3.2	2.9	.860
Killed or injured	2.6	3.6	.570
Gang	9.5	2.9	.012
Composite indices			
Crime–persons	18.2	26.4	.038
Crime–drugs	35.3	48.6	.006
Crime–weapons	4.7	7.9	.169
Crime–property	13.7	20.7	.050
Crime–public order	34.5	46.4	.013
Crime–any	48.7	57.9	.063

Note: The numbers are percentages.

show a similar pattern. Where there are statistically significant differences, those differences show that White juveniles have a higher percentage of involvement in the deviant or criminal behavior.

The data in the previous tables show race differences by the types of deviant and criminal behavior. Tables 5.9 and 5.10 show the mean number of deviant and criminal behaviors reported by juveniles by the race and ethnicity categories. For the entire sample, the juveniles reported committing, on average, about 2.07 deviant and criminal acts (Table 5.9). The model suggests there are significant race differences (F = 4.80, df = 4, 515, $p < 0.001$). To determine which specific groups are different from one another, we ran post hoc analyses.[13] The results show that Hispanic/Latinx juveniles differ significantly from White ($p = 0.001$) and Black juveniles

Table 5.9: Mean number of self-reported deviant and criminal behaviors by race

Race/ethnicity	Frequency	Std dev	Mean
Black	57	3.50	2.70
Hispanic/Latinx	246	2.37	1.52
Native American	27	3.49	2.56
White	140	3.25	2.66
Multi heritage	50	2.33	2.16
Total	520	2.87	2.07

Note: $F = 4.80$, $df = 4, 515$, $p < .001$.

Table 5.10: Mean number of self-reported deviant and criminal behaviors by race (non-White/White)

Race/ethnicity	Frequency	Std dev	Mean
Non-White	380	2.67	1.86
White	140	3.25	2.66
Total	520	2.87	2.07

Note: $F = 8.25$, $df = 1, 518$, $p < .004$.

($p = 0.037$). Table 5.10 shows the mean differences for the collapsed White and non-White race categories. Taken together, the non White juveniles reported slightly fewer than two deviant/criminal behaviors (mean = 1.86). White juveniles reported 2.66 deviant/criminal behaviors. The difference is statistically significant ($F = 8.25$, $df = 1, 518$, $p < .004$).

In short, the information from Tables 5.1–5.10 show little difference in offending between White and non-White youth.

Race and juvenile interactions with police

As we noted previously, the central focus in this chapter is to estimate deviant and criminal behavior based on the juveniles' self-reporting, rather than from police or juvenile justice records. We were also interested in what the juveniles had to say about their interaction(s) with law enforcement. In the section to follow, we present the self-report data describing the juveniles' interactions with law enforcement.

Table 5.11 shows the frequencies and percentages for the various types of interactions the juveniles reported having had with police. Over a third (34.8 percent) reported having had some interaction with police. This is a non-specific interaction. There is no indication if the encounter was positive, negative or indifferent. Aside from the non-specific interaction,

Table 5.11: Summary of self-reported interactions with police

Police interaction	Frequency	Percentage
Police – any interact	181	34.8
Police – ask help	67	12.9
Police – assist	98	18.8
Police – rude	113	21.7
Police – warning – verbal	104	20.0
Police – warning – written	54	10.4
Police – citation	62	11.9
Police – detain	70	13.5
Police – transport	37	7.1
Police – injure	23	4.4

Table 5.12: Summary of self-reported interactions with police by race

Police interaction	Black	Latino	NA/AI	Multi	White	p-value
Police – any interact	42.1	26.8	33.3	48.0	41.4	.005
Police – ask help	17.5	9.8	18.5	12.0	15.7	.283
Police – assist	15.8	15.4	25.9	22.0	23.6	.243
Police – rude	33.3	15.4	33.3	32.0	22.1	.004
Police – warning – verbal	24.6	17.5	18.5	24.0	21.4	.657
Police – warning – written	10.5	7.7	7.4	14.0	14.3	.275
Police – citation	12.3	10.6	7.4	20.0	12.1	.396
Police – detain	22.8	14.2	14.8	18.0	6.4	.024
Police – transport	5.3	8.5	18.5	8.0	2.9	.036
Police – injure	8.8	3.7	7.4	4.0	3.6	.445

Note: The numbers are percentages.

the most commonly reported interactions were receiving a verbal warning (20.0 percent), receiving assistance from an officer (18.8 percent) and asking an officer for help or assistance (12.9 percent). Interestingly, almost one fifth of the juveniles (21.7 percent) reported that the police officer was rude in the interaction. The most serious interactions with police were those that involved detainment (13.5 percent), transport to a facility (7.1 percent) or physical injury (4.4 percent).

Tables 5.12 and 5.13 show the same police interactions by race. There are several interaction types statistically related to race. Having any interaction with police ($p = 0.005$), having an interaction where the officer was rude or

Table 5.13: Summary of self-reported interactions with police by race (non-White/White)

Behavior/activity	Non-White	White	p-value
Police – any interaction	32.4	41.4	.050
Police – ask help	11.8	15.7	.242
Police – assist	17.1	23.6	.094
Police – rude	21.6	22.1	.890
Police – warning – verbal	19.5	21.4	.621
Police – warning – written	8.9	14.3	.077
Police – citation	11.8	12.1	.925
Police – detain	16.1	6.4	.004
Police – transport	8.7	2.9	.022
Police – injure	4.7	3.6	.566

Note: The numbers are percentages.

disrespectful ($p = 0.004$), being handcuffed or detained by police ($p = 0.024$) and being transported by police to a jail or detention facility ($p = .036$) are all related to race. Like the percentage differences presented previously, the statistical significance tests reported in Tables 5.12 and 5.13 are from the chi-square (χ^2) test of independence. The χ^2 test does not indicate which categories of the independent variable are different from one another.

Table 5.13 presents the interactions with police by the collapsed race categories White and non-White. There are relatively few differences. A significantly higher percentage of White juveniles have had some interaction with police (41.4 vs. 32.4 percent, $p = 0.05$). There are no differences in terms of asking for help or assistance, receiving help or assistance, or receiving a warning or citation. There are two interactions, however, that stand out: being detained by police and being transported to a jail or facility by police. The race differences for these interactions are striking. About 6.4 percent of White juveniles reported having been detained by police, compared with 16.1 percent for non-White juveniles ($p = 0.004$). Likewise, a much higher percentage of non-White juveniles (8.7 percent) reported having been transported by police compared with White juveniles (2.9 percent, $p = 0.022$). The magnitude of these differences is illustrated in Figure 5.1. The percentage differences are expressed and displayed as risk ratios. Non-White juveniles are 150 percent—two and a half times—more likely to be detained by police than Whites (RR = 2.50). The effect is even higher for being transported. Non-White juveniles have a probability of being transported by police to a jail or juvenile facility three times that of White juveniles (RR = 3.04).

Figure 5.1: Risk ratios of being detained or transported by the police for non-White juveniles (N = 520)

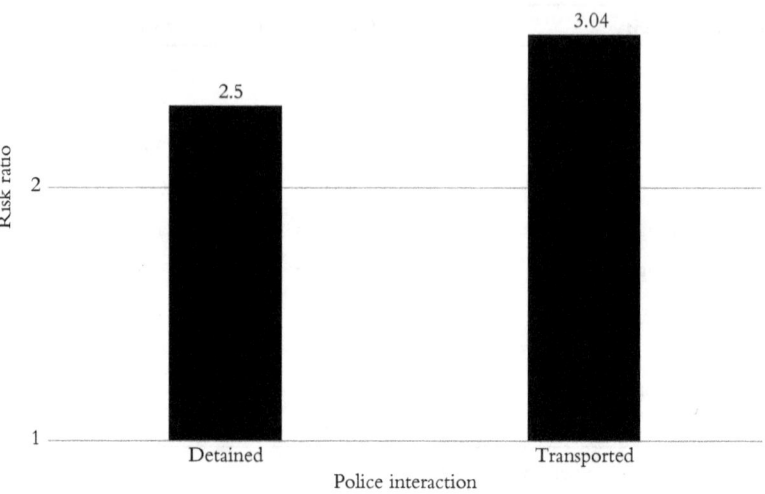

The results showing the race differences for the most consequential and severe police interactions, being detained and being transported, are striking and intriguing. We examine those differences in further detail in a later discussion. More specifically, we cross tabulate the self-report of police interaction variables detained and transported by police with the self-report behavior variables to determine if the juveniles behaving in the deviant and criminal ways are the ones being detained and transported by police. Figure 5.2 shows the results of the cross tabulations by race (White and non-White). The first column of bars shows the percentages for juveniles who were detained and reported they had engaged in deviant and criminal behaviors. Recall from Table 5.6 that 51.2 percent of the respondents self-reported having engaged in at least one of the deviant and criminal behaviors. The data show that for those detained, 90 percent of the White juveniles self-reported criminal behavior. Only 81 percent of the non-White juveniles who were detained reported having engaged in criminal behavior. The next set of percentages in the graph are for those juveniles who were detained but reported they had not engaged in any of the deviant or criminal behaviors. Ostensibly, these are juveniles who were detained without having committed a crime. These percentages are the inverse of the previous percentages. Ten percent of the White youth were detained but reported no criminal behavior. By contrast, the percentage for non-White juveniles is double (20 percent) that of White juveniles.

Examining juveniles who were transported by police to a jail or other facility shows the same pattern. One hundred percent of the White juveniles who were transported by police reported they had engaged in at least one

Figure 5.2: Detained and transported and criminal behavior by race

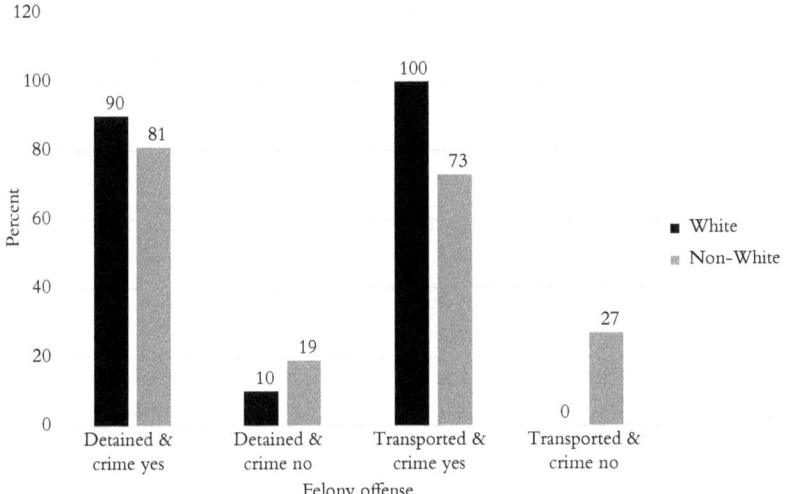

of the deviant or criminal behaviors. It follows that none (0.0 percent) of the White juveniles who were transported by police reported not having committed a crime. The non-White juveniles show a different pattern. Over a quarter (27 percent) of the non-White juveniles who were transported by police reported no criminal activity. While the differences are big (27 vs. 0.0 percent), we must point out that the number of White youths who were transported is small. We must take caution not to overanalyze the results. Still, the results are striking and consistent with the other findings.

The data show that non-White juveniles who had severe and consequential police interactions in the form of detainment and transportation to a facility were more likely to report having not committed criminal offenses. To be clear, these data are not conclusive. The data do not prove that the non-White juveniles had not committed a crime related to their interaction with law enforcement. The data are merely suggestive and fit the other patterns presented in this chapter and the other chapters.

Conclusion

We set out to determine whether non-White youth are more deviant and criminal than White youth. More specifically, we aimed to determine if non-White juvenile self-reports of criminal behavior are consistent with their overrepresentation in police encounters and the juvenile justice system. If deviance and criminality were to explain non-White juveniles' overrepresentation in the juvenile justice system, we would expect to find that non-White youth commit crimes at exceedingly higher levels

Table 5.14: Summary of deviant and criminal behavior differences by White and non-White race categories

Nature of difference	Frequency	Percent
White youth statistically significant – higher	10	47.6
Non-White youth statistically significant – higher	1	4.8
No statistically significant difference	10	47.6
Total	21	100.0

Note: The total includes the 14 individual behaviors, the six composite indices and the one mean number of reported behaviors.

than White youth. We did not find that non-White juveniles commit crimes at exceedingly higher rates. In fact, we found that White and non-White juveniles self-report relatively similar levels of deviant and criminal behaviors. Other studies have made similar findings (Paschall et al, 2001; Lauritsen, 2005). Where there were differences in self-reported offending, the differences were mostly in the direction of White juveniles offending more. On the other hand, Piquero and Brame (2008, p. 23) found "little evidence of important racial and ethnic differences in either self-reported offending (frequency or variety) or officially based arrests leading to a court referral in the year preceding study enrollment."

Table 5.14 shows a simple summary of the findings from the self-report data. We assessed race and ethnic group differences on a total of 21 indicators of deviant and criminal behavior (14 specific behaviors, six composite indices of the 14 behaviors and the total number of reported behaviors). Of the 21 indicators, ten (47.6 percent) were not statistically different between White and non-White juveniles. The remaining 11 indicators were different by race; ten of the 11 showed White juveniles with higher percentages of engaging in the deviant and criminal behaviors. Only one indicator, membership in a gang, was significantly higher for non-White juveniles.

It is worth noting that we did find evidence that some non-White groups report differences in the types of crime committed. Specifically, we found that Black and Native American juveniles reported more serious behaviors, especially related to the use of physical violence and weapon use to injure someone (see Table 5.6). Previous literature has found a similar relationship between non-White juveniles and more serious self-reported offenses (Elliot, 1994). In addition, it is important to note that we do not have a measure of the number of times a juvenile committed an offense. We used a measure of the number of different types of offenses—theft, drug crimes, weapons and so forth—but we do not have a measure of the number of times or the persistence in offending. Nevertheless, the juvenile self-report data show that non-White juveniles are not offending at rates anywhere near their representation in the justice system.

Notes

1. We are not revealing the names of the specific schools or names of the districts to protect the students, teachers and administrators from those schools and districts.
2. The Oklahoma State Department of Education's School Report Card is an indicator of a school's performance on several dimensions, as well as overall. The evaluation uses both state and federal performance and accountability criteria. The performance and accountability criteria include academic achievement, academic improvement, chronic absenteeism, progress in English language proficiency assessments, postsecondary opportunities and graduation. Each of these indicators receives a specific point value that translates to a letter grade.
3. Consent from a school required consent from the district (the superintendent's office), the individual school (the principal) and the specific teachers who taught the classes where we administered the survey.
4. The survey data of students were collected over a couple of years because the consent process took considerably longer in some of the schools.
5. At one school—the suburban school—we did not get consent to collect data from all grade levels. We got consent to collect data in junior–senior level classrooms only.
6. We administered the surveys at the schools at the beginning of two school years. In the second school year, we did not attempt to get parental informed consent at the back-to-school event. We learned in the first round of data collection that it was more efficient to seek consent from the specific students enrolled in the class selected to administer the survey.
7. If a student opted out of taking the survey after having begun the survey, the student's survey was shredded in the classroom before the student left the room.
8. All of the responses in the "Other" category actually could fit within the listed response categories. The most common responses in the "Other" category were specific Native American tribes, such as "Creek" or "Choctaw." There were also several specific Asian nationalities listed in the "Other" category responses, such as "Vietnamese."
9. The comparison of the sample demographics with those of the entire school only ensures the sample is representative in terms of those demographic characteristics. It does not guarantee the sample is representative of the main characteristics of interest, namely deviant and criminal behavior by juveniles.
10. As a simple example, suppose a study to examine the differences in income for males and females resulted in a mean difference of $8,000 with a p-value of 0.04. This p-value indicates that if gender has no effect on income (the null hypothesis), we would obtain the observed $8,000 income difference (or more) in 4 percent of studies due to random sampling error.
11. We use the common value of 0.05 as the designation for statistical significance (i.e., $p \leq 0.05$). The specific value used to establish statistical significance, and even the use of p-values at all, is contested in various scientific literatures. Some argue that an established, consistent use of a significance value is important. Moreover, researchers should strictly rely on a specified significance level such as $p \leq 0.05$ (see, for example, Mustillo et al, 2018). By contrast, others argue that the p-value is only one element of several that should be considered in the inferencing process. Relatedly, opponents of a strict use of a specified p-value argue that specified value (e.g., 0.05) is arbitrary (for an overview, see Goodman et al, 2019; Wasserstein et al, 2019). We have opted to report and highlight findings as statistically significant if the p-value is less than or equal to the traditional 0.05 value.

[12] The comparisons of means for continuous outcome data by groups is straightforward using analysis of variance (ANOVA). Like the chi-square test of independence, ANOVA determines if there are any statistically significant differences in means between two or more groups. The ANOVA, however, has many well-established post hoc tests (Bonferroni, Scheffe, Tukey, etc.) to determine which group mean differs from the other group means.

[13] We ran Tukey's Honestly Significant Difference (HSD) post hoc test. The choice of post hoc tests is somewhat arbitrary and somewhat empirical. Some tests are better suited if the groups have equal variances in the population. The Tukey HSD is one such test. We used the Levene's Test for Equality of Variances. The Levene's test suggested the group variances are equal.

6

Data Issues and the Case for Self-Report Data

> The thin blue line is stronger than the seed of evil that is planting itself.
>
> Unknown

Introduction

We have attempted to present data—lots of data—related to disproportionate minority contact (DMC) in the juvenile justice system. These data, from police interactions, court processes and outcomes, and interviews with juvenile justice officials, all come from the same location and the same time period. Our data triangulation approach to understand DMC in one place at one time shows that minority and non-White youth are disadvantaged at every point in the process, from initial contact with police to court outcomes and decisions about incarceration. These findings are only meaningful to the extent the data are accurate or valid.[1] Furthermore, the findings are more meaningful and useful to the extent the data from this one location and time period tells us something about DMC more generally. In this chapter, we examine these issues of data validity and generalizability of the findings.[2] We address these issues, in turn, with a particular focus on the validity issues related to our self-report data of juvenile deviant and criminal behavior.

Empirical comparison of self-report data and school disciplinary data

The self-report data from juveniles about their deviant and criminal behavior suggests that there are relatively few differences between White and non-White youths. Where there are differences, however, the differences suggest that White juveniles behave in ways more deviant and criminal (see Chapter 5). How accurate are the self-report data from the juveniles? Are juveniles truthful about their delinquent and criminal behavior? If not, are there differences between White and non-White juveniles? Much of our argument centers on the answers to these types of questions. If the self-report data are dismissed as inaccurate, it weakens our overall argument.[3] If, however, the self-report data paint an accurate picture of deviant and criminal behavior of juveniles, especially differences in behaviors of juveniles along racial and ethnic group lines, it strengthens our argument. Significant to our conclusion, we also explain why the official data currently used to create crime rate information are of low quality and highly biased.

Self-report vs. official data

Official reports from police, courts and prisons have long been considered a default "gold standard" of data. Other sources of data are often compared with official data as a way to evaluate the validity or quality of the other data sources. For most of the twentieth century, our basic understanding of deviant and criminal behavior was based on official data. The usefulness of official data, however, was questioned almost from the beginning of the previous century. Almost a hundred years ago, sociologist Thorsten Sellin made a point that cast doubt on the usefulness of official data for understanding deviant and criminal behavior. He noted that "the value of a crime rate for index purposes decreases as the distance from the crime itself in terms of procedure increases" (Sellin, 1931, p. 346). In simple terms: the further removed the data are from the behavior, the less useful are those data. In practical terms, Sellin was arguing that as a measure of delinquent or criminal behavior, prison data are less useful than court data. Moreover, court data are less useful than police data. The increasing distance of the data from the behavior creates what Thornberry and Krohn refer to as "layers of potential bias between the actual behavior and the data" (2000, p. 34) because the data are the product of behaviors by individuals charged with offenses, but also by behaviors of the police and court officials.

Despite the known problems with official data, self-report data of deviant and criminal behavior are still viewed with resistance and skepticism. This resistance and skepticism prevail despite considerable evidence that self-report data are valid and reliable measures of deviant and criminal behavior (Thornberry and Krohn, 2000). For more than 50 years, studies have assessed the reliability and validity of self-report deviant and criminal behavior.[4] Many of these studies make comparisons between self-reports of juveniles with and without arrest records, or those convicted or not convicted of a crime. These studies show that juveniles who have entered the juvenile justice system self-reported substantially more delinquent acts than juveniles who have not (for examples, see Erickson and Empey, 1963; Hirschi, 1969; Farrington, 1973; Hardt and Petersen-Hardt, 1977; Hindelang et al, 1981; Huizinga and Elliot, 1986). Others have examined the accuracy of self-report data by making comparisons not of groups with known differences in offending, but of individuals.[5] These data, too, show a strong relationship between self-reports and official measures of delinquency and criminality (for examples, see Hathaway et al, 1960; Blackmore, 1974; Farrington, 1977; Hardt and Petersen-Hardt, 1977; Hindelang et al, 1981; Huizinga and Elliott, 1986; Farrington, Loeber et al, 1996).[6] The relationships are especially strong as the external criterion for comparing against the self-reports is more verifiable. That is, the relationships are even stronger for self-reports of having been arrested or having been convicted (Blackmore, 1974; Farrington, 1977).

Assessment of the self-report data

We began this section with the question: how accurate are the self-report data from the juveniles? Another way to ask the question in methodological terms is: are self-reports from juveniles a valid measure of deviant and criminal behavior? Validity refers to the extent to which a measure, such as self-reports, adequately reflects the real meaning of the concept under consideration, such as deviant and criminal behavior (Maxfield and Babbie, 2018). While previous studies have demonstrated that self-reports have reasonable validity (see the previous discussion), in this section we assess the validity of the self-report data from the juveniles in our study. More specifically, we assess the criterion validity of the self-report data. Criterion validity refers to the association between a given measure and a known external criterion that is also an indicator of the concept being measured (Maxfield and Babbie, 2018).[7] We use a group criterion validity approach. We compare self-reports of delinquent and criminal behaviors from the juveniles with school-level reports of delinquent and criminal behavior. That is, we compare the rates of specific behaviors reported by the juveniles to the rates of those behaviors recorded by school administrators. If the rates reported by the juveniles are similar to the rates recorded by the school, that suggests the self-reports have a degree of validity. By contrast, if the rates are substantially different, it suggests the self-reports do not have a high degree of validity.[8]

Data collection

Self-report data

The self-report data are the same as described in the chapter assessing juvenile deviant and criminal behavior with a couple of exceptions (for a more detailed discussion of the self-report data, see Chapter 5). First, the comparison data we present in this section to assess the validity of the self-report data are limited to responses from one school. Second, and related to the first difference, we used a slightly different version of the questionnaire at the last-surveyed school site. The questionnaire was the same with one exception: when the juveniles were asked about the 14 deviant and criminal behaviors, the survey asked them to indicate whether the behavior took place at school or not at school. The analyses are limited to those behaviors that were committed while at school. Because we are comparing self-reported behaviors with those recorded by the school, we necessarily limit the data to those offenses committed at school. Obviously, the schools would have no record of behaviors and offenses that occurred at another site.

School discipline data

The external criterion we use to evaluate the self-report data are the official records of disciplinary actions recorded by school officials.[9] We requested and received disciplinary reports for two academic years to ensure we had all reports in the six months prior to the survey data collection. The disciplinary reports contain information about disciplinary incidents at the school campus. When a student commits an infraction, he or she is sent to the school office for an assessment and faces possible disciplinary action.[10] The circumstances of the infraction are recorded on an official incident report. The report includes the following information:

- student name;
- grade;
- the teacher (or school personnel) involved or witnessing the infraction;
- location (classroom, cafeteria, outside area, etc.) of the infraction;
- date and time;
- a description of the incident as written by the teacher (or school personnel involved);
- the action taken by the teacher (or school personnel);
- the action taken by the school administration.

In addition, we recorded each student's race and gender using information from school personnel (administrators, teachers and office staff). Using the list of names on the reports, the school personnel provided the student's race and gender. We also coded an additional variable from the incident reports. Trained coders coded whether the description of the incident included any of the delinquent and criminal behaviors asked in the self-report questionnaire:

- Use any tobacco product (cigarette, cigar, chewing tobacco, dip)?
- Drink any alcoholic beverage?
- Smoke/use marijuana or hash/hashish?
- Use meth, cocaine, heroin, LSD or mushrooms?

- Vandalize and/or spray-paint any property?
- Steal or shoplift any items where the total value is less than $50?
- Steal or shoplift any items where the total value is over $50?
- Break into a home or business and take things from it?
- Use a weapon or threat of force to obtain property from someone?
- Illegally possess a firearm not used for hunting?
- Get in a fight or argument which led to physical violence?
- Use a weapon to injure another person?
- Injure someone critically/seriously or kill another person?
- Are you a member of a gang?

To code the incident reports, we created a coding sheet with operational definitions for the 14 behaviors. The coders trained by using incident reports that were not used in the analyses, those reports that were for incidents that occurred after the self-report data collection. The authors monitored the training sheets and provided additional training as necessary. Once we were assured the coders understood the coding categories and operational definitions, the incident reports were coded. Despite the training and strict coding guidelines, variability in the coding is possible. We used several methods to minimize and assess coder variability. First, we used multiple coders who coded the reports independently. Second, during the coding process, we performed periodic checks to ensure the coders stayed within training guidelines. Finally, after coding was complete, we performed analyses to determine the consistency between the coders. We evaluated interrater agreement using the kappa (κ) statistic. The κ statistic evaluates the extent of agreement between two or more independent evaluations and takes into account the extent of agreement that could be expected beyond chance alone (Gwet, 2014). The interrater reliability was high (κ = 0.99). The few disagreements between coders were reconciled to achieve 100 percent agreement.

Results

As a first check of the data, we examined the distribution of general demographic characteristics from the two data sources. We examined the distribution of race, gender and grade level. The data are displayed in Table 6.1. As shown in the table, there are statistically significant differences in the distribution of race in the two data sources. White juveniles are slightly more represented in school disciplinary data (86.2 percent versus 77.0 percent, $p = .02$). Non-White juveniles are slightly underrepresented in the school disciplinary data (13.8 percent) compared with the percentage who self-reported deviant or criminal behavior at school (23.0 percent).

Table 6.1: Demographic comparisons of juvenile self-report of offenses committed at school and school administrative disciplinary report

	Self-report data N = 246	School disciplinary report N = 426	p-value
Race category			
White	23.0	13.8	0.02
Non-White	77.0	86.2	0.02
Gender			
Male	56.3	63.1	0.08
Female	43.7	36.9	0.08
Grade level			
Freshman/9th	43.2	39.4	0.33
Sophomore/10th	22.1	29.3	0.04
Junior/11th	18.5	16.7	0.56
Senior/12th	16.2	14.6	0.58

Note: The numbers are percentages.

While the race differences are statistically significant, they are not necessarily substantially significant, at least not substantively significant in terms of assessing the validity and accuracy of the self-report data. The comparison represented in Table 6.1 is for all students in the school disciplinary data, not necessarily students who have behaved in an overtly deviant or criminal way. Most of the incidents in the school disciplinary data (about 80 percent) are related to the juvenile not listening or being disruptive in the classroom. In later analyses, we narrow the data to juveniles who behaved in ways overtly deviant or criminal.

The distribution of gender is generally the same in the self-report and school discipline datasets. The differences are not statistically significant. Likewise, the distribution of grade level is generally the same in the two datasets. The only significant difference between the two data sources is for sophomores. Sophomore juveniles account for a higher percentage in the school disciplinary data (29.3 percent) compared with the percentage of sophomores who self-reported a deviant or criminal activity at school (22.1 percent).

Figure 6.1 shows the percentage comparisons of the self-report data and school disciplinary reports for behaviors that were overtly deviant or criminal. That is, the school disciplinary data in Figure 6.1 are restricted to those incidents that were for the same type of behaviors asked about in the self-report survey, the 14 deviant and criminal behaviors. Because some of the frequencies were relatively small for some of the groups,

Figure 6.1: Comparison of juvenile self-reports of offenses committed at school and school disciplinary data

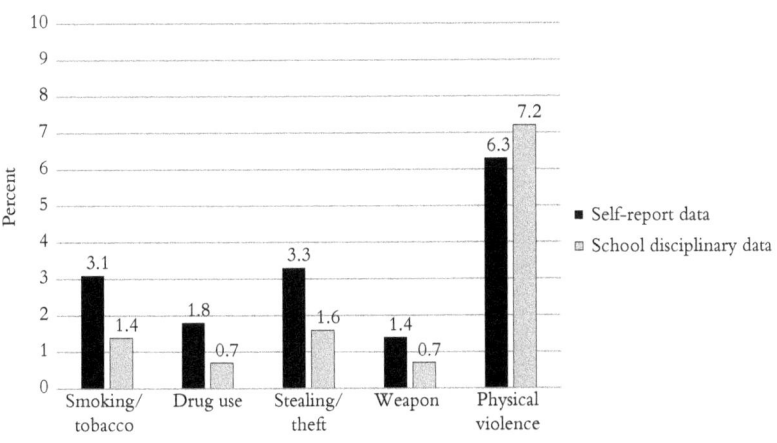

we combined the 14 deviant and criminal behaviors into five categories of behavior: (a) smoking/using tobacco products; (b) drug use, which combines the questions about alcohol, marijuana and other drugs; (c) stealing/theft, which combines the two questions about stealing items worth less than $50 and more than $50; (d) weapons-related behaviors, which combines the use of a weapon to obtain property, illegal possession of a firearm and using a weapon to injure someone; and (e) use or threat of physical violence. The school disciplinary data had no reported incidents of vandalism, breaking and entering, critically injuring someone or being a gang member.[11]

The data show several interesting trends. First, the most common infraction from both the self-report data and the school disciplinary data is the threat or use of physical violence. Just over 6 percent (6.3 percent) of juveniles self-reported physical violence behaviors, while 7.2 percent of the school disciplinary reports were for physical violence. Second, the other infractions are relatively rare. None of the other types of behaviors had percentages higher than approximately 3 percent. Third, the differences in the percentages between the self-reported behaviors and the school disciplinary data are not statistically significant. For all the behaviors other than physical violence, the percentages are actually slightly higher in the self-report data (again, the difference is not statistically significant). It is reasonable that the self-report data show higher percentages. The school disciplinary data contain only behaviors in which the juvenile was caught. It makes sense, for example, that the number of juveniles who self-reported smoking or using tobacco at school is more than double the percentage in the disciplinary data (3.1 and

Figure 6.2: Comparison of juvenile self-report of physical violence committed at school and school disciplinary data of physical violence by race

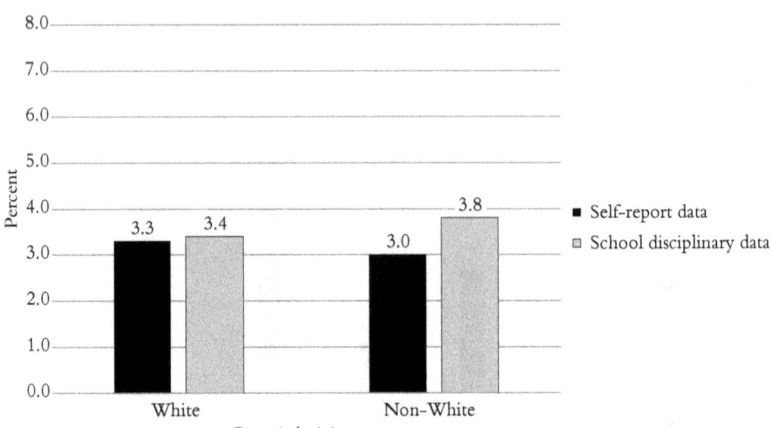

1.4 percent, respectively). It is highly probable that juveniles used tobacco more often than they got caught.

Relatively speaking, the differences between the self-report and school disciplinary data related to behaviors of physical violence are closer than those for the other behaviors. The percentage difference from the self-report data for physical violence is about 14 percent, compared with the other behaviors which have percentage differences roughly between 50 and 60 percent. This, too, seems reasonable. The use of physical violence is much less likely to go unnoticed or unreported on school grounds. Given the probability that school reports involving physical violence are the most representative of actual behavior, we examined the race and ethnicity difference for behaviors involving physical violence. Figure 6.2 shows the differences for White and non-White juveniles. Again, a couple of findings stand out. Both White and non-White juveniles self-report slightly lower percentages of behaviors involving physical violence relative to the percentages in the school disciplinary data. In the self-report data, 3.0 percent of the non-White juveniles reported committing an act of physical violence at school. The school disciplinary data show that 3.8 percent of the incidents involving physical violence involved a non-White juvenile. The difference is not statistically significant. The difference for White juveniles is even less (3.3 versus 3.4 percent). The comparisons between the two groups of data are remarkably similar for White and non-White youth.

We made the same data comparisons of behaviors involving physical violence for males and females. Figure 6.3 shows the percentages from the self-report and school disciplinary data. Males slightly under-report physical violence compared with the disciplinary reports (2.6 and 4.0 percent,

Figure 6.3: Comparison of juvenile self-report of physical violence committed at school and school disciplinary data of physical violence by gender

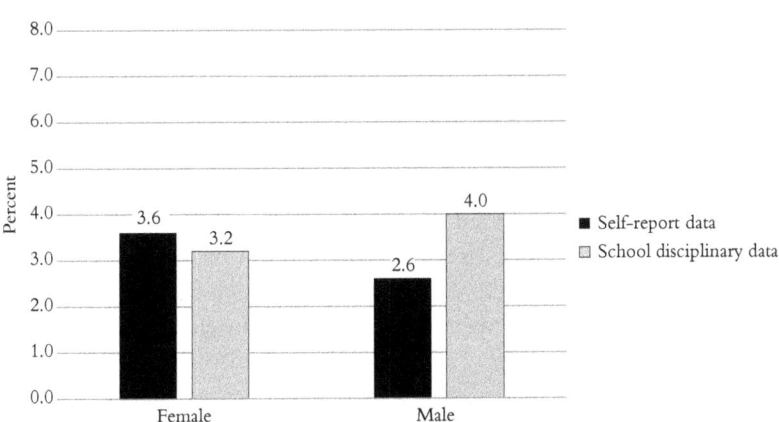

respectively). Females, by contrast, slightly over-report behaviors of physical violence compared with their numbers in the school disciplinary data. Again, these differences are not statistically significant.

The assessment of the self-report data is fairly conclusive in what it shows. Assessing the self-report data to the external criterion of the school disciplinary data showed there are no systematic race differences between the self-report data and the school disciplinary data when comparing deviant and criminal behaviors. We recognize that making group-level comparisons provides only a minimal validity assessment. Because the self-report data are anonymous, we are unable to validate self-reports at the individual level. Despite the limitations of the group-level comparisons, the school discipline data certainly are compatible with the juvenile self-report data. The assessment of the validity of the measurement of deviant and criminal behavior provides support for our more general argument—that the overrepresentation of minorities in the juvenile justice system is not a direct result of differential offending by non-White youth. Said another way, establishing the measurement validity of the self-report data provides support that the conclusions drawn from the data accurately reflect what is going on in the study group. This notion of the conclusions correctly describing the relationships among variables (e.g., cause and effect) in the study is also referred to as internal validity (Campbell and Stanley, 1963). It follows, then, that having a high degree of internal validity also makes it feasible to eliminate alternative explanations for a finding. In our case, having confidence in the validity of the juvenile self-report data increases the internal validity of the differential treatment argument. This, in turn, casts doubt on the alternative explanation of differential behavior by non-White juveniles.[12]

Generalizability of the data

It is not sufficient to establish internal validity alone. Even if the results of a study provide an accurate assessment of the relationships for the specific group under investigation, another important issue is how applicable those results are to other people, places or situations. This is the issue of generalizability or external validity (Maxfield and Babbie, 2018). Our data, after all, are not from a random sample of juveniles or court cases or juvenile justice officials from across the United States. The data, in fact, are not necessarily a representative selection of cases from the state of Oklahoma. We now take up the issue of generalizability—the extent to which the data and findings from our study tell us something about DMC more generally.

Comparisons with the state of Oklahoma

We begin by making explicit comparisons between the study data—from Oklahoma City—and data from other locations in the state of Oklahoma. The comparisons follow the same procedure that we presented for the quantitative data analyses: police interactions, court intake decisions and court dispositions. The data from other locations in the state are not always identical to our own study data. For example, the police interaction data in our study recorded whether the juvenile was Hispanic/Latinx. The police data we compare with our data did not record Hispanic/Latinx ethnicity. There are other differences as well. We make note of those in the comparisons in the coming analyses.

Table 6.2 shows the comparisons of being arrested (versus being ticketed or cited) for the study data (Oklahoma City) and two other metropolitan areas in Oklahoma—Lawton and Tulsa. Tulsa is the second most populous city in the state. Lawton is the third most populous city that is outside the Oklahoma City and Tulsa metropolitan areas.[13] The data are from 60,347 police reports from the three locations. The numbers in the table are odds

Table 6.2: Comparisons of odds ratios of arrest for race by location in Oklahoma

	Lawton	Tulsa	Oklahoma City
Black	2.12	1.98	2.21
Native American	3.41	2.43	2.47
Asian	1.04	0.68	0.82

Note: The numbers are odds ratios comparing the odds of being arrested compared with Whites for each group.

ratios (ORs). Odds ratios represent the odds that an outcome (arrest) will occur in one group (Black juveniles) compared with the odds of the outcome occurring in a different group (the reference group, e.g., White juveniles). In Table 6.2, White juveniles are the reference group, so that the odds ratios for the race categories listed in the table are compared with White juveniles. The odds ratio for Black juveniles in Oklahoma City, for example, is 2.21. This means that in Oklahoma City, Black juveniles have an odds ratio of arrest 2.21 higher than White juveniles. Previously, we noted the problems with using odds ratios as estimates of relative risk (see Chapter 3 and Chapter 4). For the current purposes, we are not specifically interested in estimating risk. Rather, we are interested in comparing the magnitude of the effects from the study data with the other locations.[14] Furthermore, note that the table does not include the ethnicity category Hispanic/Latinx. The police interaction data from Lawton and Tulsa did not have measures of ethnicity.

The odds ratios from the different locations vary slightly. For example, in the study data (Oklahoma City), the odds ratio of arrest for Black juveniles is 2.21. The odds ratios in Lawton and Tulsa are 2.12 and 1.98, respectively. The most variability in the effects is for Asian juveniles. In Oklahoma City and Tulsa, Asian juveniles have an odds ratio less than 1.0, indicating Asian juveniles have a lower odds ratio of arrest compared with White juveniles. In Lawton, however, the odds of arrest for Asian juveniles is slightly higher than for White juveniles (OR = 1.04). The general pattern of results is consistent. Across the three areas compared, Native American youth have the highest odds ratios, followed by Black youth. Asian juveniles have the lowest odds ratios in all three locations.

The comparisons of arrest data for the three locations suggest that the Oklahoma City study data are very similar to those from the other locations. There is not a central, statewide data repository for police records. The data for each city are collected and maintained by the city. As such, we were not able to make comparisons beyond those with Tulsa and Lawton. For the court processes data, however, there is a statewide data repository, the Juvenile On-Line Tracking System (JOLTS). For the court intake and disposition data we were able to compare the Oklahoma City data with those for the state as a whole. We can also make comparisons with the other metropolitan areas (Tulsa and Lawton) used in the arrest data comparisons.

Table 6.3 shows the charges associated with the referrals to juvenile court. We present data for the study area (Oklahoma City), the other metropolitan areas combined (Tulsa and Lawton) and the state as a whole. The data come from 40,985 juvenile court referrals across the state. The most obvious difference between the study data and the data for other locations is the number of felony charges in the Oklahoma City data. The percentage of felonies in Oklahoma City (60.2 percent) is almost double the percentage in the state as a whole (34.5 percent) and the other metropolitan areas

Table 6.3: Comparisons of referred offenses by location in Oklahoma

	State	Other metro locations	Oklahoma City
Felonies	34.5	33.4	60.2
Sex crimes	2.4	1.9	2.5
Against persons	6.4	7.3	11.9
Drug crimes	5.2	5.3	9.8
Weapons crimes	1.5	2.0	4.6
Property crimes	19.6	17.9	33.3
Public order	1.6	1.2	2.4
Misdemeanors	55.9	53.9	42.3
Against persons	14.8	11.3	10.7
Drug crimes	14.1	8.8	12.4
Weapons crimes	1.3	1.6	3.0
Property crimes	20.9	25.7	10.8
Public order	10.1	10.3	11.1
All others	18.8	20.5	8.3
Status offenses	15.5	15.4	7.8
Technical violations	3.3	5.1	0.5

Note: The numbers are percentages.

(33.4 percent). The difference is likely due to the interlocal agreement between the juvenile court and municipal court in Oklahoma City. That interlocal agreement specifies that the city's municipal courts can process juveniles arrested, ticketed or cited by Oklahoma City Police under the following conditions: (a) the city attorney approves, (b) the charges do not include any felonies and (c) there are no more than two misdemeanor charges. All felonies in Oklahoma City are processed through the juvenile court system. The other cities do not have a similar interlocal agreement. There is no restriction on processing felony charges against juveniles in local, municipal courts. As such, Oklahoma City has more felony charges processed through the juvenile system.[15]

Despite the differences in the overall percentages of felony (and misdemeanor) charges, the patterns and trends in the data are very similar. The most common category of felony referrals in each location is for property crimes. The second most common category of felony referrals in each location is for crimes against persons. The least common felony referrals are for crimes against the public order. For the statewide data, weapons-related crimes are actually the least common category, though it is a near tie with the crimes against the public order category (1.5 vs.

1.6 percent). The referrals for misdemeanor charges show a similar pattern, though not quite to the same degree as the felony charges. Property crimes are the most common misdemeanor charges statewide (20.9 percent) and in the other metropolitan areas (25.7 percent). In the Oklahoma City data, misdemeanor property crimes (10.8) are the third most common charge in the referrals but are very close to the most frequent category, drug crimes (12.4 percent).

Tables 6.4–6.6 show comparisons of the results from the statistical models calculating odds ratios for the various intake decisions in the juvenile court system by race. We make the same comparisons for the three sets of data: statewide, Oklahoma City and the other metropolitan areas. The tables do not include a comparison for Asian juveniles. Recall from Chapter 4 that less than 1 percent of the cases in the Oklahoma City juvenile court data were labeled as Asian.

Table 6.4 shows the comparisons of the intake decision to decline. For the entire state, Black juveniles are less likely than White juveniles to have their case declined (OR = 0.93). In the metropolitan areas, by contrast, Black juveniles are more likely to have their case declined. In Oklahoma City, the odds ratio is even higher (OR = 1.40). The case of Hispanic/Latinx youth is also different for Oklahoma City compared with the other locations. In Oklahoma City, Hispanic/Latinx juveniles are more likely than White juveniles to have their case declined (OR = 1.60). Statewide and in the metropolitan areas, Hispanic/Latinx juveniles have lower odds compared with White juveniles. There is clearly variability in the decision to decline a referral across the state. Cases in Oklahoma City are different compared with the other locations, but there are no clear patterns when comparing the state-level data and the metropolitan area data. We suspect the variability in the decision to decline may be related to policy differences, as racial outcomes remain strikingly similar.

The comparisons of the intake decision to place the referred juvenile on informal probation are presented in Table 6.5. Recall that informal probation refers to deferred prosecution or a deferred filing agreement with

Table 6.4: Comparisons of intake decision to decline by race and location in Oklahoma

Race	State	Other metro locations	Oklahoma City
Black	0.93	1.05	1.40
Asian	0.97	1.06	—
Native American	1.02	1.15	1.50
Hispanic/Latinx	0.72	0.83	1.60

Note: The numbers are odds ratios.

Table 6.5: Comparisons of intake decision for informal probation by race and location in Oklahoma

Race	State	Other metro locations	Oklahoma City
Black	0.45	0.61	0.70
Asian	1.07	1.08	—
Native American	0.97	0.73	0.38
Hispanic/Latinx	0.87	0.72	0.57

Note: The numbers are odds ratios.

Table 6.6: Comparisons of intake decision to file petition by race and location in Oklahoma

Race	State	Other metro locations	Oklahoma City
Black	1.89	1.49	1.21
Asian	0.82	0.78	—
Native American	1.09	1.21	1.40
Hispanic/Latinx	1.61	1.54	1.18

Note: The numbers are odds ratios.

specific terms and conditions for completion by the juvenile in order to avoid prosecution. The table shows that the trends for informal probation are very consistent. In all three locations, Black juveniles are less likely than White juveniles to receive informal probation. Native American and Hispanic/Latinx youth are also less likely than Whites to receive informal probation. The data for Asian youth are also consistent, though there is no comparison with the Oklahoma City data as noted previously. Asian youth are more likely than White youth to receive informal probation.

The final comparison of intake decisions is for filing a petition for prosecution. This is the most serious outcome at the intake decision point. If a petition is filed on the referral, the juvenile faces potentially serious consequences including incarceration. Like the data for informal probation, the data in Oklahoma City are very similar to the data for other locations and there is a great deal of consistency from location to location. The data show that in all three locations, non-White juveniles of color are more likely than White juveniles to have a petition filed in their case. Asian juveniles in the statewide data and the other metropolitan areas have lower odds compared with White juveniles of having a petition filed in their case.

We now turn to comparisons of the outcomes or dispositions of the cases referred to the juvenile courts. Table 6.7 shows the percentages of cases with

Table 6.7: Comparisons of disposition of referrals by location in Oklahoma

	State	Other metro locations	Oklahoma City
Transferred to adult court	0.9	0.8	0.9
Placed in OJA custody	29.5	23.6	29.0
Case dismissed	5.8	8.8	16.1
Probation	61.6	64.1	50.9
Convicted, sentenced as adult	2.0	3.6	2.9

Note: The numbers are percentages.

Table 6.8: Comparisons of odds ratios of the case dismissed by race and location in Oklahoma

Race	State	Other metro locations	Oklahoma City
Black	0.79	0.67	0.57
Asian	1.78	1.37	—
Native American	0.55	0.38	0.46
Hispanic/Latinx	0.53	0.40	0.65

Note: The numbers are odds ratios.

various dispositions. These are the same dispositions analyzed in Chapter 4. The data are from 12,205 observations from the juvenile court records. Again, the Oklahoma City data are consistent with the data for other locations. The most common outcome of the referrals is court-ordered probation, with more than 50 percent in all locations. The least common outcome in all three locations is having the case transferred to adult criminal court, less than 1 percent in all locations.

Table 6.8 shows the odds ratios of having a case dismissed by race for the three locations. The data are fairly consistent across the locations. The Oklahoma City data are almost identical in terms of general trends: Black, Native American and Hispanic/Latinx all have lower odds of having their court case dismissed compared with White juveniles. Native American juveniles have the lowest odds ratios, ranging from 0.38 (in the metropolitan areas) to 0.55 (statewide). Asian youths have the highest odds ratios, indicating higher odds of having their cases dismissed compared with White youths. Again, there are no comparisons for Asian youth in the Oklahoma City area due to the low number of Asians in the juvenile courts system in Oklahoma City.[16]

The comparisons by location for being placed on court-ordered probation are shown in Table 6.9. Again, the data show that the Oklahoma City data

Table 6.9: Comparisons of odds ratios of being placed on probation by race and location in Oklahoma

Race	State	Other metro locations	Oklahoma City
Black	0.72	0.66	0.74
Asian	0.87	0.88	—
Native American	0.83	0.88	0.97
Hispanic/Latinx	0.86	0.76	1.08

Note: The numbers are odds ratios.

Table 6.10: Comparisons of odds ratios of being placed in OJA custody by race and location in Oklahoma

Race	State	Other metro locations	Oklahoma City
Black	1.23	1.71	1.78
Asian	0.80	0.72	—
Native American	1.32	1.38	1.25
Hispanic/Latinx	1.03	1.33	1.20

Note: The numbers are odds ratios.

are very comparable to the data for the state as a whole and for the other metropolitan areas. The odds ratios show that at all locations, juveniles from all non-White race groups have lower odds of court-ordered probation compared with White juveniles. The lone exception is the case of Hispanic/Latinx juveniles in Oklahoma City. There, Hispanic/Latinx youth have slightly higher odds (OR = 1.08) of probation compared with White youth.

We now assess the most serious and consequential outcomes from the court process: incarceration. Table 6.10 shows the comparison of race and ethnic group odds ratios by the different locations. These results, like many of the previous comparisons, show strong similarities in outcomes across the locations. The Oklahoma City data show the same patterns as the other locations: again, Black, Native American and Hispanic/Latinx youth have disadvantaged outcomes compared with White youth. The odds ratios are especially high for Black youth in all three locations. The odds ratios range from 1.23 (statewide) to 1.78 (Oklahoma City).

The final comparison is for being convicted and sentenced in adult criminal court. This is the harshest possible outcome for a juvenile who enters the justice system. Only a small percentage of the juveniles in the justice system face such an outcome (about 2 percent of the total cases across the state). Table 6.11 shows the race and ethnic group comparisons for being convicted

Table 6.11: Comparisons of odds ratios of being convicted and sentenced in adult criminal court by race and location in Oklahoma

Race	State	Other metro locations	Oklahoma City
Black	3.21	3.48	3.03
Asian	0.52	0.52	—
Native American	1.51	3.24	3.88
Hispanic/Latinx	1.49	1.44	1.39

Note: The numbers are odds ratios.

and sentenced as an adult. The numbers are striking but show the same consistency as many of the other comparisons across the different locations.

Comparisons with other studies

We conclude this discussion of the data issues with a comparison with findings from other studies. Unlike the previous comparisons of our data and findings, we do not make explicit statistical comparisons. Rather, we briefly overview the existing literature on DMC. It should come as no surprise that our findings are consistent with decades of research on DMC. Our study is, to the best of our knowledge, the first to examine multiple decision points from multiple data sources in a single location. Each component of our analyses—police interactions, court processes, self-report data, interviews—is consistent with findings over time and from different locations.

Our data showed that non-White juveniles are more likely to be arrested than White juveniles. Of all the police reports involving juveniles, 19.7 percent involved a White juvenile. The percentages were almost double that for Black juveniles (35.3 percent) and for Native American juveniles (37.8). The differential arrest rates remained even after controlling for offense type and demographic characteristics. In the multivariate statistical models, non-White juveniles had risk ratios of arrest as much as 27 percent higher than White juveniles. These findings are very similar to national-level data.

Table 6.12 shows the juvenile arrest rate ratios for selected offenses. The data are 2019 national data compiled by the Office of Juvenile Justice and Delinquency Prevention (OJJDP, 2020). The rates were calculated per 100,000 juveniles. The rate ratios were calculated by dividing the per 100,000 rate for each group listed in the table by the per 100,000 rate for White juveniles. The ratio of rates compares the rates of each non-White race group with those for White youth. A ratio of 1.0 indicates the rates for the groups are equal. A rate ratio greater than 1.0 indicates the rate for the non-White group exceeds the rate for White youth. Likewise, a ratio less than 1.0 indicates the rate for that non-White group is less than the rate

Table 6.12: US juvenile arrest rate ratios compared with White juveniles per 100,000 juveniles, 2019[a]

Offense	Non-White[b]	Black	Native American	Asian
All offenses	1.8	2.4	1.5	0.3
Curfew	1.6	2.1	1.6	0.3
Disorderly conduct	2.5	3.5	1.9	0.2
Simple assault	2.1	2.9	1.3	0.3
Aggravated assault	2.3	3.2	1.7	0.3
Weapons	2.4	3.4	0.9	0.4
Drug violations	1.0	1.3	1.2	0.2
Property crime index	2.5	3.4	1.4	0.4
Violent crime index	3.2	4.5	1.4	0.4

[a] The numbers are ratios of the rates created by dividing each race category rate by the White rate.
[b] The Non-White group includes all non-White groups, including Asian juveniles.
Source: Office of Juvenile Justice and Delinquency Prevention, 2019. Statistical Briefing Book.

for White juveniles. Inspection of the ratios shows that non-White youth as a whole have higher rates for all the listed offenses.[17] The ratios for Black juveniles are consistently the highest for the non-White groups listed in the table. The arrest rates for Black juveniles for all offenses is almost two and a half times higher than for White juveniles. The ratios for individual offenses are sometimes three or four times higher than those for White juveniles. Asian juveniles have lower rates compared with White juveniles for all offenses. These data mirror those from the current study. The problem is compounded from the point of arrest. Once in the system, racial disparities grow at almost every step of the juvenile justice system (Rovner, 2016).

Conclusion

Related to the juvenile justice system, we found significant differences in intake and outcomes based on race and ethnicity. We examined four intake decisions and four outcomes in the juvenile justice process. We found overwhelming differences by race. In the front-end intake decisions, we found that non-White youths were disadvantaged in three of the four decision points. Non-White youth were less likely than White youth to receive informal probation or have their adjudication diverted.[18] Non-White youth were more likely to have a petition filed in their case compared with White youth. The only intake decision in which minorities were advantaged compared with White youth was for having a case declined for referral. We found even more consistent disadvantage for non-White youth in outcomes if a petition was filed in the case. Of the four outcomes we examined (case dismissed, court-ordered probation, remanded to Office of Juvenile Affairs [OJA] custody, and convicted and sentenced in adult criminal court), non-White youth were disadvantaged in all four outcomes. The differences were especially large for the incarceration outcomes (OJA custody and convicted/sentenced as adult). The risk ratios for these outcomes showed non-White juveniles were two or three or four times more likely to receive these sentences compared with White juveniles, even after controlling for demographic characteristics and the severity of the offenses in the charge.

Other studies consistently show similar findings. Both systematic reviews of the literature and meta-analyses suggest that the majority of studies have detected significant race differences in the juvenile justice processing of youth (Cabaniss et al, 2007).[19] The conclusion from one such systematic review was that "the research findings support the existence of disparities and potential biases in juvenile justice processing" (Pope et al, 2002, p. 5). Griggs came to a similar conclusion from a meta-analysis of published and unpublished findings of quantitative studies, suggesting that race effects are evident across multiple studies spanning more than 30 years and show "support for the differential treatment thesis" (2014, p. 211). Perhaps the best summary of our own findings and the majority of previous studies in other locations is from Rovner:

> Among those juveniles who are arrested, black youth are more likely to have their cases referred to juvenile court. Among those cases referred to court, black youth are more likely to have their cases heard (and not diverted pre-adjudication). Among those cases that are adjudicated, black youth are less likely to receive probation and more likely to be committed to secure placement in a juvenile facility. (Rovner 2016, p. 7)

Notes

[1] Certainly, the face validity of our findings is high. Our findings are consistent with 30 years of research on DMC. Individual studies (e.g., Bishop and Leiber, 2011; Leiber and Peck, 2015; Peck and Jennings, 2016), reviews of the literature (Pope and Feyerherm, 1990a, 1990b; Engen et al, 2002;) and meta-analyses (Griggs, 2014) have shown a consistent pattern of race effects in the juvenile justice system.

[2] The issues of validity and generalizability can also be framed in terms of what Campbell and Stanley (1963) refer to as internal validity and external validity. We discuss internal and external validity issues in more detail in the findings of this chapter.

[3] We believe the argument is only weakened—not somehow disproven—because even if the juvenile self-report data are not a perfectly accurate representation of deviant and criminal behavior, there is no good evidence that official sources of data, such as police and court data, are any better. In fact, some authors argue that official data may be worse than self-report data (Thornberry and Krohn, 2000, 2003).

4   Reliability is the extent to which a measurement technique yields the same result on repeated attempts. Validity is the extent to which a measurement technique actually measures the concept under consideration (Maxfield and Babbie, 2018). A measurement technique can be reliable but not have a high degree of validity. A measurement technique, however, that is not reliable by definition is not valid. Quality measurements must be both reliable and valid.

5   Making comparisons with individual-level data is preferable to group-level data. The problem of a perfect benchmark to make comparisons is still a problem. That is, if a specific juvenile self-reports that he or she has not committed a criminal offense, just because that juvenile has been arrested or convicted does not necessarily mean the juvenile committed a crime (see the discussion in Hindelang et al, 1981, pp. 97–101).

6   While the overall association between self-reports and official records is quite high, there are mixed results related to race. Some studies have found a lower association for Black males (Hindelang et al, 1981; Huizinga and Elliott, 1986). Other studies, however, have found no difference in the relationship between self-reports and race (Farrington, Loeber et al, 1996).

7   Criterion validity is also referred to as predictive validity. How well a measure predicts the external criterion determines how well the measure reflects the concept. A simple example is college entrance exams, such as the SAT. The SAT is intended to measure a high schooler's readiness for college. A known external criterion is college grades. If a student's SAT score predicted her or his grades in college, the SAT would have predictive or criterion validity.

8   We would prefer to make individual-level comparisons. That is, we would prefer to compare specific individual responses about delinquent and criminal behaviors with the recorded school administrative data for that individual. Our self-report data, however, are completely anonymous. We have no way of matching individual self-reports to individual records in the school-level data.

9   The incident reports are handwritten, physical forms. As described in the text, trained coders entered the handwritten information into computer software and coded the descriptions of the incidents.

10   Students may be sent to the office by teachers, counselors, administrators and even school staff (e.g., custodial). The infractions vary. They could be related to school policy such as inappropriate attire, behavior issues such as talking during class, or criminal behavior such as assault, drugs or theft.

11   That the disciplinary report data had no mention of gang membership is not surprising. Merely being a member of a gang is not a reportable offense. If a juvenile committed an act as part of gang membership (e.g., stealing), the incident would be reported as stealing.

12   We are not arguing that we have conclusively established internal validity. The threats to internal validity have famously been described by Campbell and Stanley (1963) and Cook and Campbell (1979). Even in highly controlled experimental designs, the threat of internal invalidity is present whenever anything other than the experimental stimulus can affect the outcome. Establishing internal validity in observational (non-experimental) studies is even more difficult.

13   Lawton, Oklahoma, is the sixth most populous city in the state. The cities of Norman, Broken Arrow, and Edmond have larger populations, but each is a major suburb of the Oklahoma City (Edmond and Norman) or Tulsa (Broken Arrow) metropolitan areas.

14   The police data from Lawton and Tulsa were analyzed using binary logistic regression. To make the comparisons, we re-analyzed our study data to obtain odds ratios rather than using the risk ratios that we presented in the chapter on police encounters.

15   Of course, it could also be the case that Oklahoma City does issue more felony charges compared with the other locations. We are unable to fully assess the degree to which that occurs.

[16] Despite not having comparisons from Oklahoma City for Asian youth, we opted to show the results from the statewide and other metropolitan data for the Asian youth because they generally mirror the patterns we found in the chapter focused on police interactions. Asian youth often have favorable outcomes compared with White youth, while Black and Brown juveniles have disadvantaged outcomes compared with White juveniles.

[17] The non-White group is comprised of all "non-White" minority groups, including Asian juveniles. Asian juveniles tend to have lower rates of arrest compared with White juveniles. If the combined non-White group included only Brown and Black juveniles, the ratios would be higher.

[18] In the chapter examining juvenile justice processes (Chapter 4), we did not present formal findings for the decision to divert a case. In the Oklahoma City data, fewer than 1 percent of all the cases (regardless of race) were diverted. There were too few cases to analyze differences by race with additional covariates in the models. We did, however, conduct bivariate analyses using the collapsed race categories of White and non-White. Those analyses show a clear disadvantage for non-White juveniles. About 0.7 percent of the White juveniles had their cases diverted, compared with 0.4 percent for non-White juveniles. The analyses show that non-White juveniles have relative risk about 40 percent lower ($RR = 0.60$) than Whites for diverted adjudication.

[19] A meta-analysis is a statistical approach using data from independent studies of the same subject. The analyses are used to determine overall trends of the relationship between a factor and an outcome (Schmid et al, 2021).

7

Police, Juvenile Court and Juvenile Specialist Interviews

> My father kept me busy from dawn to dusk when I was a kid. When I wasn't pitching hay, hauling corn or running a tractor, I was heaving a baseball into his mitt behind the barn. ... If all the parents in the country followed his rule, juvenile delinquency would be cut in half in a year's time.
>
> Bob Feller, Major League Baseball Player

Introduction

Elija Anderson's (1999) four-year ethnographic study of a poor Black area in Philadelphia, *Code of the Street: Decency, Violence, and the Moral Life of the Inner City*, should be required reading for anyone with an interest in race and inequality. Anderson explains high rates of violence among Black juveniles in high poverty neighborhoods as resulting from decades of area economic disadvantage, a disconnection and isolation from most of American society, and experienced discrimination, resulting in antisocial behavior and even violence. Based on his analysis, he categorizes individuals and families into two types or groups: decent or street. Decent people are those who have hope and strive to achieve a better life. These are the folks who embrace middle-class values. Street people are those who have lost hope for achieving middle-class values and adopt the oppositional Code of the Street, where they tend to react violently when faced with disrespect or threat and celebrate their antisocial and criminalistic values.

All of this is relevant to disproportionate minority contact (DMC). Specific to our main argument, Anderson describes most folks in these poorest of the poor, extremely violent neighborhoods as part of the group he identifies as "decent." Most of the folks embrace mainstream values. In fact, only the most extreme of the "street" folks are typically the violent criminals. Anderson's (1999) work suggests that in the most disadvantaged areas, most folks embrace mainstream values. In addition, less than 30 percent of Blacks live under the poverty line, and clearly not all of those live in ghettos like the ones studied by Anderson. Painting, with broad strokes, the number of non-White individuals residing in ghetto or barrio neighborhoods:

- Fewer than 30 percent of all Blacks live in desperately poor Black neighborhoods (Thernstrom, 2020).
- Most people in the area studied by Anderson (1999) were what he referred to as "decent" rather than "street" people.
- Even among "street" people in Anderson's study, only the fringe street people were identified as significantly criminalistic.

A mere 0.6 percent of the population commits 50 percent of violent crime in the United States (National Network for Safe Communities at John Jay College, 2021). An Orange County, California, study on juvenile crime similarly concluded that a very few individuals commit most crime; in this case, about 8 percent of juveniles were found to be chronic offenders (Orange County Probation Office, 1997). "Gun violence is highly concentrated among particular segments of the population and in particular places," with 70 percent of non-fatal gunshots occurring in areas with only 6 percent of the population (Papachristos et al, 2015, pp. 528–9). Our point is not that 0.6 percent or 8 percent is an exact number for chronic juvenile offenders in Oklahoma City, but that numerous studies show very small parts of the population to be involved in violent crime. Add to this the knowledge that Whites and non-Whites offend at basically the same rates, and, yet again, you end up with a system that treats non-Whites as more criminalistic than Whites, which is supported by pretending that crime is rampant among non-Whites (again, they offend at the same rates) and therefore non-Whites need to be supervised by the justice system more closely. In studies of DMC, there are clearly areas with high crime rates, but the point is that those are rare, yet we treat them as endemic to non-White communities and even non-White families.

To this point, we have shown the extent of minority overrepresentation in the juvenile justice system. We have shown that non-White youth are no more prone to criminal behavior than are White youth, and we have hypothesized that professionals within the juvenile justice system tend to see non-White youth as part of this small percentage who may be chronic recidivists. White youth, on the other hand, are expected to have mainstream values and are seen as unlikely to be chronic recidivists. We test this part of our hypothesis using interviews with juvenile justice professionals. For this next part of our analysis, we interviewed 83 area police officers, juvenile court officials (lawyers and judges) and juvenile specialists to determine their ideas on the causes of DMC and to hear their descriptions of the juveniles they interact with professionally.

The interviews were semi-structured with scripted questions. Scripts differed only for questions specific to occupations (police, court, juvenile specialists) but were very similar overall (see Appendix B for details about the interview guide). Follow-up questions based upon the participant's response were encouraged. The interviews were conducted by one of the authors (Ketchum) and trained interviewers. We used other interviewers so that participants were interviewed by race-concordant interviewers. White juvenile justice professionals were interviewed by a White interviewer, Black participants were interviewed by a Black interviewer and Hispanic/Latinx participants were interviewed by a Hispanic/Latinx interviewer. We encountered no Native American interview participants. The interviewers were trained over a two-week period. The interviewers received instruction on how to interview and ask follow-up questions. Part of the training included mock interviews that were monitored and analyzed by the authors.

All interviews were digitally audio recorded. These recordings were sent to a professional transcribing company, chosen from the list of those approved for use by the University of Oklahoma. Interviews were transcribed for language only and did not include information on inflection or time of pauses. In addition, the interviews were coded by three graduate students for frequency of common responses as well as for each of the frames of color-blind racism as first described by Bonilla-Silva (2001). The coders were trained until a high level of interrater reliability was achieved. These frames have become a standard measurement for subtle racism in race literature. Any disagreements in coding were discussed between the coders and one author (Ketchum).

We conducted 84 interviews with juvenile justice professionals. Each interview typically lasted about one to 1.5 hours. Of the 84 interviewees, there were 63 police officers, one juvenile court judge, eight attorneys (district attorneys and/or public defenders) and 12 juvenile specialists. The majority ($N = 57$) of the interview participants were male and 26 were female. Sixty-five of the participants were White, seven were Black, three were Latinx and seven were unknown/did not respond. The seven "unknown" race/ethnicities were interviewed by White interviewers. All participants were told that we wanted to "race match" interviewers and participants and we explained why this was important. We believe we are safe in the assumption that the seven "unknown" participants at least live their professional lives as "White."

A large majority (69.1 percent) of all interview participants live in all or mostly White neighborhoods, which is similar to the 70.4 percent who grew up in White neighborhoods. In addition, 83.1 percent identify their current life as "middle class" and 73.2 percent answered as having no close non-White friends. At the time of the interviews, 77.9 percent of the county was White non-Hispanic (55.4 percent) or White Latinx (14.7 percent). Living in all or mostly White neighborhoods and having few close non-White friends suggests that most of these juvenile justice professionals live a life of White habitus. White habitus is defined as residential and social hyper-segregation of Whites from Blacks and other non-White groups. This then results in limited opportunities to develop meaningful relationships with non-Whites (Bonilla-Silva et al, 2006).

Most of those interviewed believed the stereotypes of non-White families having significantly different value systems and lower involvement of parents, neither of which is supported by research (Carey, 2016; Ellerby et al, 2018). There was also a tendency for those who live and/or were raised in White, segregated communities to have a strong belief in racial and ethnic family differences; however, those who were raised in less segregated communities also tended to share the same stereotypes, though they were much more likely to point out that there were exceptions to these stereotypes. This suggests the need for a structural interpretation of racism in the juvenile justice system, as the interview responses on DMC tended to closely reflect the four frames of color-blind racism (detailed later in the chapter) as described by Bonilla-Silva (2001, 2003): abstract liberalism, naturalization, cultural racism and minimization of racism were all present throughout the interviews.

We will address common themes from answers in this chapter, first by listing the frequency of that response as coded and then offering examples for the reader. After examining the most common responses, we will look at the coding and examples of Bonilla-Silva's four frames of color-blind racism, in an attempt to detect if color-blind racism plays a role in DMC.

After asking demographic questions, we framed DMC for the participants and, before offering any specific potential causes for DMC, we asked a "miracle" question, to get their view of the cause of deviance and juvenile crime. We asked the juvenile justice professionals the following question: "Pretending for a moment that you had the ability, funding and support to do so (think magic or miracle if need be), what one change would you make to minimize the need for the juvenile justice system?" Presumably, their responses indicate the fundamental issue involving deviance, criminality and overrepresentation in the system. The response frequencies and percentages are listed in Table 7.1.

The "miracle" question

The miracle question does not include a racial component. We had described the purpose of the study and briefly defined DMC for participants. For this first question, we wanted to get an idea of what the juvenile justice professionals saw as the causal factors related to juvenile delinquency and crime. The question has two purposes: the first is the more straightforward, simply asking professional experts for their impression as to the cause of a major issue, within their field of expertise. The second component was a baseline perceived cause for juvenile crime, which could be compared with later questions. Specifically:

1. Pretending for a moment that you had the ability, funding and support to do so (think magic or miracle if need be), what one change would you make to minimize the need for the juvenile justice system?
2. Some have suggested that a culture of violence (one which accepts and even embraces violence as an acceptable means for one's goals) exists in many barrio and ghetto neighborhoods. In your experience, does this seem to be the case?
3. Are some races more prone to gang membership?
4. Followed by specific questions for each group: How important is a juvenile's prior record in determining how you will deal with that individual?
5. What effect, if any, does direct or overt discrimination (think old-fashioned racism) have in juveniles ending up in the juvenile justice system?
6. Is disproportional minority contact (DMC) a problem or merely a reflection of the "real world"?

On the one hand, if the responses to the miracle question strongly aligned with the specific questions on racial and ethnic differences, that suggests non-White juveniles are their frame of reference for juvenile crime. This suggests differential treatment based on problematic characteristics of non-Whites. On the other hand, if their responses to the miracle question did not match up with questions specific to racial and ethnic differences, that would raise new questions about DMC. If the professionals are referring to behavior not specific to racial/ethnic minority groups, then they are likely seeing differential involvement. The first possibility was found to be true, with respondents describing family and home life as the most common cause. This was followed up and in later questions confirmed that most

Table 7.1: Categories of responses to the one thing juvenile justice professionals would change to minimize the need for the justice system

	Frequency	Percentage
Family and home life	38	46.3
Community	3	3.7
Schools and education	15	18.3
Programs and facilities	14	17.1
Tougher sentences/more power to Office of Juvenile Justice	8	9.8
Other	2	2.4
Nothing	2	2.4
Total	82	100.0

respondents saw Black, Latinx and/or Native American families as having different family structures and different cultural values that are not consistent with those of mainstream America.

Interviewer (I):	Okay. Pretending for a moment that you had the ability, funding and support to do so (think magic or miracle if need be), what one change would you make to minimize the need for the juvenile justice system?
Respondent (R):	Better home environments for the kids that grow up, and most of the time they end up growing up in our system, to better home lives for them, more support in their homes. (White female judge/lawyer)
I:	Pretending for a moment that you had the ability, funding and support to do so (think magic or miracle if need be), what one change would you make to minimize the need for the juvenile justice system?
R:	I'd like to see parents more involved with their children. Understanding that their kids are not perfect and just be more involved. (White male police officer)
I:	Pretending for a moment that you had the ability, funding, and support to do so (think magic or miracle if need be), what is one change you would make to minimize the need for the juvenile justice system?
R:	Hmm. Well, what would I do to minimize it?
I:	Yea, minimize the need for it.
R:	Give counseling to the parents. So you need to—I mean, I don't know. There is no way to minimize it. I think it has to come from home. It has to come from your upbringing—that unfortunately will never be the case. It'll never have to be minimized because there are going to be so many juvenile offenders—because there are so many parents that don't care what their kids are doing. There are so many people that don't report what a child is doing because they're a child. So there's—okay …. (Non-White female police officer)
I:	Pretending for a moment that you had the ability, the funding and support to do so (think magic or miracle if need be) what one change would you make to minimize the need for the juvenile justice system?

R: Well, I mean most of the reasons for the juvenile justice system is poor parenting and lack of parenting and lack of supervision and things like that. So, probably the magic is everybody be a good parent to their kids. (White female judge/lawyer)

In these interviews, these professionals, like most other respondents, see a need for greater parental involvement in kids' lives. The extent of local DMC had been given to the respondents shortly before this question was asked. Their answers emphasize that non-White, especially Native American and Black, families need to increase support and create better homes for their children. The first and second are more positive in their answers, while the third and fourth appear to have lost a bit of patience with what they see as bad parents. However, the consistent message is that parents need to do better: while muddied in vagueness and perhaps unspoken suggestions of class rather than racial differences, in the eyes of these respondents the overrepresentation of these children in the juvenile justice system was due to the parents not doing enough to raise their children correctly. There was a common disconnect, with participants responding about juvenile crime without directly addressing the racial overrepresentation.

In the next interview, unless his daughter is non-White, which is never mentioned, the White male police officer in the next example shows avoidance as he ignores race in his response. He takes a situation, probably familiar to many parents with teens and preteens, revolving around his daughter's friend's postings on Facebook. He was not the only participant to avoid mentioning the racial differences that make up DMC. Like others, he generalizes the issue, introducing his own family experience as an example of the problems that parents face. He essentially boils juvenile crime down to parents' lack of involvement in their children's social media presence, ignoring the racial differences. It is likely this this officer does not really blame Facebook for the overrepresentation of non-White youth in the very system he works within, rather this appears to be an attempt to minimize and avoid discussing the racial disparities in the juvenile justice system. As noted, none of the respondents discussed previously actually mentioned race. Were it not for the ability to look at responses to further questions, one could assume that these responses were truly color-blind. Bonilla-Silva (2001, p. 179) refers to this as "verbal pirouettes," where an individual goes to great verbal lengths to answer while dancing around the issue of racism without addressing it.

I: Okay. Pretending for a moment that you had the ability, funding and support to do so (think magic or miracle if need be), what one change would you make to minimize the need for the juvenile justice system?

I: I know it's kind of loaded there, so many avenues you could go.

R: What change to eliminate the need for the juvenile justice system?
I: Yeah, what one change would you make to minimize the need for juvenile justice system?
R: I guess if you're talking about having the money and having the resources, um, it would be parental education and getting parents to be more involved in their kids' lives and knowing what their kids are doing and are up to. I know with social media being the way it is—Facebook, Twitter. Um, you know, I have two kids in high school, I know their—I'm friends on their Facebook, I have their passwords to their Facebook, I can get in and see what's going on on their Facebook. But it amazes me that, just for instance, one of my children's friends posted something the other day on one of their other friend's sites about a rant about how stupid her mom is and this, that, and the other, and ended with something to the effect of, "Yeah, well I could say the same thing about you, you stupid whore." So, you know, obviously, in the grand scheme of things you are talking about juvenile delinquency, you know, calling your mom a whore on Facebook is small compared to committing a violent crime, but the fact is obviously this girl's mom has no idea what her daughter is doing on Facebook and to me that's just embarrassing.
I: For both.
R: You know, as a girl, I would be embarrassed posting something like that about my mom. And as the mom I would just be absolutely, totally embarrassed that my daughter is calling me a whore on Facebook. So I just—I think that would be the one place where we've got to get—we've got to educate parents to get them to pay more attention to what their kids are doing and being more, you know, involved in their kids' lives. (White male police officer)

The next respondent, a juvenile specialist, also sees the problem as one of family differences, but he looks to corporal punishment to solve juvenile delinquency. Despite decades of evidence that corporal punishment does not work, some respondents argued for it as a solution to juvenile delinquency or DMC (Novick and Novick, 2020).

I: Pretend for a moment that you had the ability, funding and support to do so (think magic or miracle if need be), what one change would you make to minimize the need for the juvenile justice system?
R: I know this is crazy, but if I could get rid of something or I could get rid of whatever I want?
I: You can do whatever you want, magic—(Both laughing)

R: I want probably, this is going to sound crazy, but I would probably get rid of, like, this child abuse law, and even though there is some kids that really did get beat down, but there are also some parents that are totally scared of their—they will not even smack their hand, they are so scared to go to jail. And a lot—I think medication has replaced discipline, and right now I think we're just creating a bunch of drug addicts, cause pretty much all these kids are on medication. Oh, I'm sad; here, pop this. Oh, I'm angry; pop this. I'm like, the pill doesn't work by itself, you have to have something with it, and I used to get whoopings when I was little and look at me. (Laughing) I didn't get beat. I think maybe we could do some training with the parents, but not all the time is it the parents' fault. We do have some good parents, but we have a lot of parents where I'm the threat, you know, if you don't go to school, I'm going to call, you know, your office. If you don't do this I'm going to call. I'm like, well, what happens when he gets dismissed or she gets dismissed, you can't call me no more. So I would probably create some program, I would take away the child abuse law. But of course, you can't just punch your kid in the face, but I have—probably some training on disciplining, disciplining your kid. That would probably be my main focus. And you have to start that early, you can't wait until your kid is 7 years old and now you're going to tell him he can't do this, and you've been telling him he can do this all of this time. So I would probably focus somewhere with the parent. (Non-White male juvenile specialist)

The following participant, a non-White male police officer, also avoids the topic of minority overrepresentation (DMC) by painting the issue as a universal one. Having access to police and court data, we see no evidence of similar overrepresentation of wealthy kids, and his response does more to "bury the lead" by giving a color-blind response to a racial issue.

I: Pretending for a moment that you had the ability, funding and support to do so (think magic or miracle if need be), what one change would you make to minimize the need for the juvenile justice system?

R: There is no one thing you can do. I mean, if it is, I'd be rich right now.

I: What are a couple things that you think, you know, probably isn't likely that you could, but ....

R: To what? Stop juvenile crime?

I: Yes.

R: Sterile [sic] some people so they couldn't have babies, strict [sic] the laws. I mean, you have parents that are rich that let their kids get away with stuff. I mean, there's no one thing you can do. (Non-White male police officer)

Research shows a picture of non-White families that is much different than that seen by those working in the juvenile justice system. The media shows non-White families, especially Black and Native American, as "broken"; Blacks are overrepresented in photos accompanying articles on poverty, education issues and social programs (Rodgers and Robinson, 2017). It is no surprise that non-Whites are often seen as broken despite widely available research showing few differences. The media still portray Black fathers as missing, confounding "not living with children" with "not participating in their lives" (Rodgers and Robinson, 2017).

A 25-year longitudinal study (Chetty et al, 2020) shows that, controlling for income and neighborhood, Black boys have lower economic success than White boys. This study found no difference between Black and White girls. The same study found that the income gap for Latinx is shrinking as their intergenerational mobility more closely resembles that of Whites rather than that of Blacks or Native Americans. The study concludes that parental involvement, class differences and neighborhood differences mean little compared with gender and race differences. Simply being a Black or Native American boy is enough to severely limit one's odds of success in society (Chetty et al, 2020). When interviewed about this topic noted Harvard sociologist and expert on the economic struggles of Black men, William Julius Wilson, highlighted the significance of the Chetty study: "That is a pathbreaking finding. They're not talking about the direct effects of a boy's own parents' marital status. They're talking about the presence of fathers in a given census tract" (New York Times, 2019).

Black fathers tend to be more involved in their children's lives than any other racial/ethnic group, including White fathers, whether they live with them or not. This remains true for both younger and older children (Jones and Mosher, 2013; Ellerbe et al, 2018). Both Black and Latinx families recognize the value that a college education can bring their children, with non-White families typically sharing the same hopes and dreams for their children and instilling in them a belief in the value of education and supporting them through their college careers (Cabrera and La Nasa, 2000; Knight et al, 2004; Ceja, 2006; Perna, 2006; Liou et al, 2009; Rios-Agular and Kiyama, 2012; Martinez et al, 2013). Black and other non-White families are not very different from White families, except when racialized institutions, such as mass incarceration of non-Whites, impose structural differences. The claim that non-White families cause DMC and other criminality becomes a feedback loop where family structure is claimed to be the cause of crime, which results in children from those families being brought into the justice system, which in turn shows that there is a problem with these non-White children who are overrepresented in the system, which suggests the family is somehow the problem ... and on, and on, and on the self-replication goes, despite it being based on false assumptions from the beginning.

Bonilla-Silva (2018) describes color-blind racism as "a curious racial ideology. Although it engages, as all ideologies do, in 'blaming the victim,' it does so in a very indirect, 'now you see it, now you don't' style that matches the character of the new racism" (p. 74). Color-blind racism is racism with plausible deniability. In many ways it is worse than Jim Crow racism as it not only discriminates but also tries to gaslight the very victims of discrimination. Blacks, Latinx and Native Americans are told they are not equal because they are still doing something wrong. Until recently, some people were publicly declaring this a post-racial era, though the Trump era seems to have put an end to that idea (Hannah-Jones, 2016). The concern with the inaccurate label of a post-racial society lay in the responsibility of failure in society, yet again resting upon the victims of racial inequality. Feagin (2006) emphasized the role of framing in maintaining the racialized system of oppression in the United States. He defined White racial frames as "an organized set of racialized ideas, stereotypes, emotions, and inclinations to discriminate" (Feagin, 2006, p. 25). He argued that Whites develop early racial frames (White racial frames) that are deeply held and that allow them to conclude that, within any given situation, Whites are superior to other groups and deserve preferential treatment in the United States. Bonilla-Silva (2018) provided a more nuanced explanation of frames of thought developed and used by Whites to describe racial issues in seemingly nonracial ways. He identified four frames: (a) abstract liberalism, (b) naturalization, (c) cultural racism and (d) minimization. While each frame is found in political racial discourse, it is the frame of abstract liberalism (e.g., justice) that has been most prominent in debates over affirmative action. As described by Feagin and Bonilla-Silva, these frames are more than just passive–aggressive reactions of minorities demanding to be recognized in society. These frames are mechanisms that buoy the structure of dominance maintained by Whites in the US. Blumer (1958) highlighted the role of politicians and interest groups in creating this type of system by espousing narratives in public discourse that produce and reproduce racism and prejudice. Accordingly, while frames of thought are important because they help individuals deal with complicated issues, we look at frames of communication produced by elite entities who have the ability to establish the lines of discussion for the masses.

Four frames of color-blind racism

Bonilla-Silva broke color-blind racism into four frames or patterns/styles of supporting racism while trying to seem as if one is not. The four frames of color-blind racism (Bonilla-Silva, 2018) are:

- **Abstract liberalism**—"Equal opportunity is part of abstract liberalism—or—regarding each person as an individual with choices—and using the liberal principles for whites having the right of choosing to live in segregated neighborhoods or sending their children to segregated schools. This claim requires ignoring the multiple institutional and state-sponsored practices behind segregation, and being unconcerned about these practices' negative consequences" (p. 28). This would include blaming absent Black fathers while ignoring the impact of locking up most young adult Black males in many communities or ignoring the impact of White habitus in DMC.
- **Naturalism**—"Naturalization is a frame that allows whites to explain away racial phenomena by suggesting they are natural occurrences for example—whites can claim 'segregation' is natural because people from all backgrounds gravitate toward likeness. Although these statements can be interpreted as 'racist' and as contradicting the colorblind logic—they are used to reinforce the myth of nonracialism. How? by suggesting these preferences are almost biologically driven and typical of all groups in society, preferences for primary associations with members of ones' race are rationalized as nonracial because 'they (racial minorities) do it too'" (p. 28). Naturalization sets up segregation as normal and impossible to change. It takes a social construction—race—and pretends it is instead a biological drive and thus something innate that cannot be changed.
- **Cultural racism**—"Cultural racism is a frame that relies on culturally based arguments" (p. 28). Arguing the existence of a non-White culture of violence is an example of cultural racism. It is a means of suggesting others are simply different and not particularly inclined or able to adopt our mainstream, White values, real or imagined.
- **Minimization of racism**—"Minimization of racism is a frame that suggests discrimination is no longer a central factor affecting minorities' life chances ('it's better now than in the past' or 'There is discrimination, but there are plenty of jobs out there.' This frame allows whites to accept facts such as the racially motivated murder of James Byrd Jr. in Jasper TX" (p. 29). The Proud Boys are seen as a fringe exception, not as the leaders and coordinators of the January 6, 2021, terrorist attack on Washington, DC. Racists aren't the problem, but racist individuals sometimes cause problems. This argument is used when Whites are committing criminal acts, but if non-Whites are doing the same, the frame is swapped to cultural racism. In many ways, minimization and cultural racism are two

sides of the same racist coin, with one using the group level to explain the shortcomings of non-Whites on a macro level and the other side explaining White racism only at the individual or micro level.

Unpacking color-blind racism

The following officer works in a special "Crimes Against Children" unit with the police department. His frustrations with working in what must be an emotionally very difficult specialization are clear, but he also echoes the stereotypes of non-White families, without ever identifying these families as being mostly non-White. We have included multiple questions and responses, which are sequential, but with other topics omitted. This is a longer section of interview to give the reader a broader idea of this officer's thought process. We also want to use parts of this interview to begin to unpack the different frames of color-blind racism that it uses.

I: Okay. Pretending for a moment that you had the ability, funding and support to do so (think magic or miracle if need be), what one change would you make to minimize the need for the juvenile justice system?

R: Required parenting classes for people to be taught. I mean, not everybody had great parents and so at some point we have to find a way to break that chain and change that. The problem in juvenile justice is that some of the juvenile offenders we see are—that they are generational. Their parents were troublemakers as children and they didn't have good parents. At some point, we have to find a way in our country to get back to the basis of—everybody wants to holler "kids first" and "children first," but the children will benefit when we make it a "families first." When the family becomes an organized unit of hierarchy of discipline and learning and teaching from the parents' viewpoint about what's right and what's wrong, how to appropriately discipline your children, how to guide them, how to be respectful. Kids learn from example. They will very much try to live up to expectations that are given them. If those expectations are unreasonable, too high standards, then they will rebel and they'll feel a failure and they won't be able to [inaudible]; but if there are no expectations put on them other than get out of my way and leave me alone, then they have nothing to try to attain. (White male police officer)

In this first part, we have a few things to address. First, knowing that non-Whites are overrepresented, without regard to reason, this officer has painted, clearly if indirectly, non-White parents as typically being far worse parents than are White parents. In his view, non-White parents simply are not good at parenting and the result of their failure is highly criminalistic children. He uses a cultural racism frame for his miracle question response.

I: Yeah, tell me about your position within the police force: are you a patrol officer, do you work with a special unit? Then tell me a little about what kind of work situation you find yourself interacting with juveniles.

R: I work specifically in the Crimes Against Children unit. I'm a 21-plus-year veteran of the police department; I worked in patrol for over 15 years; I've been assigned to the Crimes Against Children unit now for five and a half years. We interact with juveniles—largely as victims, of course. All my cases involve juvenile victims of 12 years of age and under, but many of our cases also deal with juvenile offenders and that is an unfortunate thing; as I said before, we are seeing more and more of those cases. But we work cases involving abuse of children, from physical abuse, sexual abuse, neglect aspect, up to and including child homicide has occurred in abuse.

I: Is there a person or office that makes the decision about an individual case, which results in you working with the juvenile?

R: Again, all my cases are juvenile, whether it is a victim or a suspect.

This section is pretty straightforward, with an objective answer from the officer. These first two sections we have lifted from his interview are mild in terms of racism.

I: Right. You have answered this question, but I'll tell you what it is: finally, what role have you seen difficult family issues play? You've pretty much talked a lot about that.

R: That is the biggest issue, you know, regardless of race, a child that grows up in a single parent home—especially—and I've known some fantastic people that have succeeded and done well in a single parent house. But if you take a single parent home that doesn't have a good parent to start with, or that is in difficult situations, it makes it even worse. Because two parents staying together in a bad situation is not going to be great either. But the parenting, the upbringing, that these children get, the things they are taught for right and wrong, the character that is instilled in them by their parents will have a bigger effect on the juvenile justice system than any other single factor. You know, we joke in this office all the time because we see the moms that are spitting out their fourth, fifth or sixth kid and they don't have custody of any of them. That in the United States you have to take a test

	to get a driver's license, you have to test and be approved to do a number of things, but you don't have to have a test to make a baby and become a parent.
I:	Right, Right.
R:	So until we do a better job as a society—and I'm not talking sex education on how to not get pregnant—until we do a better job teaching people morals, ethics and how to live their life right, we are only gonna get worse, and that goes back directly to when we get away from what God has instituted as right.
I:	Right.
R:	The world is going to go to hell, literally.
I:	Right.
R:	We were given some very specific rules about what we should and should not do. In God's word he tells us how to be parents. He tells us how to be the people we should be, and until we as a country and as a nation and as a people return to that it is only gonna get worse and uglier, and we are gonna lose more kids to the juvenile justice system.
I:	Right.
R:	… go out there and make a baby. Doesn't make you a good parent, doesn't make you a mom or a dad. It just makes you a—this is a really coarse-sounding term, but the term we use here is they are breeders. They're not parents; they make babies that they don't care for. I've got files here, a whole stack of files right there, of people that aren't caring about their kids properly. The kids are being victimized, they are being beaten, they are being sodomized, they are raped, they are being killed by people who are capable of making babies, but they are not capable of being a parent.

We don't want to minimize the pain and frustration of working with kids who are victims and/or perpetrators, and there is a part of this that appears to be the venting of that frustration. The concern comes with the fact that he is talking mostly about non-Whites without ever naming that. Not only is the entire interview about racial overrepresentation in the juvenile justice system, but he uses common code words, talking about single parent families, mothers with children with different fathers, mothers not having custody of their children. These are not just non-White specific; these descriptions are Black specific. As we noted earlier, Black fathers, on average, are slightly more involved in the lives of their children than fathers overall. Multiple relationships resulting in children with different fathers is an outgrowth of justice policies in Black neighborhoods, yet that fact is ignored by the officer, who instead makes it a cultural flaw of Blacks. He then moves into more of an old-fashioned racist description as he shifts Blacks from "people" and "families" to "breeders," which echoes the long treatment of Blacks as subhuman and animalistic. He carefully avoids naming race by utilizing graceful verbal pirouettes to make it clear he is referring to the Black community, in very coarse terms, without actually naming the community.

I: Right. Have you witnessed any other cultural problems, other than language, that your department has run into, such as tribal issues, or cultural issues within certain racial or ethnic groups?

R: We have some. You know, it is funny, here in Oklahoma, where we have 39 recognized tribes, and tribal issues—Oklahoma City police department doesn't really have to deal with those much. Your tribal reservation—we don't actually have "reservation" reservations in Oklahoma like they do in other states, it is outlying outside of primarily Oklahoma City. Some of the things we do see, culturally, occasionally, we will see some medicinal things or whatever from cultures, especially the Oriental population. Things, well, called cupping or coining that they do for medicinal that shocks the normal American peoples: "Oh my God, what are they doing to that child!" One of the things that we do see that is directly affected in our unit is the juveniles that are offended sexually with our Hispanic culture. It seems—and I know our domestic violence deals with it a lot too, because of the male-dominated society that they come from—but sexually, in Mexico, it seems from what we are seeing up here is that traditionally they still take wives or take the child brides so to speak. In our country a hundred years ago, prime marrying age was 14, and now it's a crime and we investigate that. But the families that are moving up here from Mexico, we still see that, adult males 20–30 years old having sex with these teenage girls, very young, 14–15 years old.

I: Because it is culturally accepted there?

R: Because it is culturally accepted there, and even younger kids, because even though it may not be 100 percent culturally accepted, there is such a male-dominated society that nobody ever says anything. I don't think there is anywhere in the world where it is just okay to go have sex with a very small child; however, it happens, but nobody ever deals with it so it's perceived by these suspects as being not such a big deal, and so we do see some of that.

This section of the interview relies strongly upon cultural racism. The officer seems to have little interaction with Native Americans, and the demographics support that few Native Americans live in Oklahoma City. Aside from the odd use of the term "Orientals," he appears to see Asians as culturally odd but fairly harmless, as he references "strange" medical treatments unique to

Asians. When he moves on to Latinx, he repeatedly refers to a tendency toward pedophilia, specifically of Latinx men with young teen Latinx girls, as a large problem which is culturally accepted. This classic example of cultural racism is followed with, "I don't think there is anywhere in the world where it is just okay to go have sex with a very small child; however, it happens, but nobody ever deals with it so it's perceived by these suspects as being not such a big deal, and so we do see some of that." This makes it unclear whether it is culturally acceptable or not, in his eyes. It is also worth pointing out that this is not a Latinx issue, as 25 states, including Oklahoma, have no minimum age requirement for marriage, though many of those states do require parental consent.

I: Is disproportional minority contact (DMC) a problem or merely a reflection of the "real world"?

R: I think it's a reflection of the real world, and you know, not saying that any one race is more prone to criminal activity, like I said, we're reactionary, and so real world and its historical problems that we have caused as a society is why you see that. I mean, you can go all the way back to days of slavery, I believe—and I don't know what studies there are to support this, but in the days of slavery, when the households were broke into different and, you know, the fathers were sold here, and mother sold there, and kids grown up, and it becomes a generational—well, this kid grew up without a dad and had no [inaudible] and it's just perpetuated through the times that—you know, I think it all goes back to the cultural raisings that are there. But I don't think it's disproportionate as far as the contacts, I think it is just a reflection of society.

I: Okay, well, this concludes the questions. Is there anything on the juvenile justice system or the impact of race or ethnicity on the juvenile justice system that you would like to add?

R: Not as far as race goes. Again, juvenile justice system deals with what comes through their door. We are dealing with how we are called and respond.

In the final section of the interview, the officer again relies heavily on a cultural racism framing as he explains that missing fathers are simply a continuation of cultural norms acquired while Blacks were being held as slaves. First, this should clear up any lingering doubts about his focus on describing Blacks in most cases, and it is an odd way of shifting blame squarely onto the shoulders of Black families. He then follows it up with a minimization of racism, seemingly washing his hands, and those of his department, of any racial bias, by explaining that is just the way things are, which implies true objectivity in all aspects of policing, which the evidence does not support.

Is there a "culture of violence"?

When asked if there is a culture of violence surrounding Black and Latinx youth, we received a resounding "yes" from the participants. Table 7.2 shows the frequencies and percentages of responses. Sixty-seven of the 75 who answered the question answered that there is a Black and Latinx culture of violence. In fact, unique to all (non-background) questions, 35 of the 67 participants (46.7 percent) who answered in the affirmative answered "yes," "yes, yes" or "yeah" with no further follow-up. Almost 47 percent of those who responded felt so strongly about its existence that they only needed to affirm it, which to them is only what is patently obvious. Only one person said only "no," using the same finality in his response (non-White male police officer), and only eight respondents, in total, stated there is no culture of violence in poor Black or Latinx neighborhoods.

I: Some have suggested that a culture of violence (one which accepts and even embraces violence as an acceptable means for one's goals) exists in many barrio and ghetto neighborhoods. In your experience, does this seem to be the case?
R: No. (Non-White male police officer)

This officer offered detailed explanations for every other DMC question, but he was clear in stating there is no racial/ethnic culture of violence. Another officer gave a more detailed explanation, one that strongly mirrors the conclusions of this study.

I: Okay. Some have suggested that a culture of violence (one which accepts and even embraces violence as an acceptable means for one's goals) exists in many barrio and ghetto neighborhoods. Is this your experience?
R: Violence with juveniles is?
I: That exists in many barrio and ghetto neighborhoods, that it is a culture of violence and that it is acceptable to use violence to get to your goals.
R: You know—it is definitely a perception. I would say the percentage is smaller than what a lot of people perceive. I think there is that small percentage that is involved in the violence and the gangs, but it may be a smaller percentage than what the public perceives. (White male police officer)

When asked if there is a culture of violence in Black (ghetto) or Latinx (barrio) neighborhoods, 89 percent of respondents said yes. This could potentially be a misunderstanding where the participants missed or misunderstood the terms

Table 7.2: Is there a culture of violence in barrio and ghetto neighborhoods?

	Frequency	Percentage
No	8	10.7
Yes	67	89.3
Total	75	100.0

"ghetto" and "barrio"; however, we found pretty much the same numbers when we asked about each racial/ethnic group individually. When asked if Asians, Blacks, Latinx, Native Americans or Whites are the most prevalent group having contact with the system, 45.8 percent responded that Black youth are the most overrepresented group, and 32.5 percent stated that Latinx are the most overrepresented. That is, 79.3 percent chose Black or Latinx as the most problematic juveniles, with a few others answering that both are equally so in a metropolitan area with a White population making up almost 68 percent of the population. Clearly, non-White youth are seen as more criminalistic by most juvenile justice professionals.

I: Right. Some have suggested that a culture of violence (one which accepts and even embraces violence as an acceptable means for one's goals) exists in many barrio and ghetto neighborhoods. In your experience, does this seem to be the case?

R: So does a culture of violence exist in barrio and ghetto neighborhoods? It just depends on what your definition of "culture of violence" is. Do I see violence in those neighborhoods? Yes. Do I see violence in White neighborhoods? Yes. Do I see people who gravitate towards violence? I see that in every type of race. I don't know that I would necessarily agree that there's this strong culture, that violence is preferred over other means of conflict resolution, so …. (White male police officer)

I: Some have suggested that a culture of violence (one that accepts and even embraces violence as an acceptable means for one's goals) exists in many barrio and ghetto neighborhoods. In your experience, does this seem to be the case?

R: I would say it's not just limited to that, it's—I would say it's everywhere.

I: Right, you think it's like their culture, like they've just grown up that way, learning that?

R: Now is—is that a specific question for the Hispanic community, is that?

I: No, I think it's in general in minorities, like that's kind of very broad.

POLICE, JUVENILE COURT AND JUVENILE SPECIALIST INTERVIEWS

R: Yeah, I don't—I would—I don't see it just as being in minority community, I would say it's in every, every race.
I: Every race?
R: Yes. (White female police officer)

I: Some have suggested that a culture of violence (one which accepts and even embraces violence as an acceptable means for one's goals) exists in many barrio and ghetto neighborhoods. In your experience, does this seem to be the case?
R: I'm sorry, can you repeat the question, I was distracted for a minute.
I: Sure. Some have suggested that a culture of violence (one which accepts and even embraces violence as an acceptable means for one's goals) exists in many barrio and ghetto neighborhoods. In your experience, does this seem to be the case?
R: With the gangs, yes. Yeah, that is pretty evident. That's another thing, like I said with the—what they want is the same. Everybody wants the same thing, a sense of belongingness, a sense of family, and gangs offer that. They offer, "Hey, we're gonna be your brothers and your sisters," and, well, the police department is trying to counter that by saying, "Hey, look, you don't need that. We will be your family." You know, if you're not getting it at home, which I feel like that's where it starts.
I: Oh, definitely.
R: I really think there could be more done in educating parents on how to teach their children, starting with the character model, you know, Character First, you know, or even some variation of that, and it really works. I think it's tough being a parent, because you're really not given a book on it, you do what you were raised to do.
I: Exactly.
R: So that cycle continues, and there is no doubt that that influences, so it's up to us to teach them that, you know, "Hey, we can be your family. We can teach you the same thing, offer you same thing, only better. We'll offer you a future that doesn't involve you going to prison or going against your conscience and stealing," or, you know. A lot of these gangs will "jump you in," where it is very violent or they want to see what you are made of, that kind of thing, and have you do something that—to see if you ....
I: Prove yourself.
R: Yeah, prove yourself to them; it is sad, but it's true, it exists, it's out there.
I: Yeah. So, some have suggested that a culture of violence, which is here described as one that, which accepts and even embraces violence

R: Yes.
I: Okay.
R: Yes. Yes. They will resort to crime to obtain, you know, things that they can't find a way to obtain otherwise. (White male police officer)

The idea of a "culture of violence" among racial and ethnic minorities appears to be an attempt to deflect racial and ethnic differences in the juvenile justice system. Cultural racism has long served as an excuse for harsh, differential treatment and that is continued in the OKC juvenile justice system. Cultural racism allows individuals to treat non-Whites as more likely to be criminals, and simultaneously to ignore the fact that juvenile crime is strikingly similar among racial and ethnic groups.

The role of gang membership

Oklahoma generally, and Oklahoma City more specifically, are hotbeds for White supremacist groups (Medina et al, 2018), yet few juvenile justice professionals saw gangs as a White issue. By a more than two to one majority, participants responded that some races are more prone to gang membership. Table 7.3 shows the frequencies and percentages of responses.

When asked, one by one, if the racial/ethnic group mentioned was more prone to gang membership, Blacks (64 percent) and Latinx (60 percent) were seen as the most likely to belong to gangs, while Asians (2 percent) and Whites (2 percent) were unlikely to be seen as having high levels of gang membership. Interestingly, no participants thought Native American youth are prone to gang membership. Table 7.4 shows the frequencies and percentages of responses.

The following White male officer was in the minority in his responses, as he describes gang activity as having economic motivations rather than being race/ethnic-based. He mostly describes non-Whites, but he is consistent with literature in suggesting that many gangs are multiracial/multiethnic. He is also in the minority in pointing out White membership in gangs; however,

Table 7.3: Are members of some races more prone to gang membership?

	Frequency	Percentage
No	22	28.9
Yes	54	71.1
Total	76	100.0

Table 7.4: Perceptions of being prone to gang membership for specific race groups

	Asian	Black	Hispanic/ Latinx	Native American	White
No	97.6	36.1	39.8	100.0	97.6
Yes	2.4	63.9	60.2	0.0	2.7

he does not appear to be referencing White supremacist gangs but rather White members of what were once more strictly race/ethnic-based gangs.

I: Okay. Are there times when using labels or stereotypes within the juvenile justice system, such as gang affiliation, benefits the larger community?

R: No, because not all—not all these kids are in gangs. Out of the majority of the children that I deal with, you know, I'm going to say 80 to 90 percent are not into a gang, there are not any gang affiliation or anything like that; they are influenced by gangs though, but they're not a member of a gang, not a full-fledged member. And the reason why I'm saying that is, I've seen these kids wanting to be into a gang and the gang uses these children to commit a crime and then, that's it, you know, it's, "Okay, you did what you did, we don't want you in our gang now." So, I— that's where the stereotype and labeling comes from, is, "Oh, they're gang members." Well, no, they just want to be in a gang, but they're not a full-fledged gang banger, so, yeah, it's—it's hard to get a number down.

I: Okay.

R: I—we know where our hardcore gangs are, you know, where our Latino gangs and our African American gangs and we even have some Chinese gangs (laughs), so you know, because that is a big influence. The Oriental communities coming in, and they're— that can mean a bigger influence in that, and along with your Hispanics, so—that's why I keep saying, you know, minority for me is not just, you know, a Black and White issue, it's a Black and Hispanic and Oriental and sometimes Indian, because we're living [in] a state with Indians, so—so it's kind of hard for me to ….

I: Just pick?

R: Yeah, to select—be selective, I guess.

I: Okay. So have you observed any racial or ethnic differences in gang participation? In other words, are some racial or ethnic groups more likely to belong to gangs?

R: No.

I: No?

R: I'm going to say it's more likely a social economic issue with gangs.
I: Okay.
R: Not racial and ethnic. Yes, your race—your gangs are defined by race, but I've seen Crips with Hispanic members in it, I've seen Bloods with Hispanic members, I've seen GBC, which is your Latino gang, with Black members in it and White members, so yeah, I—I've not—I think it's more of a social economic setting that causes your gangs because, you know, I'm—in the community I live, it's ethnically diverse and we don't have any gangs in our neighborhood and in my area and that's like, okay, it tells me that it's got to be ….
I: The areas.
R: Yeah, the areas that they live in, and it goes back to the parents not caring, and these kids are trying to identify with a group instead of, you know, getting out on their own, because they know if they're, if they're on their own, they get picked on by these bullies and it just goes—it just is a downward spiral after that. (White male police officer)

The next respondent, a White male public defender, had more information on how race and ethnicity and gang membership works in the metropolitan area.

I: Is gang affiliation significant as a factor in juvenile delinquency or crime rates?
R: Yes.
I: How do you think that that is?
R: Many of my clients are gang members. They are gang members for a variety of reasons: socioeconomic, single parent households or no parent households—and I say "no parent households," yeah, they have a mother or they have a father.
I: But they're not ….
R: But they're not the mother or father, they have their own problems. Many of them are alcoholic or drug or they are, they're working so much that they're an absentee parent. The kids see other people in the neighborhoods wearing new clothes or having new shoes or new cars.
I: And they get that from the gangs?
R: Yeah, and they get that from the gangs, they—they make money selling drugs or they make, you know. … But more fundamentally, the gangs provide, or the kids think the gangs provide—I don't think the gangs really provide, but the kids think the gangs provide identity, love, somebody who cares about

them. Well, I talk to a lot of kids who are in jail or in detention, and one of the questions that I'll ask them is, "Well, you know, where are your boys now? They've—they've, of course, come and put money on your books?" "Well, no." "Will they come and visit you?" "Well, no." "Well, they're taking care of your mama at home, aren't they? They're going by and taking out the trash and cutting the yard?" "No." And that's one of the things I talk about with the kids is, you know, all these people who you say love you and that you have love for your—your "homies" or your "bros" or whatever their—their term for them is, "Well, where are those guys now?"

I: Right.

R: And sometimes it takes them a while to get that, but gangs are—gangs are an incredible feeder for our system.

I: Have you observed any racial or ethnic differences in gang participation? In other words, are some racial or ethnic groups more likely to belong to gangs?

R: Yes, Black and Hispanics tend to be—belong to gangs more than Whites, not that Whites aren't, I certainly represent Whites who are members of the Southside Locos and the GBCs and the Bloods and the Crips, okay. Our gang population has not stayed pure, you know, the Mexican gangs, if you go farther west, tend to be almost exclusively Hispanic—they're not here; the Bloods and the Crips tended at one time to be almost exclusively Black—they're not. So, yes, there are—there are gangs—I have not seen the proliferation of the White supremacists or the skinheads into street gangs here in Oklahoma City; they may be—they may exist, we just haven't seen them. I know from my years downtown working with adult population that those gangs are in the adult prisons, but they have not seemed to—that's not something I hear about in juvenile court.

I: Juvenile.

R: It's Bloods, Crips, GBCs, it's those gangs.

I: Okay. Gangs are often portrayed as highly racialized, such as Black, Latino, Native American and neo-Nazi White gangs. Is this portrayal pretty accurate or are gangs less about race and ethnicity than the public might think?

R: They're less about ethnicity, at least here. I think the farther you get from the west coast, the more ….

I: Integrated?

R: The more integrated they get. The neighborhoods that the gangs were born out of in—at least the Hispanic gangs in Los Angeles, really, are His—they're—they're Hispanic neighborhoods that are overwhelmingly Hispanic, so there's not—there was not

I: the opportunity for interracial—Although I know from—My undergraduate's from the University of New Mexico. Paul Steel, who was the criminal justice professor there, was a professor of mine. One of his areas of expertise was gangs; he was actually born in Los Angeles and grew up in the—in the neighborhoods where the gangs were spawned; well, he's—he's Anglo. He was from the neighborhood so he had some credibility with those people and was able to study them a little more.

I: Oh, I see.

R: So, there were some Anglos in the gangs, but because the—the neighborhood was so heavily Hispanic, it just ….

I: It didn't happen.

R: It didn't happen as much as it does in our mixed-race neighborhoods. (White male public defender)

His analysis of gangs is largely consistent with what we know of gangs in the area, but he makes one especially interesting point when he references White gangs. He points out the racial/ethnic fluidity in most area gangs, which includes some White membership. He then notes that there is a large White supremacist gang membership in the state prison system, but he does not see them in the juvenile end. This is clearly something that needs more research as it is unclear if police are looking for White juvenile gang activity or if White gang membership skews older, with a later start, than in the other juvenile/street gangs. We see no evidence suggesting gangs are not a larger issue for the Black and Latinx communities in the area; however, the question of White supremacist gang membership being low or ignored is interesting. There is also the inconsistent reporting of Whites as members of historically Black and Latinx gangs, with some noting it and others seemingly unaware of White gang membership.

Most participants simply described gangs as non-White issues. The following non-White male officer managed to describe, in some detail, every major racial and ethnic group's gang problems, with the notable exception of Whites, despite others mentioning White gang members.

I: Have you observed any racial or ethnic differences in gang participation? In other words, are some racial or ethnic groups more likely to belong to gangs?

R: No, all racial or ethnic groups have gangs. The Asians have gangs that do home invasion where the take the driver license, they'll rape a child, the daughter, 'cause they know the parents won't report it because they'll lose face. You have Native American gangs. You have Black gangs. You have Mexican gangs. Everybody has a gang. (Non-White male police officer)

Most participants saw gangs as a Black and/or Latinx issue only.

I: Have you observed any racial or ethnic differences in gang participation? In other words, are some racial or ethnic groups more likely to belong to gangs?

R: I believe the Blacks, African Americans and Hispanic are mostly attracted to gangs or most likely to belong to a gang, as well as some Asian. (Non-White male police officer)

I: Have you observed any racial or ethnic differences in gang participation? In other words, are some racial or ethnic groups more likely to belong to gangs?

R: Yeah. Pretty much, for the kids that come through here, most of our minority men are in gangs, Hispanics and Blacks. Yeah, a very, very, very high percentage of them. You know, some of them maybe not be as active or might consider themselves wanna-bes, but to me a wanna-be is a gonna-be. If you want to be in it, you're eventually gonna be in it, so yeah, yeah, very high. (Non-White male juvenile specialist)

I: Okay, good. Have you observed any racial or ethnic differences in gang participation? In other words, are some racial or ethnic groups more likely to belong to gangs?

R: I would say a majority of, here in Oklahoma City, you're going to have more Hispanic and Black gang members than you would White or pretty much any other race. Now, there are some Native Americans that are coming, especially within the Hispanic gangs. Now, I'm not saying White kids aren't involved, because they are, it's just a majority, you know, most of the population with the gang members are going to be of that ethnicity that I have seen. (Non-White male juvenile specialist)

Prior juvenile record

When asked about the significance of a juvenile's prior record in their treatment, responses fell into a similar pattern of circular logic, where non-Whites are over-policed, leading to a greater likelihood of non-Whites having a prior record, which in turn gives reason to over-police non-Whites (see frequencies and percentages in Table 7.5).

I: Okay. How important is a juvenile's prior record in determining how you will deal with that individual?

R: Again, it depends on the case and the prior record. I would say it's always important. It's always important, but a history of petty offences might not increase a risk factor with a specific juvenile, but a history of some violent offences would. So, it is important. It is important. (White male judge)

I: Okay, that's interesting. How important is a juvenile's prior record in determining how you will deal with that individual?

R: It's very important; one of my areas is youthful offender law where the kids have committed very serious crimes. When I make a decision what to do with them, whether or not they have exhausted the resources of our system, one of the major factors is the contacts they've had with the juvenile justice system. And it becomes almost self-defeating when the kids just continue to commit new crimes. And you do everything you can but there are, unfortunately, some juvenile delinquents who I do not believe will ever, no matter how much they are being—no matter how much intervention we—we give them, get it. They are too mired in their behaviors to ever get it. And I have several on my caseload where I am just waiting them out until they are too old to be in my courtroom anymore, and it's tragic and I hate it, but I can't—at some point in time, I have to look at these—at these delinquents and go, "I can't do anything else for you," and that's very frustrating.

I: Only focus on the ones that you can maybe …?

R: Yes. (White female district attorney)

Prior record can be a useful tool for helping juveniles, but only if prior record means the same thing across racial/ethnic lines. On the one hand, if DMC is due to differential involvement, then prior record is not problematic in any way. On the other hand, if differential treatment is the major cause of DMC, then prior record will only multiply the severity of DMC. Simply put, our analysis shows juveniles committing crimes at the same rate across racial/ethnic

Table 7.5: Importance of a juvenile's prior record in determining how juvenile justice officials deal with the juvenile

	Frequency	Percentage
Not very important	19	23.2
Somewhat important	14	17.1
Very important	49	59.8
Total	82	100.0

Table 7.6: Does direct or overt discrimination play a role in juveniles ending up in the juvenile justice system?

	Frequency	Percentage
No	45	57.0
Yes	34	43.0
Total	79	100.0

Table 7.7: Is disproportionate minority contact a problem?

	Frequency	Percentage
No	55	73.3
Yes	20	26.7
Total	75	100.0

lines, yet official police and court data show non-Whites being arrested and charged more often. Take a simple example of two kids, one Black and one White. Each has committed three crimes of the same severity. Using the area odds of arrest from earlier, the Black kid is likely to be arrested two to three times for the same amount of crime that the White kid will only be arrested for once. Again, they have committed the same amount of crime and of the same severity, yet one will be treated as a recidivist, perhaps, while the other will be treated as a first-time offender. A year later both kids get caught for a crime again. The White kid is on his second charged crime while the Black kid is now on his third or fourth charge. There is no difference in their actions, but under differential treatment, Black, Latinx and Native American kids are more likely to be arrested and charged, despite committing no more crime than White kids. And because prior record is so important in the juvenile justice system, differential treatment is compounded.

Views of racism and DMC

Our final interview questions to be addressed in this chapter are related to one another. We asked: "What effect, if any, does direct or overt discrimination (think old-fashioned racism) have in juveniles ending up in the juvenile justice system?" and "Is disproportionate minority contact (DMC) a problem or merely a reflection of the 'real world'?" The frequencies and percentages of responses to the two questions are presented in Table 7.6 and Table 7.7, respectively.

I: What effect, if any, does direct or overt discrimination—think old-fashioned racism—have in juveniles ending up in the juvenile justice system?

R: I think, now, different times, different generation, that old-fashioned racism does not contribute to putting kids in jail or even getting them help. That's not my generation, and so, for me, old-fashioned racism doesn't exist. So I don't think it has an effect on whether or not kids or any type of different ethnic groups, whether or not they go to jail or get incarcerated or have dealings with the justice system. So I don't think that contributes.

I: Okay. Is disproportional minority contact—DMC—a problem or merely a reflection of the real world?

R: Um, I want to say it's a reflection, because the way the city's split up—it's divided into four quadrants, and you can see different types of socioeconomic groups live in different quadrants of the city. So, you could say, it could be twisted so that a White officer patrolling in northeast Oklahoma City, which is a predominantly Black neighborhood, if he took the city as a whole and all of his contacts were, if he said it was 90 percent, 95 percent contacts with Black, the Black culture or the Black community, then it could be construed as being, his contacts are—but in the south of Oklahoma City, the majority of the contacts up there are Hispanic, could be due to the neighborhood that the officer patrols in. Um, so, um, so the question is?

I: Is it a problem?

R: No.

I: Or is it just a reflection of the real world?

R: I think it—I think it's just a reflection of the world that we live and the community that we live in. And the community that we serve. (White male police officer)

I: Okay. What effect, if any, does direct or overt discrimination—think old-fashioned racism—have in juveniles ending up in the juvenile justice system? This doesn't directly deal with you.

R: I don't think there is—you mean is there racism or is there profiling or anything?

I: Yeah, what effect does direct racism have on juveniles ending up in the juvenile system?

R: I don't think it does. I mean, I haven't seen it. I've never seen profiling or racism with my job. Everybody is treated equally. You know, a lot of times there is just so many calls and—anyway.

I: Okay. Is disproportional minority contact—DMC—a problem or merely a reflection of the "real world"?

R: Well, any type of crime or whatever is an issue. Why is it taking place? I don't know, I mean, I don't know as far as at the time of arrest. Well, and all through the system, I don't believe that there

> is profiling or racism that is causing it, by any means. No matter what the ethnic group is, I mean as far as committing crime—a crime is a crime, and I think I speak for all officers in that case, it doesn't matter—male, female, or what ethnic background—a crime is a crime. (White male police officer)

The frames of color-blind racism have proven to be pretty consistent throughout the interviews. From the background sections, we found that almost all the juvenile justice professionals lived lives steeped in White habitus, where their sole reference for non-Whites was in their justice system work. This is perhaps more important than White habitus found in other areas of society. Your average suburban elementary school teacher or engineer who lives a life marked by White habitus may not typically interact casually with non-Whites and is unlikely to see non-Whites in criminal circumstances as their main contact with non-Whites, as is true for many of the juvenile justice professionals. Naturalism was often the best frame to explain their questions revolving around neighborhood and friends.

When addressing issues of criminal activity, cultural racism and abstract liberalism were the common frames for explaining how broken non-Whites are, as compared with Whites. Non-Whites are seen as having different values and poor parenting skills, which leads to lives of crime for many of their children. Different values, such as describing Black and Latinx as embracing a culture of violence, clearly reflect cultural racism. Poor parenting skills may also include cultural racism but also embodies abstract liberalism as there is no acknowledgment of official justice policies that directly impact the family lives of Blacks and others. Rather than see the racism in over-policing Black communities, cultural shortcomings and economic inequality are blamed.

When asked about the clear overrepresentation of non-Whites, minimalization of racism was applied. Many acknowledged that some racism may exist, though many also denied it existed at all. Most, however, claimed that racism was not much of an issue, despite the overwhelming overrepresentation of non-Whites in the system.

Final thoughts

There is a final point we would like to address in this chapter, but we didn't include any measure for it in our study, as it simply had not occurred to us. There were more than a few responses, such as the one that follows, that read more like bullying.

I: Okay. Pretending for a moment that you had the ability, funding and support to do so (think magic or miracle if need be), what one

> change would you make to minimize the need for the juvenile justice system?
>
> R: I would reinstitute corporal punishment in the school systems and teach—because most children spend most of the day in the accompaniment of other adults, whether it be in school or daycare or whatever. I would want to re-institute a little bit more respect taught in schools; without that—I mean, without that corporal punishment, like I grew up with, it just—they don't respect themselves, they don't respect other adults, they come to me on the streets and they think, "Well, I can just talk to you like I talk to my teacher," and then they're in for a rude awakening when that doesn't happen. (White male police officer)

Bullying can clearly be a component of racism, but we didn't think much of it until two events that took place after our data collection brought it to our attention. In the first, a local police department, where both of the authors have former students working, was given the task to take over the school resource officer positions in an overwhelmingly White, relatively affluent school district. Multiple officers contacted the authors with very similar comments about how patrol officers were not thrilled to be patrolling schools, but, interestingly, the common question from officers during the initial announcement was if they could teach kids who didn't show them respect a lesson. The second incident involved a male Latinx training officer for a large department who was a guest in a class we co-teach. This officer is nearing retirement and wants to start a second career as a teacher in a public school. He loves working with kids and spent a lot of time explaining to our class how important it was to him to be a positive role model for non-White youth in urban schools. Less than ten minutes later, in response to a student question, he explained how non-White kids often don't know how to show respect to officers and that he likes to arrest "smart-ass" kids to teach them respect, and he trains his officers to do the same. We then asked if that wasn't counter to his desire to help urban kids, as prior record is a major concern in how they are treated by the juvenile system and it seems that would further hurt the very same kids he wants to help. The consensus after he left the class (after answering further questions) was that it had never occurred to him. We will discuss this a bit more, and what further questions it may suggest, in the next chapter.

8

Conclusion and Discussion

> Defeating racism, tribalism, intolerance, and all forms of discrimination will liberate us all, victim and perpetrator alike.
> Ban Ki-moon, former Secretary-General
> of the United Nations

Disproportionate minority contact (DMC) is about a difference in the ratio of non-White kids versus White kids who are caught and punished for delinquent behavior (Figure 8.1). DMC has never been about Black, Latinx and Native American kids being more delinquent or criminalistic than White kids. DMC has always been about a racially skewed focus on the small number of juvenile crimes that are solved. The problem with measuring DMC is that we, as researchers and policymakers, are using bad data. We incorrectly assume that arrest and conviction rates give an objective, proportional picture of criminal activity, despite all evidence to the contrary. Like the recent racial incident in the *Journal of the American Medical Association* (JAMA), too often it is assumed that professionals are above having racial bias, be it purposeful or simply negligent. Given that there is overwhelming evidence of racial inequality—differential treatment of non-Whites—in all areas of society, to even suspect differential involvement we must first assume that race works differently in the justice system than it does in the rest of society. Arrest reports are not "clean" data but are written by the arresting officer, whose own career may be judged, among other factors, based on the reports he or she writes. One does not need to be a "bad actor" to frame oneself in a better light, rather that should be expected as a common bias.

According to 2015 FBI data, 46 percent of the violent crimes and 19 percent of the property crimes reported to police in the United States were cleared (Gramlich, 2017). As noted earlier, just over half of 1 percent of the US population (0.6 percent) is responsible for half of the violent crime in the US (National Network for Safe Communities at John Jay College,

Figure 8.1: Depiction of DMC

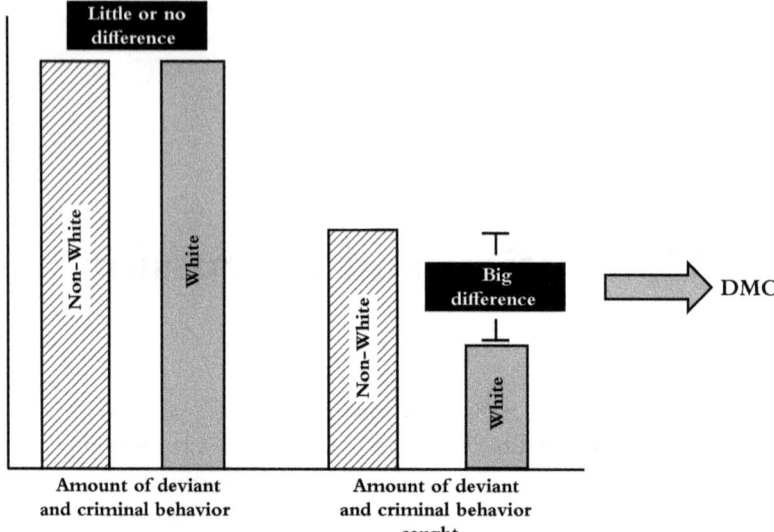

2021). We also know that White and non-White kids commit crimes at pretty much the same rate, both by category of crime and by severity, and that police, lawyers, judges and juvenile specialists all tend to see non-White juveniles and their families as more problematic and as much more likely to embrace criminality as acceptable, despite literature showing non-White families to be strikingly similar to White families.

The authors are both middle-aged White guys. Both have a background in researching inequality, but neither has ever experienced discrimination in any meaningful way. Our Whiteness showed as we were speculating about where, on the differential treatment to differential involvement continuum, the cause of DMC would fall. We figured it would be 70–80 percent differential treatment and 20–30 percent differential involvement. One of the authors has been studying this for more than a decade and a half and still expected differential involvement to be a significant cause of DMC. We were incredibly wrong. DMC is caused—exclusively—by differential treatment. We fell into the same trap—trying to place some of the responsibility on non-Whites—that we are now trying to help others avoid. Non-White kids are the victims. Period. Full stop.

One could argue that there is a small, low single digit, differential involvement component to DMC; however, the number of non-White chronic offenders is very small compared with the rest of the non-White population, and typically very geographically isolated, and it is a separate phenomenon. DMC research is conflating these two very different issues and hiding the over-policing of minority children as artifacts of examining the few chronic offenders. Keep in mind that *all* non-White youth suffer from differential treatment. They are all looked at as likely or potential criminals in a way that does not apply to White kids as a group. All children of color are seen as potentially a problem, whereas White children need to provide a reason to be seen that way.

DMC and police

In our self-report survey, juveniles attending public schools were anonymously surveyed. This is helpful in learning how the "on track" non-White kids, who make up the vast majority of the non-White youth population, compare with White youth. Juveniles either not enrolled or not regularly attending public school were not included, nor were those attending a private school or those home schooled. It is possible that students who have dropped out of school may be more likely to be chronic offenders; however, as Piquero and Brame note: "Therefore, despite the existence of considerable evidence about race and crime in the extant literature, virtually nothing is known about these patterns in samples of serious adolescent offenders" (2008, p. 23). Martinez (2002) and Anderson (1999) address the issues that increase crime rates in the poorest of non-White neighborhoods. While their work is not specific to DMC, there is significant overlap. It is impossible to ignore high crime rates in poor minority communities, and there is obviously an overrepresentation of non-Whites in delinquent and criminal acts in these neighborhoods. However, "crime rates" are not the same as the "number of criminals." That distinction is important as non-White and White kids offend at approximately the same rate. Only about 1 percent of juveniles in the area served by the public schools surveyed are not enrolled in school, according to the urban school district records. This is only slightly higher than the suburban schools and about the same as the rural school. The neighborhoods served by the urban school are considered "high crime" areas but are not among the worst in the city. There is not enough information to determine if the kids who are not enrolled in school are much more likely to be chronic offenders, especially given that Latinx who immigrated to the US as children are much more likely than their peers to be working full time to help support their family (Dennis et al, 2005, p. 229). Those living in barrios and ghettos as described by Martinez (2002) and Anderson (1999) make up a very small percentage of Latinx and Blacks living in the US. And in the communities studied by each, most of the folks are no more criminalistic than other groups.

Our point is that the few individuals who are chronic offenders are being used as an excuse to treat all other Black, Latinx or Native American youth, including all those not living in those poorest neighborhoods, as if they are all chronic offenders. In our sample, White kids actually had more interactions with police. In initial police contact, White juveniles in the study had more contact with police than any other group, though much of this was seen as positive contact, such as assisting or visiting juveniles, rather than investigating them. However, non-White juveniles, who had strikingly similar rates of criminal activity and strikingly similar types of criminal activity, were detained two and a half times as often as were the White juveniles. At the next police decision point, the decision to transport a juvenile in police custody, non-Whites were three times as likely to be transported than were the White juveniles. When we describe DMC as two issues masquerading as one, these are the two very different groups—one group consisting of the few chronic offenders in the poorest non-White neighborhoods, the second being the bulk of the non-White kids in these same geographic areas. The behavior of the first group, the chronic offenders, best lends itself to criminological theories that incorporate the societal inequality that led to the creation of these barrios and ghettos. The first group is where strain and similar theoretical frameworks appear to be best suited for understanding these kids. The second group consists of the much larger number of juveniles, including the rest of the kids in those poor neighborhoods, as well their cohorts from suburban and rural neighborhoods. For this larger group, DMC is solely an issue of differential treatment, and to minimize or eliminate DMC there is a need to change how and how often police interact with non-White juveniles.

The police data used are an accurate measurement of results at decision points in the juvenile justice system. The concern is that these data are often used to determine crime rates when that is not what they are measuring. Police data, unlike court data, are self-report data without the benefit of anonymity. Quite the opposite: an officer must often defend her or his data to superiors and/or court personnel. Police arrest data are a very precise and accurate measure of arrests. But arrests are not the same as crimes, nor are they the same as convictions. Report and arrest data are often used as a proxy to measure crime, which may be appealing to researchers as the data are prevalent and relatively easy to access.

As an example, the university that employs the authors has put in place programs and policies to increase the university's retention rate. This goal, shared by all public colleges and universities in the state, is driven by the state legislature. The idea suggests that improving the quality of teaching, combined with programs and strategies that identify and assist students who are at risk of not graduating, can help these "at-risk" students graduate. The goal seems worthy of support, and the university has increased its retention rate. What remains unclear is the extent to which these programs have helped. Is the increase in retention due to these programs, or, as some have suggested, is the increase do instead to grade inflation and/or a lowering of academic rigor? Furthermore, does the increased retention rate mean the university is better educating the students, or just that it has gotten better at graduating them? Does giving higher grades, resulting in more students passing, equate with "better teaching?" This "correlation does not imply causation" warning is equally applicable to police data: much as in the example of retention rates, police data may be a poor measure for criminality of Whites and non-Whites but instead be measuring the extent of bias in the juvenile justice system. Police data are accurate only as a measurement of police involvement. Programs designed to change the behavior of statistically normal non-White juveniles are not only doomed to failure but are objectively racist.

The police department included in this study does not collect data on initial police contact, which severely limits our knowledge of the decisions made before any formal action was taken and gives us no information about contact that did not result in official interaction. Policing tends to allow a significant amount of professional discretion in much of the initial contact. Initial police contact, unless under order by a court, city, county or state law, is rarely recorded. As noted in Chapter 2, this discretion often results in differential treatment of non-Whites. Initial police contact resulting from bias or racism, at an individual level, is easily explained away. It is not until enough quality data are available that one can determine if a pattern exists. As shown earlier, there are numerous studies documenting differential treatment based upon race and ethnicity in all facets of social life. There is simply no rational reason to expect this does not also happen to non-White juveniles in the juvenile justice system. Future studies are needed to determine the extent of differential treatment in initial police contact with juveniles, as it is likely this may be a largely undocumented starting point of DMC.

The interviews with area police, juvenile court attorneys and judges, and juvenile specialists give further insight into differential treatment. Everyone working as a judge or lawyer in the area juvenile court volunteered to participate in our interviews. Only those who were out of the office for the few days that court personnel were interviewed were not included in the interviews. The same was true for juvenile specialists working for the Office of Juvenile Affairs. Both of these groups are small compared with the much larger area police department, which employs more than 1,100 officers. As with the other interviews, only those who volunteered to be interviewed participated. There was no incentive offered. We coordinated with a very helpful Chief of Police who placed a lieutenant in charge of helping us find volunteers. Requests were made, by the lieutenant, at daily briefings for patrol officers and to units specializing in working with juveniles.

The most significant information we gleaned from the interviews was not what was said, but what was mostly left unsaid. Very few professionals attributed DMC to forces outside the control of the families, such as police and/or court actions and decisions, or general social and economic inequality. For most, the idea that DMC may be due to differential treatment was never acknowledged. In fact, it was often countered with adamant descriptions of the problems with non-Whites. For the vast majority of participants, DMC was simply due to non-White differential involvement in crime. As detailed in the previous chapter, participants' responses frequently referred to culturally unique family structures and values. Missing fathers were blamed, when Black fathers spend more time with their kids than do White fathers, though fathers from of all racial/ethnic groups are fairly similar in this area. Broken families were blamed, without acknowledging the overrepresentation of non-Whites in the prison system, something that at least most police officers who were interviewed should be aware of, as they are in the front end of that process. Non-White families were seen as embracing a culture of violence, also with little evidence in support.

When addressing issues of criminal activity, two of the frames of racism, cultural racism and abstract liberalism, were most often used to explain the overrepresentation of non-Whites. Non-Whites are seen as having different values and poor parenting skills, which leads to lives of crime for many of their children. References to different values, such as describing Black and Latinx as embracing a culture of violence, clearly reflect cultural racism. The attribution of poor parenting skills may also include cultural racism but also embodies abstract liberalism, as there is no acknowledgment of official justice policies that directly impact the family lives of Blacks and others. Rather than seeing racism in the over-policing of Black communities, cultural shortcomings and economic inequality are blamed.

Juvenile courts and DMC

Nationwide, DMC pretty consistently increases at each decision point, culminating in non-Whites being most severely overrepresented at the most severe point, waiver/certification to adult court. Placement in a juvenile detention facility, one step lower in severity than waiver/certification, shows extensive minority overrepresentation (Peck and Jennings, 2016). An exception to this trend, but not one that changes the overall higher-end outcomes, is the adjudication point. Judges and/or district attorneys (DAs) consistently attempt to correct racial overrepresentation at this point (Secret and Johnson, 1977; Bishop and Frazier, 1988; Lieber and Jamieson, 1995; Bishop et al, 2010). One of the DAs who participated in our interviews stated that she often declines to prosecute non-White juveniles due to obvious racial bias in the police reports.

Our findings are consistent with other studies in that our highest level of overrepresentation, as mentioned earlier, occurs at the decision point to waive/certify a youth to be tried as an adult. This decision is rare, happening in only 2.9 percent of area juvenile cases, but within this group non-Whites were three times as likely as Whites to be tried as an adult. Similarly, those found guilty and sentenced to a secure facility were also much more likely to be non-White. It is worth mentioning that Black youth were, by far, the most likely to see this result. Of minor note, Peck and Jennings refer to a **correction effect** as a measure taken by judges. In the county in this study a correction effect was also found, but it was at the DA level, rather than the judge level. This is probably due simply to procedural differences, as the result is very much the same as reported by Peck and Jennings (2016), with cases for non-Whites 33 percent more likely to be dismissed than cases for White youth.

Court-ordered probation was a bit of a mixed bag in terms of racial outcomes. Black youth were disadvantaged in the rate of court-ordered probation, yet Latinx were slightly advantaged compared with their White counterparts. While there are trends to suggest that non-Whites are treated differently than Whites at most decision points in the juvenile justice system, there are within-group differences among non-Whites.

Recommendations

First and foremost, the concept of DMC needs to be reworked into its two components. The bulk of DMC is a result of discrimination. As noted previously, overall White and non-White juveniles commit deviant and criminal acts very similarly in terms of type of crime and frequency of crime. This study, consistent with others, as noted earlier, shows an overrepresentation of non-Whites at almost every decision point. Given those two pieces of information, differential treatment fueled by racial bias, be it overt racism, institutional racism or accidental racial ignorance, is clearly the driving force in DMC and it needs to be addressed from that perspective. Instead, society and the justice system tend to blame the victims and seek to modify the behavior of non-White juveniles, while ignoring the same behavior from White juveniles. Society, at least "White" society, appears to avoid challenging White privilege and risk or seeing White society as the cause of DMC (DiAngelo and Dyson, 2018).

DMC must be split into (a) the larger area of racial bias resulting in minority overrepresentation within the juvenile justice system and (b) the smaller area of concentrated pockets of extreme poverty in non-White areas, resulting from a racialized social system, which leads to higher rates of chronic criminality by a few individuals in a few areas. The first requires structural changes in policing and the juvenile court system. The second involves both social change, to alleviate extensive poverty along racial lines, as well as individualized rehabilitation, based on proven methods.

Juvenile courts would appear to be the easiest place to make changes, especially given that there is a common, if largely ineffective, "correction effect" in place. Oklahoma City court personnel tend to work together as a single unit, and based upon interviews and observations from a previous study (Ketchum, 2008), most individuals genuinely see their goal as helping juveniles. Most welcome changes, and there are few political pressures as to how juveniles need to be treated in the court system. The sticking point is their perspective of differential involvement as a major contributor to DMC. Given the current baseline of White juvenile crime and delinquency and that there has been no outcry regarding a White juvenile crime issue, it seems that simply treating non-White kids, in the court system, the same as White kids are treated would free up resources, with no reason to expect any increase in criminal activity. The solution for DMC in the courts is painfully simple, politically achievable and the most likely of these recommendations to be embraced, as courts are already taking some measures in an attempt to meaningfully reduce DMC.

Policing needs to change. Just the fact that the US tends to police more aggressively than any other wealthy country is evidence enough that a different way of policing is possible, and even desirable. Most programs aimed at reducing DMC try to change the behavior of the non-White kids. This will never significantly reduce DMC, as evidenced by decades of trying to "fix" the non-White kids, because they simply are not "broken." With very few exceptions, the issue is not one of non-White youth being more delinquent or criminalistic, but of differential treatment by the police.

Changes in policing are arguably more difficult to achieve than changes in the juvenile court, as the number of parties involved, even at the local level, is substantially increased. Police also have much greater latitude, and their Fraternal Order of Police unions (FOP) have been loath to limit individual officer discretion by increasing oversight, nor are the FOP amenable to holding officers more accountable for differential treatment by race. Anecdotally, the authors and their students were told by four different officers, just days before the national Black Lives Matter (BLM) marches, that the Oklahoma City Police Department had no problems with race and that BLM would never protest in Oklahoma City as they had no reason to do so due to fantastic police–citizen relations. On May 31, a massive BLM protest was held in Oklahoma City, resulting in protesters being shot with teargas and rubber bullets. Numerous arrests were made (KOCO, 2020). Police departments tend to be entrenched in doing things the way they have always done them. Prior to the teargas, rubber bullets and arrests in Oklahoma City, officers "took a knee" with protesters in an empty show of solidarity. As long as police see civilians as needing to be subservient to their orders and whims, given that this is much more pronounced with non-White civilians, change will be difficult.

The authors agree with many of the principles espoused by those who want to "defund the police." Police are the ultimate generalists, in areas where being a generalist can cause damage. Both nationally and locally, we need more well-paid social workers and juvenile specialists. We need more investment and research into programs designed to treat juveniles and reduce recidivism. We need police who consistently are seen as advocates for and as working for the community. We need a police department that looks like the area it serves in terms of gender, race and ethnicity. Most importantly, we need police who do not embrace unsupported stereotypes of non-White children and their families. We need police to have the same starting point, in terms of expectations, for both White and non-White children and teens.

Future research

Largely anecdotally, we heard in the interviews, from officers in a local police department known personally to the authors, as well as in classroom discussions featuring officers, a reoccurring theme of the need for the public to show respect to the police. By respect, it is clear they mean civilians speaking respectfully to officers and following all directions without question. We do not have a measure of this, but it begs future research. In order to reduce racial bias, it may be worth looking deeper into the motivations of officers when making racially biased decisions. Are the officers acting fully or primarily out of racism, or is it an authoritarian drive that is easier to carry out with those who have the least power in society? In the end, both are rooted in racism; however, to reduce the extent of racist decisions at both the individual level and the department level, each of the causes may require entirely different interventions.

We concur with Piquero and Brame (2008) when they state the need for research on race and chronic juvenile offenders. This group makes up the smaller portion of DMC, yet a greater understanding of the details of this phenomenon is necessary to effectively reduce the problem. Much like the 50-plus-year debate between proponents of differential involvement and differential treatment, there are still too many theoretical disagreements regarding race and chronic offending. Perhaps part of this is due to the confounding of two issues as one, under the umbrella of DMC.

APPENDIX A

Juvenile Self-Report Questionnaire

Please do not write your name or any identifying information on the survey

Background/demographic questions

Please tell us a little about yourself.

1. Are you
    a) male
    b) female

2. As of today, how old are you? _____

3. What grade are you in?
    a) 7th grade
    b) 8th grade
    c) 9th grade
    d) 10th grade
    e) 11th grade
    f) 12th grade

4. Do you qualify for the free lunch program at school?
    a) yes
    b) no
    c) unsure/don't know

5. Who do you live with?
    a) birth or adoptive Mother and Father
    b) birth or adoptive Mother only
    c) birth or adoptive Father only

APPENDIX A

    d) family member other than Mother or Father
    e) other non-family member such as foster family or family friend

6. What racial/ethnic group or groups do you belong to? (mark all that apply)
    a) Asian
    b) Black
    c) Latino
    d) Native American/American Indian
    e) White
    f) Other

7. Using your answer to the last question as a reference, for the racial/ethnic group you identify with, do you believe your skin tone/shade of skin is: (*Note: This question is designed to examine if being darker or lighter than average within your racial/ethnic group is an advantage/disadvantage/neither)
    a) darker than average
    b) about average
    c) lighter than average

8. What racial/ethnic group do most people assume you belong to, at least at first impression?
    a) Asian
    b) Black
    c) Hispanic
    d) Native American/American Indian
    e) White
    f) Other

9. Did you attend Crooked Oak Schools last school year?
    a) Yes
    b) No

Questions about activity

The following questions are about activities in which you may or may not have participated. For the following questions, please indicate (X) if you participated in any of the following activities.

10. Did you use any tobacco product (cigarette, cigar, chewing tobacco, Skoal or Copenhagen type dip)?	At school	Location other than school	# Times the police were involved?	# Times you were issued a citation?	# Times you were arrested?
During summer vacation?	NA	_____	_____	_____	_____
In the last 6 months?	_____	_____	_____	_____	_____

11. Did you drink any alcoholic beverage?	At school	Location other than school	# Times the police were involved?	# Times you were issued a citation?	# Times you were arrested?
During summer vacation?	NA	_____	_____	_____	_____
In the last 6 months?	_____	_____	_____	_____	_____

12. Did you smoke/use marijuana or hash/hashish?	At school	Location other than school	# Times the police were involved?	# Times you were issued a citation?	# Times you were arrested?
During summer vacation?	NA	_____	_____	_____	_____
In the last 6 months?	_____	_____	_____	_____	_____

13. Did you use meth, cocaine, heroin, LSD or mushrooms?	At school	Location other than school	# Times the police were involved?	# Times you were issued a citation?	# Times you were arrested?
During summer vacation?	NA	_____	_____	_____	_____
In the last 6 months?	_____	_____	_____	_____	_____

14. Did you vandalize and/or spray-paint any property?	At school	Location other than school	# Times the police were involved?	# Times you were issued a citation?	# Times you were arrested?
During summer vacation?	NA	_____	_____	_____	_____
In the last 6 months?	_____	_____	_____	_____	_____

15. Did you steal or shoplift any items where the total value is less than $50?	At school	Location other than school	# Times the police were involved?	# Times you were issued a citation?	# Times you were arrested?
During summer vacation?	NA	_____	_____	_____	_____
In the last 6 months?	_____	_____	_____	_____	_____

16. Did you steal or shoplift any items where the total value is over $50?	At school	Location other than school	# Times the police were involved?	# Times you were issued a citation?	# Times you were arrested?
During summer vacation?	NA	_____	_____	_____	_____
In the last 6 months?	_____	_____	_____	_____	_____

17. Did you break into a home or business and take things from it?	At school	Location other than school	# Times the police were involved?	# Times you were issued a citation?	# Times you were arrested?
During summer vacation?	NA	_____	_____	_____	_____
In the last 6 months?	_____	_____	_____	_____	_____

18. Did you use a weapon or threat of force to obtain property from someone?	At school	Location other than school	# Times the police were involved?	# Times you were issued a citation?	# Times you were arrested?
During summer vacation?	NA	_____	_____	_____	_____
In the last 6 months?	_____	_____	_____	_____	_____
In the last week?					

19. Did you illegally possess a firearm not used for hunting?	At school	Location other than school	# Times the police were involved?	# Times you were issued a citation?	# Times you were arrested?
During summer vacation?	NA	_____	_____	_____	_____
In the last 6 months?	_____	_____	_____	_____	_____

20. Did you get in a fight or argument which led to physical violence?	At school	Location other than school	# Times the police were involved?	# Times you were issued a citation?	# Times you were arrested?
During summer vacation?	NA	_____	_____	_____	_____
In the last 6 months?	_____	_____	_____	_____	_____

21. Did you use a weapon to injure another person?	At school	Location other than school	# Times the police were involved?	# Times you were issued a citation?	# Times you were arrested?
During summer vacation?	NA	_____	_____	_____	_____
In the last 6 months?	_____	_____	_____	_____	_____

22. Did you injure someone critically/seriously injured or kill another person?	At school	Location other than school	# Times the police were involved?	# Times you were issued a citation?	# Times you were arrested?
During summer vacation?	NA	_____	_____	_____	_____
In the last 6 months?	_____	_____	_____	_____	_____

23. Are you a member of a gang?
    a) No
    b) Yes, but not very active
    c) Yes, an active member

Questions about interactions with police

The following questions are about situations in which you may or may not have experienced [sic]. For the following questions, choose yes or no for each question as it applies to you in the last 6 months.

APPENDIX A

	At school		Location other than school	
24. Have you had any interaction or communication with a police or law enforcement officer?	Yes	No	Yes	No
25. Have you asked any law enforcement officer for help?	Yes	No	Yes	No
26. Has a police or law enforcement officer provided assistance to you?	Yes	No	Yes	No
27. Have you had any interaction with a police officer where the officer was rude or disrespectful to you?	Yes	No	Yes	No
28. Has a police officer given you a verbal warning?	Yes	No	Yes	No
29. Has a police officer given you a written warning?	Yes	No	Yes	No
30. Has a police officer given you a ticket or citation?	Yes	No	Yes	No
31. Have you been detained, questioned or handcuffed by the police?	Yes	No	Yes	No
32. Have you been transported by police car to a detention facility, juvenile hall, jail, etc.?	Yes	No	Yes	No
33. Have you been physically struck or injured by a police officer?	Yes	No	Yes	No

APPENDIX B

Interview Guide for Judges, Police Officers and Juvenile Specialists

Contact information for interview participants

(Please leave this sheet with the interview participant)

If you have concerns or complaints about the research, the researchers conducting this study, Dr. Paul Ketchum can be contacted at [redacted] or Dr. John Duncan at [redacted].

If you have any questions about your rights as a research participant, concerns, or complaints about the research and wish to talk to someone other than individuals on the research team or if you cannot reach the research team, you may contact the University of Oklahoma – Norman Campus Institutional Review Board (OU-NC IRB) at [redacted].

Interview question sheet

Introduction

I have turned on the tape recorder. To assist with accurate recording of your responses, this interview will be recorded on an audio recording device. You have the right to refuse to allow such recording without penalty. Please respond that you do or do not consent to audio recording.

> NOTE TO INTERVIEWER: *Should the participant not consent to audio recording of the interview, please turn off the recorder immediately and thank them for their time.*

The following is information which the University of Oklahoma's Institutional Review Board, which is the agency which oversees the protection of study participants, requires you to have before deciding whether to participate in this study.

APPENDIX B

You are being asked to volunteer for this research study. This study is being conducted at the University of Oklahoma. You were selected as a possible participant because of your role as a professional in the juvenile justice system.

I am going to give you some information about the study and please ask if you have any questions or don't understand any part of this information.

The purpose of this study is to examine the extent and possible causes for minority overrepresentation in the juvenile justice system. There are a few different parts to this study. We are analyzing juvenile delinquency data from different agencies and will include survey information from juveniles in public schools. The part that you are being asked to participate in today are interviews with juvenile justice professionals including police officers, juvenile specialists, juvenile court attorneys, and juvenile court justices.

If you agree to be in this study, you will be asked to answer questions regarding your background, for general demographic purposes and specific questions about possible contributing factors to minority overrepresentation at many stages of the juvenile justice system.

This interview should take about an hour to complete, though that may vary with the length of your responses.

Participation in the study has no known significant risks, though addressing issues about racial or ethnic inequality may be uncomfortable for some participants. There are no direct benefits to you from participating in this study.

In published reports, there will be no information included that will make it possible to identify you without your permission. Research records will be stored securely, and only approved researchers will have access to the records.

There are organizations that may inspect and/or copy your transcribed interview for quality assurance and data analysis. These organizations include the Office of Juvenile Affairs, which is sponsoring this research, and the OU Institutional Review Board.

You will not be reimbursed for your time and participation in this study.

Participation in this study is voluntary. If you withdraw or decline participation, you will not be penalized or lose benefits or services unrelated to the study. If you decide to participate, you may decline to answer any question and may choose to withdraw at any time.

If you have concerns or complaints about the research, the researchers conducting this study, Dr. Paul Ketchum can be contacted at [redacted] or Dr. John Duncan at [redacted].

If you have any questions about your rights as a research participant, concerns, or complaints about the research and wish to talk to someone other than individuals on the research team or if you cannot reach the research team, you may contact the University of Oklahoma – Norman Campus Institutional Review Board (OU-NC IRB) at [redacted].

You have been given a copy of this contact information. If not, please pause the interview and ask for a copy.

Again, I will remind you that this interview is strictly voluntary and that you may refuse to answer any question at any time and furthermore, that you may stop this interview at any time.

We are not making a written record of this consent, at it would be the only way to link you to participation in this study. For that reason, I will ask for a verbal confirmation that you understand the information presented to you.

Do you agree to participate in this study?

NOTE TO INTERVIEWER: Should the participant not consent to participate in the study, please turn off the recorder immediately and thank them for their time.

Then we will begin. I will ask you scripted questions, though I may deviate from the script to pursue relevant information. I encourage you to give detailed answers rather than a simple yes or no answer.

There will be three main sections to this interview. First, I will ask some background questions about you. Next, we will cover some general juvenile justice issues and finally we will discuss the impact of race and ethnicity in the juvenile justice system.

Background

- Describe your family's socioeconomic standing, when you were growing up. Were you poor, lower middle class, middle class, upper middle class, professional class such as doctors and lawyers or were [sic]wealthy?
- What did/does your father do for a living?
- What did/does your mother do for a living?
- As a child, what were your dreams and expectations for your future?
- Do you recall what your parents' dreams and expectations were for you?
- What was your childhood neighborhood like? If you had more than one, please describe the one you most identify with.
- Did you live in the city, suburb, or country? Did the neighbors all know each other and how often did they interact with one another? In other words, describe the character of your childhood neighborhood.
- What was the racial and ethnic makeup of your neighborhood?
- What were the socioeconomic characteristics of your neighborhood like? Did most of your neighbors seem to have similar incomes as your family? Think back to things like the size of the houses, add-ons like pools, types and number of cars owned, etc.

- How would you characterize your current economic standing? Poor, lower middle class, middle class, upper middle class, professional class or are you simply very, very rich?
- Please describe the character of your current neighborhood.
- What is the racial and ethnic makeup of your current neighborhood?
- Are the socioeconomic characteristics of your neighborhood pretty similar to your childhood home?
- Do you interact with any of the neighbors; Do you consider any of the neighbors to be your friend; Do you interact with any of the minorities in your neighborhood?
- Do you consider any of the minorities in the neighborhood to be your friend?
- What kinds of activities do you do with these friends?

General juvenile justice

- Let's deal with the juvenile justice system in general for a moment. Do you think protecting members of society from the actions of juvenile offenders and maintaining the extra protection of juvenile offenders afforded by the juvenile justice system are mutually exclusive? If there is a conflict, which takes priority? Could you explain?
- Do most people have an accurate picture of the scope and significance of juvenile delinquency and crime? Overestimate? Underestimate?
- Pretending for a moment that you had the ability, funding and support to do so (think magic or miracle if need be), what one change would you make to minimize the need for the juvenile justice system?
- Are there legitimate reasons for being selectively harsh on a particular juvenile offender, such as stacking multiple offences for one incident? Without being overly specific, could you provide me with any examples?
- Tell me about your position within the police force, are you a patrol officer, do you work with a special unit, etc. Then please tell me a little about what kind of work situations you would find yourself interacting with juveniles.
- Is there a person or office that makes the decision about an individual case which results in you working with a juvenile?
- Do you work in a single community or do you work different areas of the city?
- Do you get to know any of the juveniles you interact with? If so, how might that happen?
- In the time that you have worked in the juvenile justice system, has the focus on juveniles changed in any way? (If so, how?)

Race

- Let's move the discussion to race and ethnicity. Just so that you know what this research is looking at, we are, of course looking at arrest and incarceration data, but through these interviews with police, lawyers, judges and juvenile specialists we are also trying to gain insight from those who actually work with juvenile offenders, regarding possible social influences which may combine with race or ethnicity, possibly contributing to minority overrepresentation. Do you record a juvenile's race or ethnicity on any paper work? If so, do you know the options listed or do you come up with you [sic] own description?
- How do you choose which race or ethnicity to list? Do you ask the juvenile? Do you take your best guess?
- For purposes of this interview I will frequently refer to minority overrepresentation in the juvenile justice system as "disproportional minority contact" or "DMC" which is the term used by the Office of Juvenile Justice and Delinquency Prevention (OJJDP). An overwhelming amount of data reveals that disproportionate minority contact occurs at almost every point in the juvenile justice system. However, there is also a large body of research that shows that DMC differs dramatically from jurisdiction to jurisdiction. The purpose of this interview is to gain insights from those who work within the juvenile justice system, in an effort to understand how race and/or ethnicity becomes a factor, be it direct or indirect. From your experience, are minority youths overrepresented in official contact with your department?
- How significant is the overrepresentation? In other words, is there a lot of overrepresentation, a little, or somewhere in between?
- Which group or groups are most overrepresented (or "represented" if the participant states that there is no overrepresentation)?
- Is this from your own experience and observations or are you familiar with official numbers for your department?
- Let us address the issues outside of direct influence of the juvenile justice system. What effects, if any have you seen a lack of quality educational resources play in DMC? *(Probe for examples)*
- What about the accompanying socioeconomic conditions such as poverty, substance abuse, few job opportunities and high crime rates? *(Probe for examples)*
- Some have suggested that a culture of violence (one which accepts and even embraces violence as an acceptable means for ones [sic] goals) exists in many barrio and ghetto neighborhoods. In your experience, does this seem to be the case?
- Do you think DMC can be largely explained by class? In other words, is DMC a reflection of poverty?

- What role have you seen difficult family issues play? *(Probe for examples)*
- What percentage, approximately, of juveniles that you have contact with, do not have English as their first language?
- What other primary languages have you run into?
- What resources do you have to deal with parents and juveniles who don't speak English fluently?
- Have you witnessed any other cultural problems, other than language that your department has run into, such as tribal issues, or cultural issues with certain racial or ethnic groups?
- Are there times when using labels or stereotypes within the juvenile justice system, such as gang affiliation, benefits the larger community?
- Have you observed any racial or ethnic differences in gang participation? In other words, are some racial or ethnic groups more likely to belong to gangs?
- What effect, if any, does direct, or overt discrimination (think old-fashioned racism) have in juveniles ending up in the juvenile justice system?
- Is disproportional minority contact (DMC) a problem or merely a reflection of the "real world"?
- This concludes the questions. Is there anything on the juvenile justice system or the impact of race or ethnicity on the juvenile justice system that you would like to add?
- Thank you for your assistance in this research. Please don't hesitate to contact me with any questions which you may have.

Bibliography

Acolin, A. and Vitiello, D. (2018). "Who owns Chinatown: Neighborhood preservation and change in Boston and Philadelphia." *Urban Studies*, 55(8), pp. 1690–710.

Agnew, R. (2002). *Criminological theories: Past and present*, 2nd ed. Los Angeles, CA: Roxbury Park.

Akers, R., Krohn, M., Radosevich, M. and Lanza-Kaduce, L. (1981). "Social characteristics and self-reported delinquency: Differences in extreme types," in Jenson, G. F. (ed.), *Sociology of delinquency*. Beverly Hills, CA: SAGE Publications, pp. 48–62.

Akinyemiju, T. F., Soliman, A. S., Johnson, N. J., Altekruse, S. F., Welch, K., Banerjee, M., Schwartz, K. and Merajver, S. (2013). "Individual and neighborhood socioeconomic status and healthcare resources in relation to black-white breast cancer survival disparities." *Journal of Cancer Epidemiology*, 490472. https://doi.org/10.1155/2013/490472

Alexander, M. and West, C. (2012). *The New Jim Crow: Mass Incarceration in the Age of Colorblindness*. New York, NY: The New Press.

American Civil Liberties Union. (2014). "Black, Brown and targeted: A report on Boston Police Department street encounters from 2007–2010." ACLU Foundation of Massachusetts. Available at: https://www.aclum.org/sites/default/files/wp-content/uploads/2015/06/reports-black-brown-and-targeted.pdf

Anderson, E. (1999). *Code of the street: Decency, violence, and the moral life of the inner city*. New York, NY: W. W. Norton and Company.

Archambault, I., Janosz, M., Morizot, J. and Pagani, L. (2009). "Adolescent behavioral, affective, and cognitive engagement in school: Relationship to dropout." *Journal of School Health*, 79(9), pp. 408–15.

Armour, J. and Hammond, S. (2009). *Minority youth in the juvenile justice system: Disproportionate minority contact*. Washington, DC: National Conference of State Legislatures.

Austin, J. (1995a). "The overrepresentation of minority youths in the California juvenile justice system: Perceptions and realities," in Kempf-Leonard, K., Pope, C. E. and Feyerherm, W. (eds.), *Minorities in juvenile justice*. Thousand Oaks, CA: SAGE Publications. pp. 200-220.

Austin, J. (1995b). "Racial disparities in the confinement of juveniles: Effects of crime and community social structure on punishment," in Leonard, K. K., Pope, C. and Feyerherm, W. (eds.), *Minorities in juvenile justice*. Thousand Oaks, CA: SAGE Publications. pp. 221–43.

Austin Office of Police Oversite, Office of Innovation and Equity Office. (2020). "Analysis of the Austin Police Department's Racial Profiling Report." City of Austin, Texas. Available at: http://www.austintexas.gov/edims/pio/document.cfm?id=334984

Badger, E., Miller, C. C., Pearce, A., and Quealy, K. (2018). "Extensive Data Shows Punishing Reach of Racism for Black Boys." March 17. *The New York Times*. Available at: https://www.nytimes.com/interactive/2018/03/19/upshot/race-class-white-and-black-men.html

Badolato, G. M. B., Boyle, M. D., McCarter, R., Zeoli, A. M., Terrill, W. and Goyal, M. K. (2020). "Racial and ethnic disparities in firearm-related pediatric deaths related to legal intervention." *Pediatrics*, 146. doi: 10.1542/peds.2020-015917

Balko, R. (2014). "How municipalities in St. Louis County, Mo., profit from poverty." September 3. *Washington Post*. Available at: https://www.washingtonpost.com/news/the-watch/wp/2014/09/03/how-st-louis-county-missouri-profits-from-poverty/

Barkan, S. E. and Cohn, S. F. (1994). "Racial prejudice and support for the death penalty by whites." *Journal of Research in Crime and Delinquency*, 31(2), pp. 202–9.

Barkan, S. E. and Cohn, S. F. (2005). "Why whites favor spending more money to fight crime: The role of racial prejudice." *Social Problems*, 52(2), pp. 300–14.

Barlow, M. H. (1998). "Race and the problems of crime in Time and Newsweek cover stories, 1946–1995." *Social Justice*, 25, pp. 149–83.

Barshay, J. (2020). Research looks at college graduation rates by race and ethnicity two states. *Hechinger Report*. Available at: https://hechingerreport.org/another-way-to-quantify-inequality-inside-colleges/

Baumgartner, F. R. (2018). *Suspect citizens: What 20 million traffic stops tell us about policing and race*. Cambridge: Cambridge University Press.

Bayer, C., Ferreira, F. and Macmillan, R. (2017). "Racial and ethnic price differentials in the housing market." *Journal of Urban Economics*, 102(C), pp. 91–105.

BBC News. (2017). "Venezuela TV shows 'US citizens confessing over failed coup'." May 7. Available at: https://www.bbc.com/news/world-latin-america-52568475

Bennett, W. J., Dilulio, J. J. and Walters, J. P. (1996). *Body count: Moral poverty–and how to win America's war against crime and drugs*. New York, NY: Simon & Schuster.

Bernard, T. J. (1992). *The cycle of juvenile justice*. New York, NY: Oxford University Press.

Bertrand, M. and Sendhil, M. (2004). "Are Emily and Greg More Employable Than Lakisha and Jamal? A Field Experiment on Labor Market Discrimination." *American Economic Review*, 94(4), pp. 991–1013.

Bishop, D. (2005). "The role of race and ethnicity in juvenile justice processing," in Hawkins, D. and Kempf-Leonard, K. (eds.), *Our children, their children: Confronting racial and ethnic differences in American juvenile justice*. Chicago, IL: University of Chicago Press, pp. 23–82.

Bishop, D. M. and Frazier, C. E. (1988). "The influence of race in juvenile justice processing." *Journal of Research in Crime and Delinquency*, 22(2), pp. 309–28.

Bishop, D. M. and Frazier, C. E. (1996). "Race effects in juvenile justice decision-making: Findings of a statewide analysis." *Journal of Criminal Law and Criminology*, 86(2), pp. 392–413.

Bishop, D. M. and Leiber, M. J. (2011). "Racial and ethnic differences in delinquency and justice system responses." In Bishop, D. M. and Feld, B. C. (eds.), *The Oxford handbook of juvenile crime and juvenile justice*. New York, NY: Oxford University Press, pp. 445–84.

Bishop, D. M., Leiber, M. J. and Johnson, J. D. (2010). "Contexts of decision making in the juvenile justice system: An organizational approach to understanding minority overrepresentation." *Youth Violence and Justice*, 8(3), pp. 213–33.

Blackmore, J. (1974). "The relationship between self-reported delinquency and official convictions amongst adolescent boys." *British Journal of Criminology*, 14(2), pp. 172–6.

Blumer, H. (1958). "Race Prejudice as a Sense of Group Position." *Pacific Sociological Review*, 1(1), pp. 3–7.

Bobo, L. and Kluegel, J. (1993). "Opposition to race-targeting: Self-interest, stratification ideology or racial attitudes?" *American Sociological Review*, 58(4), pp. 443–64.

Bolton, K. and Feagin, J. (2004). *Black in Blue: African-American Police Officers and Racism* (1st ed.). Oxford: Routledge.

Bond, C. and Williams, R. (2007). "Residential Segregation and the Transformation of Home Mortgage Lending." *Social Forces*, 86(2), pp. 671–98.

Bonilla-Silva, E. (2001). *White supremacy and racism in the post-civil rights era*. Boulder, CO: Lynne Rienner Publishers.

Bonilla-Silva, E. (2003). *Racism without racists: Color-blind racism and the persistence of racial inequality in the United States*. Lanham, MD: Rowman and Littlefield.

Bonilla-Silva, E. (2018). *Racism without racists: Color-blind racism and the persistence of racial inequality in America*. Lanham, MD: Rowman and Littlefield.

Bonilla-Silva, E., Goar, C. and Embrick, D. G. (2006). "When Whites flock together: The social psychology of White habitus." *Critical Sociology*, 32(2–3), pp. 229–53. doi: 10.1163/156916306777835268

Borowski, S. (2012, June 12). "The origin and popular use of Occam's razor." American Association for the Advancement of Science. Available at: https://www.aaas.org/origin-and-popular-use-occams-razor

Bound, J., Schoenbaum, M. and Waidmann, T. (1995). "Race and education differences in disability status and labor force attachment." NBER Working Paper Series, 5159.

Bradley, S. and Lenton, P. (2007). "Dropping out of post-compulsory education in the UK: An analysis of determinants and outcomes." *Journal of Population Economics*, 20(2), pp. 299–328.

Braveman, P., Egerter, S., and Williams, D. R. (2011). "The social determinants of health: coming of age." *Annual Review of Public Health*, 32, 381–98. https://doi.org/10.1146/annurev-publhealth-031210-101218

Bridges, G. S. and Steen, S. (1998). "Racial disparities in official assessments of juvenile offenders: Attributional stereotypes as mediating mechanisms." *American Sociological Review*, 63(4), pp. 554–70.

Bridges, G. S., Conley, D. J., Engen, R. L. and Price-Spratlen, T. (1995). "Racial disparities in the confinement of juveniles: Effects of crime and community social structure on punishment," in Leonard, K. K., Pope, C. and Feyerherm, W. (eds.), *Minorities in juvenile justice*. Thousand Oaks, CA: SAGE Publications, pp. 128-152.

Brown, S., Lee, S., Brown, T. A. and Waddell, B. E. (2010). "Effect of race on thyroid cancer care in an equal access healthcare system." *American Journal of Surgery*, 199(5), pp. 685–9.

Bush, B. (2019). "Columbus police use force disproportionately against minorities, study finds." August 21. *Columbus Dispatch*. Available at: https://www.dispatch.com/news/20190821/columbus-police-use-force-disproportionately-against-minorities-study-finds

Cabaniss, E. R., Frabutt, J. M., Kendrick, M. H. and Arbuckle, M. B. (2007). "Reducing disproportionate minority contact in the juvenile justice system: Promising practices." *Aggression and Violent Behavior*, 12(4), pp. 393–401.

Cabrera, A. F. and La Nasa, S. M. (2000). "Understanding the college-choice process." *New Directions for Institutional Research*, 2000(107), pp. 5–22. doi: 10.1002/ir.10701.

Campbell, D. T. and Stanley, J. C. (1963). *Experimental and quasi-experimental designs for research*. Boston, MA: Houghton Mifflin Company.

Carden, K. (2016). "American Indian access to health care services in Oklahoma Post Affordable Care Act." Available at: https://shareok.org/handle/11244/47049

Carey, R. L. (2016). "'Keep that in mind ... you're gonna go to college': Family influence on the college going processes of Black and Latino high school boys." *Urban Review*, 48(5), pp. 718–42.

Casey, C., Glasberg, D. S. and Beeman, A. (2011). "Racial disparities in access to mortgage credit: Does governance matter?" *Social Science Quarterly*, 92(2), pp. 782–806.

Cashman, H. (2018). *Queer, Latinx, and bilingual: Narrative resources in the negotiation of identities*. New York, NY: Routledge.

Ceja, M. (2006). "Understanding the role of parents and siblings as information sources in the college choice process of Chicana students." *Journal of College Student Development*, 47(1), pp. 87–104. doi: 10.1353/csd.2006.0003

Center for Children's Law and Policy. (2015). *Racial and ethnic disparities reduction practice manual*. Washington, DC: Center for Children's Law and Policy.

Chai, C. A. (2014). "The impact of stereotypical Asian crimes on juror decision-making: Punishing the model minority." Doctoral Dissertation, University of Wyoming. Proquest.

Chambliss, W. (1995). *Power, politics and crime*. Boulder, CO: Westview Press.

Charish, C., Davis, S. and Damphousse, K. (2004). *Race/ethnicity and gender effects on juvenile system processing*. Oklahoma City, OK: Oklahoma Office of Juvenile Affairs.

Charles, C. Z., Roscigno, V. J. and Torres, K. C. (2007). "Racial inequality and college attendance: The mediating role of parental investments." *Social Science Research*, 36(1), pp. 329–52. doi: 10.1016/j.ssresearch.2006.02.004.

Chetty, R., Hendren, N., Jones, M. R. and Porter, S. R. (2020). "Race and economic opportunity in the United States: An intergenerational perspective." *Quarterly Journal of Economics*, 135(2), pp. 711–83.

Childs, K. K., Sullivan, C. J. and Gulledge, L. M. (2010). "Delinquent behavior across adolescence: Investigating the shifting salience of key criminological predictors." *Deviant Behavior*, 32(1), pp. 64–100.

CNA. (2019). Racial bias audit of the Charleston, South Carolina, Police Department. City of Charleston. Available at: https://bloximages.newyork1.vip.townnews.com/postandcourier.com/content/tncms/assets/v3/editorial/c/98/c9836a0e-e3b6-11e9-9b2d-ffb3c58d9204/5d9254e3cddbd.pdf.pdf

Coates, R. (2007). "Racism in the USA and globally," in Gallagher, C. (ed.), *Rethinking the color line: Readings in race and ethnicity*, 3rd ed. New York, NY: McGraw Hill.

Coates, T. (2013). "Understanding out-of-wedlock births in Black America: Revisiting the controversial Moynihan Report." June 21. *The Atlantic*. Available at: https://www.theatlantic.com/sexes/archive/2013/06/understanding-out-of-wedlock-births-in-black-america/277084/

Cohen, L. and Kluegel, J. (1978). "Determinants of juvenile court dispositions: Ascriptive and achieved factors in two metropolitan courts." *American Sociological Review*, 43(2), pp. 162–76.

Cole, D. (2000). *No equal justice: Race and class in the American criminal justice system*. New York, NY: New Press.

Collins, S. (1996). *Black Corporate Executives (Labor and Social Change)*. Philadelphia, PA: Temple University Press.

Collins, B. and Zadrozny, B. (2021). "Extremists made little secret of ambitions to 'occupy' Capitol in weeks before attack." Jan 8. *NBC News*. Available at: https://www.nbcnews.com/tech/internet/extremists-made-little-secret-ambitions-occupy-capital-weeks-attack-n1253499

Collins, J. W., Jr, David, R. J., Handler, A., Wall, S. and Andes, S. (2004). "Very low birthweight in African American infants: the role of maternal exposure to interpersonal racial discrimination." *American Journal of Public Health*, 94(12), 2132–8. https://doi.org/10.2105/ajph.94.12.2132

Cook, T. D. and Campbell, D. T. (1979). *Quasi-experimentation: Design and analysis issues for field settings*. Boston, MA: Houghton Mifflin Company.

Crowell, C. (2018). "Redlining settlement fails to provide strong penalties." June 7. *Philadelphia Tribune*. Available at: https://search.proquest.com/docview/2056424335?accountid=1296

The Daily Progress. (2020). "Report finds racial disparity at almost every level of local criminal justice system." January 30. Available at: https://dailyprogress.com/dailyprogress/report-finds-racial-disparity-at-almost-every-level-of-local-criminal-justice-system/article_8c1dad70-7e3a-565b-a98c-f9bc4a189862.html

Dannefer, D. and Schutt, R. K. (1982). "Race and juvenile justice processing in court and police agencies." *American Journal of Sociology*, 87(5), pp. 1113–32.

Darling-Hammond, L. (2013). "Inequality and school resources: What it will take to close the opportunity gap," in Stombler, M. and Jungels, A. M. (eds.), *Focus on social problems: A contemporary reader*. New York, NY: Oxford University Press, pp. 4–12.

Davies, H. T. O., Crombie, I. K. and Tavakoli, M. (1998). "When can odds ratios mislead?" *British Medical Journal*, 316(9), pp. 989–91.

Dekker, R. (2018). "Racial disparities in childbirth." Available at: https://evidencebasedbirth.com/racial-disparities-child-birth/

DeLuca, S., Clampet-Lundquist, S. and Edin, K. (2016). *Coming of age in the other America*. New York, NY: Russell SAGE Foundation.

Denbeaux, M., Kearns, K. and Ricciardelli, M. (2016). Racial profiling report: Bloomfield Police and Bloomfield Municipal Court. Elsevier. Available at: https://papers.ssrn.com/sol3/papers.cfm?abstract_id=2760382

Dennis, J. M., Phinney, J. S. and Chuateco, L. I. (2005). "The role of motivation, parental support, and peer support in the academic success of ethnic minority first-generation college students." *Journal of College Student Development*, 46(3), pp. 223–36. https://doi.org/10.1353/csd.2005.0023

DiAngelo, R. (2018). *White fragility: Why it's so hard for white people to talk about racism*, Reprint ed. Boston, MA: Beacon Press.

Dixon, T. L., Schell, T. L., Giles, H. and Drogos, K. L. (2008). "The influence of race in police–civilian interactions: A content analysis of videotaped interactions taken during Cincinnati police traffic stops." *Journal of Communication*, 58(3), pp. 530–49.

Donnelly, E. A. (2017). "The disproportionate minority contact mandate." *Criminal Justice Policy Review*, 28(4), pp. 347–69.

Downs, K. (2016). "FBI warned of White supremacists in law enforcement 10 years ago. Has anything changed?" 21 October. PBS NewsHour. Available at: https://www.pbs.org/newshour/nation/fbi-white-supremacists-in-law-enforcement

D'Souza, D. (1995). *The end of racism*. New York, NY: Free Press.

Du Bois, W. E. B. (1968). *The souls of black folk: Essays and sketches*. New York, NY: Johnson Reprint Corporation.

Du Bois, W. E. B. (2007). *The Negro*. New York, NY: Cosimo Classics.

Duggan, P. (2019). "A disproportionate number of D.C. police stops involved African Americans." September 9. *Washington Post*. Available at: https://www.washingtonpost.com/local/public-safety/a-disproportionate-number-of-dc-police-stops-involved-african-americans/2019/09/09/6f11beb0-d347-11e9-9343-40db57cf6abd_story.html

Duran, R. J. and Posadas, C. E. (2013). "Disproportionate minority contact in the land of enchantment: Juvenile justice disparities as a reflection of White over-color ascendancy." *Journal of Ethnicity in Criminal Justice*, 11(1–2), pp. 93–111.

Duran, R. J. and Posadas, C. E. (2016). "The policing of youth on the U.S.–Mexico border: A law enforcement perception of leniency." *Race and Justice*, 6(1), pp. 57–83.

Duran, R. J., Posadas, C. E. and Mata, J. O. (2008). Juvenile Justice Project Las Cruces, New Mexico: Disproportionate Minority Contact Assessment Study. Technical Report.

Earl, T., Saha, S., Lombe, M., Korthuis, P. T., Sharp, V., Cohn, J., Moore, R. and Beach, M. C. (2013). "Race, relationships, and trust in providers among Black patients with HIV/AIDS." *Social Work Research*, 37(3), pp. 219–26.

Eberhardt, J., Davies, P., Purdie-Vaughns, V. and Johnson, S. (2006). "Looking deathworthy: Perceived stereotypicality of Black defendants predicts capital-sentencing outcomes." *Psychological Science*, 17(5), pp. 383–6.

Edwards, F., Esposito, M. H. and Lee, H. (2018). "Risk of police-involved death by race/ethnicity and place, United States, 2012–2018." *American Journal of Public Health*, 108(9), pp. 1241–8.

Edwards, F., Lee, H. and Esposito, M. (2019). "Risk of being killed by police use of force in the United States by age, race–ethnicity, and sex." *Proceedings of the National Academy of Sciences of the United States of America*, 116(34), pp. 16793–8.

Eitle, D., Turner, R. J., & Eitle, T. M. (2003). "The Deterrence Hypothesis Reexamined: Sports Participation and Substance Use among Young Adults." *Journal of Drug Issues*, 33(1), pp. 193–221. https://doi.org/10.1177/002204260303300108

Ellerbe, C. Z., Jones, J. B. and Carlson, M. J. (2018). "Race/ethnic differences in nonresident fathers' involvement after a nonmarital birth." *Social Science Quarterly*, 99(3), pp. 1158–82.

Elliott, D. S. (1994). "1993 serious violent offenders: Onset, developmental course, and termination. The American Society of Criminology 1993 Presidential Address." *Criminology*, 32(1), pp. 1–21.

Elliott, D. S., Huizinga, D. and Menard, S. (1989). *Multiple problem youth: Delinquency, substance use and mental health problems*. New York, NY: Springer-Verlag.

Engen, R. L., Steen, S. and Bridges, G. S. (2002). "Racial disparities in the punishment of youth: A theoretical and empirical assessment of the literature." *Social Problems*, 49(2), pp. 194–220.

Enquirer editorial board (2019). "Editorial: Racial disparities in police stops demands attention." December 20. *Cincinnati Enquirer*. Available at: https://eu.cincinnati.com/story/opinion/2019/12/20/editorial-racial-disparities-police-stops-demands-attention/2666685001/.

Epp, C. R., Maynard-Moody, S. and Haider-Markel, D. P. (2014). *Pulled over: How police stops define race and citizenship*. Chicago, IL: University of Chicago Press.

Erickson, M. L. and Empey, L. T. (1963). "Court records, undetected delinquency, and decision-making." *Journal of Criminal Law, Criminology, and Police Science*, 54(4), pp. 456–69.

Fagan, J., Piper, E. and Moore, M. (1987). "Violent delinquents and urban youth." *Criminology*, 24(3), pp. 439–71.

Farrington, D. P. (1973). "Self-reports of deviant behavior: Predictive and stable?" *Journal of Criminal Law and Criminology*, 64(1), pp. 99–110.

Farrington, D. P. (1977). "The effects of public labelling." *British Journal of Criminology*, 17(2), pp. 112–25.

Farrington, D. P., Barnes, G. C. and Lambert, S. (1996). "The concentration of offending in families." *Legal and Criminological Psychology*, 1(1), pp. 47–63.

Farrington, D. P., Loeber, R., Stouthamer-Loeber, M., Van Kammen, W. B. and Schmidt, L. (2003). "Self-reported delinquency and a combined delinquency seriousness scale based on boys, mothers, and teachers: Concurrent and predictive validity for African-Americans and Caucasians." *Criminology*, 34(4), pp. 493–517.

Feagin, J. (2006). *Systemic Racism: A Theory of Oppression*. New York, NY: Tayor and Francis Group.

Federal Bureau of Investigation. (2019). National Crime Information Center (NCIC) Missing Person and Unidentified Person Statistics. Available at: https://www.fbi.gov/file-repository/2019-ncic-missing-person-and-unidentified-person-statistics.pdf/view

Federal Interagency Forum on Child and Family Statistics. (2019). *America's children: Key national indicators of well-being*. Washington, DC: US Government Printing Office.

Feld, B. C. (1995). "The social context of juvenile justice administration: Racial disparities in an urban juvenile court," in Kempf-Leonard, K., Pope, C. E. and Feyerherm, W. (eds.), *Minorities in juvenile justice*. Thousand Oaks, CA: SAGE Publications.

Feld, B. C. (1999a). "A funny thing happened on the way to the centenary: Social structure, race and the transformation of the juvenile court." *Punishment and Society*, 1(2), pp. 187–214.

Feld, B. C. (1999b). *Bad kids: Race and the transformation of the juvenile court*. New York: Oxford University Press.

Feyerherm, W. (1995). "The DMC initiative: The convergence of policy and research themes," in Kempf-Leonard, K., Pope, C. E. and Feyerherm, W. (eds.), *Minorities in juvenile justice*. Thousand Oaks, CA: SAGE Publications.

Frankel, A. (2019). "1st Circuit: In criminal justice system, transparency (still) trumps juror privacy." January 22. *Reuters*. Available at: https://www.reuters.com/article/legal-us-otc-jury/1st-circuit-in-criminal-justice-system-transparency-trumps-juror-privacy-idUSKCN1PG2KH

Frazier, C. E. and Cochran, J. (1986). "Detention of juveniles: Its effects on subsequent juvenile court processing decisions." *Youth and Society*, 17(3), pp. 286–385.

Frazier, C. E. and Bishop, D. M. (1995). "Reflections on race effects in juvenile justice," in Kempf-Leonard, K., Pope, C. E. and Feyerherm, W. (eds.), *Minorities in juvenile justice*. Thousand Oaks, CA: SAGE Publications.

Free. M. (1996). *African Americans and the Criminal Justice System*. New York, NY: Garland Publishing.

Gabbidon, S. L. (2003). "Racial profiling by store clerks and security personnel in retail establishments: An exploration of 'shopping while Black.'" *Journal of Contemporary Criminal Justice*, 19(3), pp. 345–64.

Geller, A., Fagan, J., Tyler, T. and Link, B. G. (2014). "Aggressive policing and the mental health of young urban men." *American Journal of Public Health*, 104(12), pp. 2321–7. doi: 10.2105/ajph.2014.302046.

Ghent, A. C., Hernández-Murillo, R. and Owyang, M. T. (2014). "Differences in subprime loan pricing across races and neighborhoods." *Regional Science and Urban Economics*, 48, pp. 199–215.

Glover, K. (2009). *Racial profiling: Research, racism, and resistance*. Lanham, MD: Rowman and Littlefield.

Gomes, H. S., Maia, A. and Farrington, D. P. (2018). "Measuring offending: Self-reports, official records, systematic observation and experimentation." *Crime Psychology Review*, 4(1), pp. 26–44.

Goodman, W. M., Spruill, S. E. and Komaroff, E. (2019). "A proposed hybrid effect size plus p-value criterion: Empirical evidence supporting its use." *American Statistician*, 73(sup1), pp. 168–85.

Gottfredson, M. and Hirschi, T. (1990). *A general theory of crime*. Stanford, CA: Stanford University Press.

Goyal, M. K., Kuppermann, N., Cleary, S. D., Teach, S. J. and Chamberlain, J. M. (2015). "Racial Disparities in Pain Management of Children With Appendicitis in Emergency Departments." *JAMA Pediatrics,* 169(11), 996–1002. doi:10.1001/jamapediatrics.2015.1915

Graham, P. C. (2018). "Housing crisis for Black Americans is a 'de jure' issue." October 20. *Charlotte Post*. Available at: https://search.proquest.com/docview/2136843125?accountid=12964

Gramlich, J. (2017). "Most violent and property crimes in the U.S. go unsolved." 1 March. *Pew Research Center*. Available at: https://www.pewresearch.org/fact-tank/2017/03/01/most-violent-and-property-crimes-in-the-u-s-go-unsolved/

Greenwood, B. N., Hardeman, R. R., Huang, L. and Sojourner, A. (2020). "Physician–patient racial concordance and disparities in birthing mortality for newborns." *Proceedings of the National Academy of Sciences*, 117(35), 21194–200. https://doi.org/10.1073/pnas.1913405117

Griggs, J. (2014). *The effect of race on pretrial detention in the juvenile justice system: A meta-analysis*. Doctoral dissertation, University of Connecticut. Available at: http://OpenCommons@UConn

Grim, R. and Lacy, A. (2019). "Pete Buttigieg says marijuana arrests signify 'systemic racism.' His South Bend police fit the bill." 26 November. *The Intercept*. Available at: https://theintercept.com/2019/11/26/pete-buttigieg-south-bend-marijuana-arrests/

Gwet, K. L. (2014). *Handbook of inter-rater reliability: The definitive guide to measuring the extent of agreement among raters*, 4th ed. Gaithersburg, MD: Advanced Analytics.

Hamparian, D., Leiber, M., Morton, R. and Community Research Associates. (1997). *Disproportionate confinement of minority juveniles in secure facilities: 1996 national report*. Washington, DC: US Department of Justice, Office of Justice Programs, Office of Juvenile Justice and Delinquency Prevention.

Hannah-Jones, N. (2016). "Choosing a School for My Daughter in a Segregated City." July 3. *The New York Times*. https://www.nytimes.com/2016/06/12/magazine/choosing-a-school-for-my-daughter-in-a-segregated-city.html

Hardt, R. H. and Petersen-Hardt, S. (1977). "On determining the quality of the delinquency self-report method." *Journal of Research in Crime and Delinquency*, 14(2), pp. 247–61.

Harris, A. G., Henderson, G. R. and Williams, J. D. (2005). "Courting customers: Assessing consumer racial profiling and other marketplace discrimination." *Journal of Public Policy and Marketing*, 24(1), pp. 163–71.

Hart, R. (2021). "Figures show stark difference between arrests at D.C. Black Lives Matter protest and arrests at Capitol Hill." January 7. *Forbes*. Available at: https://www.forbes.com/sites/roberthart/2021/01/07/figures-show-stark-difference-between-arrests-at-dc-black-lives-matter-protest-and-arrests-at-capitol-hill/?sh=5409aa915706

Hathaway, S. R., Monachesi, E. D. and Young, L. A. (1960). "Delinquency rates and personality." *Journal of Criminal Law, Criminology, and Police Science*, 50(5), pp. 433–40.

Hawkins, D., Laub, J. and Lauritsen, J. (1998). "Race, ethnicity, and serious juvenile offending," in Loeber, R. and Farrington, D. M. (eds.), *Serious and violent juvenile offenders: Risk factors and successful interventions*. Thousand Oaks, CA: SAGE Publications.

Hawkins, D. F., Kempf-Leonard, K. and Bishop, D. M. (2005). "The role of race and ethnicity in juvenile justice processing," in Hawkins, D. F. and Kempf-Leonard, K. (eds.), *Our children, their children: Confronting racial and ethnic differences in American juvenile justice*. Chicago, IL: University of Chicago Press, pp. 23–82.

Hawkins, J., Herrenkohl, T., Farrington, D., Brewer, D., Catalano, R., Harachi, T. and Cothern, L. (2000). *Predictors of youth violence*. Washington, DC: US Department of Justice, Office of Justice Programs, Office of Juvenile Justice and Delinquency Prevention.

Hendricks, J. and Byers, B. (eds.). (2000). *Multicultural perspectives in criminal justice and criminology*, 2nd ed. Springfield, IL: Charles C. Thomas Publisher.

Hennigan, W. J. and Bergengruen, V. (2021). "Insurrectionists openly planned for weeks to storm the Capitol. Why were police so easily overwhelmed?" January 7. *Time*. Available at: https://time.com/5927215/capitol-hill-police-riots-unprepared/

Henry, K. L., Cavanagh, T. M. and Oetting, E. R. (2011). "Perceived parental investment in school as a mediator of the relationship between socio-economic indicators and educational outcomes in rural America." *Journal of Youth and Adolescence*, 40(9), pp. 1164–77.

Herrnstein, R. and Murray, C. (1994). *The bell curve: Intelligence and class structure in American life*. New York, NY: Free Press Paperbacks.

Hindelang, M. J., Hirschi, T. and Weis, J. G. (1981). *Measuring delinquency*. Beverly Hills, CA: SAGE Publications.

Hinton, E. (2017). *From the war on poverty to the war on crime: The making of mass incarceration in America*. Harvard, MA: Harvard University Press.

Hirschi, T. (1969). *Causes of delinquency*. Berkeley, CA: University of California Press.

Horton, A., Tran, A. B., Steckelber, A. and Muyskens, J. (2020). "Military helicopters descended on protesters in Washington, D.C. as a 'show of force'. Here's how close they got." 23 June. *Washington Post*. Available at: https://www.washingtonpost.com/graphics/2020/investigations/helicopter-protests-washington-dc-national-guard/

Hsia, H. and Hamparian, D. (1998). *Disproportionate minority confinement: 1997 update*. Washington, DC: US Department of Justice, Office of Justice Programs, Office of Juvenile Justice and Delinquency Prevention.

Huang, F. L. (2019). "Alternatives to logistic regression models in experimental studies." *Journal of Experimental Education*, 87, pp. 1–12. doi: 10.1080/00220973.2019.1699769

Huizinga, D. and Elliot, D. S. (1986). "Reassessing the reliability and validity of self-report delinquent measures." *Journal of Quantitative Criminology*, 2(4), pp. 293–327.

Huizinga, D. and Elliott, D. S. (1987). "Juvenile offenders: Prevalence, offender incidence, and arrest rates by race." *Crime and Delinquency*, 33(2), pp. 206–23.

Humes, E. (1996). *No matter how loud I shout*. New York, NY: Touchstone.

In re Gault, 387 U.S (1967).

In Re Winship, 397 U.S. 358 (1970).

Jackson, R. and Pabon, E. (2000). "Race and treating other people's children as adults." *Journal of Criminal Justice*, 28(6), pp. 507–15.

Johnson, B. D. and Betsinger, S. (2009). "Punishing the Model Minority: Asian-American criminal sentencing outcomes in federal district courts". *Criminology*, 47(4), 1045–90. https://doi.org/10.1111/j.1745-9125.2009.00169.x

Johnson, E. (2019). "Racial inequality, at college and in the workplace." October 18. *Inside Higher Education*. Available at: https://www.insidehighered.com/news/2019/10/18/racial-inequality-college-and-workplace

Jolliffe, D. and Farrington, D. P. (2014). "Self-reported offending: Reliability and validity," in Bruinsma, G. and Weisburd, D. (eds.), *Encyclopedia of criminology and criminal justice*. New York, NY: Springer, pp. 4716–23.

Jones, J. and Mosher, W. (2013). *Fathers' Involvement With Their Children: United States, 2006–2010*. National Health Statistics Report Number 71. Available at: https://www.cdc.gov/nchs/data/nhsr/nhsr071.pdf

Joseph, J. (1995). *Black youths, delinquency, and juvenile justice*. Westport, CT: Greenwood Publishing Group.

Juszkiewicz, J. (2000). *Youth crime/adult time: Is justice served? Building blocks for youth*. Washington, DC: Pretrial Services Resource Center.

Kaba, M. (2020). "Opinion: Yes, we mean literally abolish the police." June 13. *New York Times*. Available at: https://www.nytimes.com/2020/06/12/opinion/sunday/floyd-abolish-defund-police.html

Kahn, J. (2017). "Science is complex—so is race." *American Journal of Bioethics*, 17(9), pp. 56–8.

Kakar, V., Voelz, J., Wu, J. and Franco, J. (2018). "The Visible Host: Does race guide Airbnb rental rates in San Francisco?" *Journal of Housing Economics*, 40 (25–40). https://doi.org/10.1016/j.jhe.2017.08.001

Kamin, D. (2020). "Black homeowners face discrimination in appraisals." August 25. *New York Times*. Available at: https://www.nytimes.com/2020/08/25/realestate/blacks-minorities-appraisals-discrimination.html

Kaur, H. C. (2019). "Black kids go missing at a higher rate than White kids. Here's why we don't hear about them." November 3. *CNN News*. Available at: https://www.cnn.com/2019/11/03/us/missing-children-of-color-trnd/index.html

Kaur, H. C. (2020). "Videos often contradict what police say in reports. Here's why some officers continue to lie." June 6. *CNN News*. Available at: https://edition.cnn.com/2020/06/06/us/police-reports-lying-videos-misconduct-trnd/index.html

Kempf-Leonard, K., Sontheimer, K. and Sontheimer, H. (1995). "Racial disparities in the confinement of juveniles: Effects of crime and community social structure on punishment," in Kempf-Leonard, K., Pope, C. E. and Feyerherm, W. (eds.), *Minorities in juvenile justice*. Thousand Oaks, CA: SAGE Publications.

Ketchum, P. (2008). "Where are all the White kids? The effects of race in juvenile court decision making." Doctoral Dissertation, Texas A&M University. Proquest.

Khuu, B. P., Lee, H. Y., Zhou, A. Q., Shin, J. and Lee, R. (2016). "Healthcare providers' perspectives on parental health literacy and child health outcomes among Southeast Asian American immigrants and refugees." *Children and Youth Services Review*, 67, pp. 220–9.

Kiang, L., Huynh, V. W., Cheah, C. S. L, Wang, Y. and Yoshikawa, H. (2017). "Moving beyond the model minority." *Asian American Journal of Psychology*, 8(1), pp. 1–6.

Kim, J. and Bushway, S. D. (2018). "Using longitudinal self-report data to study the age–crime relationship." *Journal of Quantitative Criminology*, 34(2), pp. 367–96.

Kim, L., Whitaker, M., O'Halloran, A., Kambhampati, A., Chai, S. J., Reingold, A., et al. COVID-NET Surveillance Team (2020). "Hospitalization rates and characteristics of children aged <18 years hospitalized with laboratory-confirmed COVID-19". *Morbidity and Mortality Weekly Report*, 69(32), pp. 1081–8. https://doi.org/10.15585/mmwr.mm6932e3

King, C., Chen, J., Dagher, R. K. Holt, C. L., Thomas, S. B. (2015). "Decomposing differences in medical care access among cancer survivors by race and ethnicity." *American Journal of Medical Quality*, 30(5), pp. 459–69.

Kirk, D. S. (2006). "Examining the divergence across self-report and official data sources on inferences about the adolescent life-course of crime." *Journal of Quantitative Criminology*, 22(2), pp. 107–29.

Kirschenman, J. and Neckerman, K. (1991). "We'd love to hire them, but …: The meaning of race for employers," in Jencks, C., Peterson, P. E. (eds.), *The urban underclass*. Washington, DC: Brookings Institution.

Knight, M. G., Norton, N. E., Bentley, C. C. and Dixon, I. R. (2004). "The power of black and Latina/o counterstories: Urban families and college-going processes." *Anthropology & Education Quarterly*, 35(1), pp. 99–120. doi: 10.1525/aeq.2004.35.1.99

KOCO (2020). "Law enforcement vehicle burned, tear gas deployed as protest intensifies in Oklahoma City." May 31. Available at: https://www.koco.com/article/protesters-gather-saturday-night-in-oklahoma-city-in-response-to-george-floyds-death/32720663#

Kozol, J. (1991). *Savage inequalities: Children in America's schools*. New York, NY: Crown Publishers.

Krisberg, B., Schwartz, I., Fishman, G., Eisikovits, Z., Guttman, E. and Joe, K. (1987). "The incarceration of minority youth." *Crime and Delinquency*, 33(2), pp. 173–205.

Krivo, L. J. and Kaufman, R. L. (2004). "Housing and wealth inequality: Racial-ethnic differences in home equity in the United States." *Demography*, 41(3), pp. 585–605.

Lardiero, C. (1997). "Of disproportionate minority confinement." *Corrections Today*, 59, pp. 14–15.

Lauritsen, J. L. (2005). "Racial and ethnic differences in juvenile offending," in Hawkins, D. F. and Kempf-Leonard, K. (eds.), *Our children, their children: Confronting racial and ethnic differences in American juvenile justice*. Chicago, IL: University of Chicago Press, pp. 83–104.

Lee, J. (2020). "How student debt worsens racial inequality." *GBPI*. Available at: https://gbpi.org/how-student-debt-worsens-racial-inequality/

Leiber, M. J. (2002). "Disproportionate minority confinement (DMC) of youth: An analysis of state and federal efforts to address the issue." *Crime and Delinquency*, 48(1), pp. 3–45.

Leiber, M. J. and Jamieson, K. M. (1995). "Race and decision making within juvenile justice: The importance of context." *Journal of Quantitative Criminology*, 11(4), pp. 363–88.

Leiber, M. J. and Fox, K. C. (2005). "Race and the impact of detention on juvenile justice decision making." *Crime and Delinquency*, 51(4), pp. 470–97.

Leiber, M. J. and Mack, K. (2003). "The individual and joint effects of race, gender, and family status on juvenile justice decision-making." *Journal of Research in Crime and Delinquency*, 40(1), pp. 34–70.

Leiber, M. J. and Peck, J. H. (2015). "Race, gender, crime severity, and decision-making in the juvenile justice system." *Crime and Delinquency*, 61(6), pp. 771–97.

Leiber, M. J., Bishop, D. and Chamlin, M. B. (2011). "Juvenile justice decision-making before and after the implementation of the disproportionate minority contact (DMC) mandate." *Justice Quarterly*, 28(3), pp. 460–92.

Lewis, D. O., Shanok, S. S., Cohen, R. J., Kligfeld, M. and Frisone, G. (1980). "Race bias in the diagnosis and disposition of violent adolescents." *American Journal of Psychiatry*, 137(1), pp. 1211–16.

Libassi, C. J. (2018). "The neglected college race gap: Racial disparities among college completers." *Center for American Progress*. Available at: https://www.americanprogress.org/issues/education-postsecondary/reports/2018/05/23/451186/neglected-college-race-gap-racial-disparities-among-college-completers/

Liou, D. D., Antrop-Gonzalez, R. and Cooper, R. (2009). "Unveiling the promise of community cultural wealth to sustaining Latina/o students' college-going information networks." *Educational Studies*, 45(6), pp. 534–55. doi: 10.1080/00131940903311347

Liu, A. and Xie, Y. (2016). "Why do Asian Americans academically outperform Whites? The cultural explanation revisited." *Social Science Research*, 58(1), pp. 210–26.

Loeber, R., Farrington, D. P., Pardini, A. E. and Ahonen, S. D. (2018). "Constancy and change in the prevalence and frequency of offending when based on longitudinal self-reports or official records: Comparisons by gender, race, and crime type." *Journal of Developmental and Life-Course Criminology*, 1(2), pp. 150–68.

Long, S. and Freese, J. (2001). *Regression models for categorical dependent variables using Stata*. College Station, TX: Stata Corporation.

Lundetra, K. (2011). "Does parental educational level predict drop-out from upper secondary school for 16- to 24-year-olds when basic skills are accounted for? A cross country comparison." *Scandinavian Journal of Educational Research*, 55(6), pp. 625–37.

Lynch, J. (2002). *Trends in juvenile violent offending: An analysis of victim survey data*. Washington, DC: US Department of Justice, Office of Justice Programs, Office of Juvenile Justice and Delinquency Prevention.

Lyons, K. (2019). "Racial disparities in traffic stops down, but minority drivers often treated differently." June 25. *CT Mirror*. Available at: https://ctmirror.org/2019/06/25/racial-disparities-in-traffic-stops-down-but-minority-drivers-often-treated-differently/

Maahs, J. (2001). *Maternal risk factors, early life events, and deviant outcomes: Assessing antisocial pathways from birth through adolescence*. Rockville, MD: National Criminal Justice Reference Service.

MacDonald, J. and Lattimore, P. (2010). "Count models in criminology," in Piquero, A. R. and Weisburd, D. (eds.), *Handbook of quantitative criminology*. New York: Springer, pp. 683–98.

MacIntosh, T., Desai, M. M., Lewis, T. T., Jones, B. A. and Nunez-Smith, M. (2013). "Socially-assigned race, healthcare discrimination and preventive healthcare services." *PLOS ONE*, 8(5), p. 64522.

Males, M. (2015). "San Francisco's disproportionate arrest of African American women persists." *CJCJ*. Available at: http://www.cjcj.org/uploads/cjcj/documents/disproportionate_arrests_in_san_francisco.pdf

Males, M. and Macallair, D. (2000). *The color of justice: An analysis of juvenile adult court transfers in California. Building blocks for youth*. Washington, DC: Justice Policy Institute.

Martin, J. (1970). *Towards a political definition of delinquency*. US Department of Health, Education and Welfare. Washington, DC: US Government Printing Office.

Martinez, M. A., Cortez, L. J. and Sáenz, V. B. (2013). "Latino parents' perceptions of the role of schools in college readiness." *Journal of Latinos and Education*, 12(2), pp. 108–20. doi: 10.1080/15348431.2012.745402

Martinez, R. (2002). *Latino Homicide: Immigration, Violence, and Community*. New York, NY and London: Routledge.

Massey, D. and Nancy D. (1993). *American apartheid: segregation and the making of the underclass*. Cambridge, MA: Harvard University Press.

Mather, K. (2015). "LAPD found no bias in all 1,356 complaints filed against officers." December 15. *Los Angeles Times*. Available at: https://www.latimes.com/local/lanow/la-me-ln-lapd-biased-policing-report-20151215-story.html

Mauer, M. (1999). *The sentencing project*. New York, NY: New Press.

Maxfield, M. G. and Babbie, E. R. (2018). *Research methods for criminal justice and criminology*, 8th ed. Stamford, CT: Cengage Learning.

Mazumder, B. (2014). "Black-White differences in intergenerational mobility in the United States," *Economic Perspectives*, 38, 1–18.

McCarthy, B. and Smith, B. (1986). "The conceptualization of discrimination in the juvenile justice process: The impact of administrative factors and screening decision on juvenile court dispositions." *Criminology*, 24(1), pp. 41–64.

McGuire, D. (2002). "Cumulative disadvantage as an explanation for observed disproportionality with the juvenile justice system: An empirical test." *Juvenile and Family Court Journal*, 53(1), pp. 1–17.

McKeiver v. Pennsylvania, 403 U.S. 528 (1971).

McNutt, L., Wu, C., Xue, X. and Hafner, J. P. (2003). "Estimating the relative risk in cohort studies and clinical trials of common outcomes." *American Journal of Epidemiology*, 157(1), pp. 940–3.

McShane, M. and Williams, F., III (eds.). (2003). *Encyclopedia of juvenile justice*. Thousand Oaks, CA: Pine Forge Press.

Medina, R. M., Nicolosi, E., Brewer, S. and Linke, A. M. (2018). "Geographies of organized hate in America: A regional analysis." *Annals of the American Association of Geographers*, 108(4), pp. 1006–21. doi: 10.1080/24694452.2017.1411247.

Mills, C. W. (1997). *The racial contract*. Ithaca, NY: Cornell University Press.

Miracle, V. (2020). "LAPD officers accused of falsifying reports, wrongly classifying people as gang members." January 7. *ABC News*. Available at: https://abc7.com/5821095/

Mitchell, B. and Franco, J. (2018). "HOLC 'redlining' maps: The persistent structure of segregation and economic inequality." *NCRC*. Available at: https://ncrc.org/holc/

Mitchell, O. (2009). "Is the war on drugs racially biased?" *Journal of Crime and Justice*, 32(2), pp. 49–75.

Morris, S., Shanklin, F. and Carter, A. (1993). *Equal justice under law: A report on the overrepresentation of minority children in the Oklahoma juvenile justice system*. Oklahoma City, OK: Oklahoma Commission on Children and Youth.

Moynihan, P. (1965). *The Negro family: The case for national action*. Washington, DC: Office of Policy Planning and Research, US Department of Labor.

Mustillo, S., Krieger, N., Gunderson, E. P., Sidney, S., McCreath, H., and Kiefe, C. I. (2004). "Self-reported experiences of racial discrimination and Black-White differences in preterm and low-birthweight deliveries: The CARDIA Study." *American Journal of Public Health*, 94(12), 2125–31. https://doi.org/10.2105/ajph.94.12.2125

Mustillo, S. A., Lizardo, O. A. and McVeigh, R. M. (2018). "Editors' comment: A few guidelines for quantitative submissions." *American Sociological Review*, 83(6), pp. 1281–3.

NAACP. (2017). "It matters if you are Black or White: Racial disparities in the handling of complaints against North Charleston officers." Available at: https://www.naacpldf.org/files/about-us/NAACP%20LDF%20report%20on%20North%20Charleston%20Police%20Dept%20FINAL%20July%202017.pdf

Nafiu, O. O., Mpody, C., Kim, S. S., Uffman, J. C. and Tobias, J. D. (2020). "Race, postoperative complications, and death in apparently healthy children." *Pediatrics*, 146(2). doi: 10.1542/peds.2019-4113.

National Advisory Committee on Racial, Ethnic and Other Populations. (2014). *Race and Hispanic origin research working group: Final report.* Washington, DC: United States Census Bureau.

National Council on Crime and Delinquency. (2007). *And justice for some: Differential treatment of youth of color in the justice system.* Oakland, CA: National Council on Crime and Delinquency.

National Highway Traffic Administration. (2018). "Risky driving." March 16. Available at: https://www.nhtsa.gov/risky-driving

National Network for Safe Communities at John Jay College. (2021, February 24). "Group violence intervention." February 24. *National Network for Safe Communities (NNSC)*. Available at: https://nnscommunities.org/strategies/group-violence-intervention/

National Panel on Juvenile Crime. (2000). "Race, crime, and juvenile justice: The issue of racial disparity," in McCord, J., Widom, C. S. and Crowell, N. A. (eds.), *Juvenile crime, juvenile justice.* Washington, DC: National Academy Press.

Neckerman, K., & Kirschenman, J. (1991). "Hiring strategies, racial bias, and inner-city workers." *Social Problems,* 38(4), 433-47. doi:10.2307/800563

New York Times. (2019, August 22). "*Perspective:* For black men, growing up rich may not help." August 22. *Tampa Bay Times.* https://www.tampabay.com/opinion/perspective/Perspective-For-black-men-growing-up-rich-may-not-help_166508831/

Nichols, J. D. (2004). "An exploration of discipline and suspension data." *Journal of Negro Education*, 73(4), pp. 408–23.

Nittle, N. K. (2019). "How racism affects minority students in public schools." *ToughtCo.* Available at: https://www.thoughtco.com/how-racism-affects-public-school-minorities-4025361

Novick, J. and Novick, K. K. (2020). "Why won't they learn: Unconscious underpinnngs of corporal punishment." *Psychoanalytic Study of the Child*, 73(1), pp. 62–72.

OJJDP (Office of Juvenile Justice and Delinquency Prevention). (2010). *Oklahoma juvenile justice profile: 2010. Statistical briefing book.* Washington, DC: Department of Justice, Office of Justice Programs.

OJJDP (Office of Juvenile Justice and Delinquency Prevention). (2015). "Literature review: A product of the model programs guide." Washington, DC: US Department of Justice, Office of Justice Programs.

OJJDP (Office of Juvenile Justice and Delinquency Prevention). (2019). "The Decline in Arrests of Juveniles Continued Through 2019" Available at: https://www.ojjdp.gov/ojstatbb/snapshots/DataSnapshot_UCR2019.pdf

OJJDP (Office of Juvenile Justice and Delinquency Prevention). (2020). *Statistical briefing book*. Available at: https://www.ojjdp.gov/ojstatbb/special_topics/qa11501.asp?qaDate=2019

Oliver, M. and Shapiro, T. (2006). *Black wealth/White wealth: A new perspective on racial inequality*. New York, NY: Routledge.

Omi, M. and Winant, H. (1994). *Formation in the United States: From the 1960's to the 1990's*, 2nd ed. New York, NY: Routledge.

Oquendo, A. R. (1995). "Re-imagining the Latino/a race." *Harvard Blackletter Law Journal*, 12(1), pp. 93–7.

Orange County Probation Office. (1997). "8 percent problem study findings". OCgov.com. Available at: https://www.ocgov.com/gov/probation/about/8percent/findings

Oregon Criminal Justice Commission. (2019). *Statistical transparency of policing report per House Bill 2355*. Available at: https://www.oregon.gov/cjc/CJC%20Document%20Library/STOP_Report_Final.pdf

Pager, D. (2003). "The Mark of a Criminal Record." *American Journal of Sociology*, 108(5), pp. 937–75.

Pager, D. and Shepherd, H. (2008). "The Sociology of Discrimination: Racial Discrimination in Employment, Housing, Credit, and Consumer Markets." *Annual Review of Sociology*, 34, pp. 181–209.

Papachristos, A. V., Wildeman, C. and Roberto, E. (2015). "Tragic, but not random: The social contagion of nonfatal gunshot injuries." *Social Science & Medicine*, 125, pp. 139–50. https://doi.org/10.1016/j.socscimed.2014.01.056

Paradies, Y., Ben, J., Denson, N., Elias, A., Priest, N., Pieterse, A., Gupta, A., Kelaher, M., & Gee, G. (2015). "Racism as a Determinant of Health: A Systematic Review and Meta-Analysis." *PlOS One*, 10(9), e0138511. https://doi.org/10.1371/journal.pone.0138511

Paschall, M. J., Ornstein, M. L. and Flewelling, R. L. (2001). "African American male adolescents' involvement in the criminal justice system: The criterion validity of self-report measures in a prospective study." *Journal of Research in Crime and Delinquency*, 38(2), pp. 174–87.

Peck, J. H. and Jennings, W. G. (2016). "A critical examination of 'being Black' in the juvenile justice system." *Law and Human Behavior*, 40(3), pp. 219–32.

Peeples, F. and Loeber, R. (1993). "Families, race and juvenile delinquency: A study of neighborhood contexts," in Huizinga, D., Loeber, R. and Thornberry, T. (eds.), *Urban delinquency and substance abuse*. Washington, DC: US Department of Justice, Office of Justice Programs, Office of Juvenile Justice and Delinquency Prevention.

Perna, L. W. (2006). "Studying college access and choice: A proposed conceptual model," in Smart, J. C. (ed.), *Higher education handbook of theory and research*. Cambridge, MA: Springer, pp. 99–157.

Perry, A. M., Rothwell, J. and Harshbarger, D. (2018). "The devaluation of assets in black neighborhoods." *Brookings College*. Available at: https://www.brookings.edu/research/devaluation-of-assets-in-black-neighborhoods/

Pettit, B. and Western, B. (2004). "Mass imprisonment and the life course: Race and class inequality in U.S. incarceration." *American Sociological Review*, 69(2), pp. 151–69.

Phelan, J. C., & Link, B. G. (2015). "Is Racism a Fundamental Cause of Inequalities in Health?" *Annual Review of Sociology*, 41(1), 311–30. https://doi.org/10.1146/annurev-soc-073014-112305

Pierson, E., Simoiu, C., Overgoor, J., Corbett-Davies, S., Jenson, D., Shoemaker, A. et al. (2020). "A large-scale analysis of racial disparities in police stops across the United States." *Nature Human Behaviour*, 4(7), pp. 736–45. doi: 10.1038/s41562-020-0858-1

Piliavin, I. and Briar, S. (1964). "Police encounters with juveniles." *American Journal of Sociology*, 70(2), pp. 206–14.

Piper, M. E., Cook, J. W., Schlam, T. R., Jorenby, D. E., Smith, S. S., Bolt, D.M. and Loh, W. Y. (2010). "Gender, race, and education differences in abstinence rates among participants in two randomized smoking cessation trials." *Nicotine & Tobacco Research*, 12(6), pp. 647–57. Available at: https://doi.org/10.1093/ntr/ntq067

Piquero, A. R. (2008). "Disproportionate minority contact." *The Future of Children*, 18(2), pp. 59–79.

Piquero, A. R., & Brame, R. W. (2008). "Assessing the Race–Crime and Ethnicity–Crime Relationship in a Sample of Serious Adolescent Delinquents." *Crime & Delinquency*, 54(3), pp. 390–422. https://doi.org/10.1177/0011128707307219

Pittman, C. (2020). "'Shopping while Black': Black consumers' management of racial stigma and racial profiling in retail settings." *Journal of Consumer Culture*, 20(1), pp. 3–22.

Pizarro, J., Chermak, S. and Gruenewald, J. (2007). "Juvenile 'super-predators' in the news: A comparison of adult and juvenile homicides." *Journal of Criminal Justice and Popular Culture*, 14(1), pp. 85–111.

Poe-Yamagata, E. (2000). *And justice for some: Differential treatment of minority youth in the justice system*. Washington, DC: Youth Law Center.

Pope, C. E. and Feyerherm, W. (1990a). "Minority status and juvenile justice processing, Part I." *Criminal Justice Abstracts*, 22(2), pp. 327–36.

Pope, C. E. and Feyerherm, W. (1990b). "Minority status and juvenile justice processing, Part II." *Criminal Justice Abstracts*, 22(3), pp. 527–42.

Pope, C. E. and Feyerherm, W. (1991). *Minorities in the juvenile justice system*. Washington, DC: US Department of Justice, Office of Juvenile Justice and Delinquency Prevention.

Pope, C. E. and Snyder, H. (2003). *Race as a factor in juvenile arrests*. Washington, DC: US Department of Justice, Office of Justice Programs, Office of Juvenile Justice and Delinquency Prevention.

Pope, C. E., Lovell, R. and Hsia, H. M. (2002). *Disproportionate minority confinement: A review of the research literature from 1989 through 2001*. Washington, DC: Office of Juvenile Justice and Delinquency Prevention.

Pope, C. E., Lovell, R. and Hsia, H. M. (2003). *Synthesis of disproportionate minority confinement (DMC) literature (1989–1999)*. Washington, DC: US Department of Justice, Office of Juvenile Justice and Delinquency Prevention.

Poston, B. and Chang, C. (2019). "Analysis: LAPD searches Blacks and Latinos more often." June 5. *Los Angeles Times*. Available at: https://www.latimes.com/local/lanow/la-me-lapd-searches-20190605-story.html

Pryor, M., Buchanan, K. S. and Goff, P. A. (2020). "Risky situations: Sources of racial disparity in police behavior." *Annual Review of Law and Social Science*, 16(1), pp. 343–60.

Puzzanchera, C. and Hockenberry, S. (2015). *Disproportionate minority contact databook*. Washington, DC: Office of Juvenile Justice and Delinquency Prevention.

Quigley, A. (2019). "Racial disparities, search rates decline in Burlington police traffic stops." July 30. *VTDigger*. Available at: https://vtdigger.org/2019/07/30/racial-disparities-search-rates-decline-in-burlington-police-traffic-stops/

Raizada, A., Stys, A., Stys, T. and Petrasko, M. (2014). "Ethnic differences in coronary artery calcium scores between Native Americans and Caucasians in the Midwest." *Journal of the American College of Cardiology*, 63(12), p. 1162.

Reeves, R. V. and Halikias, D. (2017). "Race gaps in SAT scores highlight inequality and hinder upward mobility." *Brookings*. Available at: https://www.brookings.edu/research/race-gaps-in-sat-scores-highlight-inequality-and-hinder-upward-mobility/

Reinarman, C., Passas, N., & Agnew, R. (2000). "The Future of Anomie Theory." *Contemporary Sociology*, 29(1), pp. 252. https://doi.org/10.2307/2654956

Rios-Aguilar, C. and Kiyama, J. M. (2012). "Funds of knowledge: An approach to studying Latina(o) students' transition to college." *Journal of Latinos and Education*, 11(1), pp. 2–16. doi: 10.1080/15348431.2012.631430

Rodgers, N. and Robinson, R. (2017). "How the news media distorts black families." December 29. *Washington Post*.

Rodriguez, N. (2007). "Juvenile court context and detention decisions: Reconsidering the role of race, ethnicity, and community characteristics in juvenile court processes." *Justice Quarterly*, 24(4), pp. 629–56.

Rodriguez, N. (2010). "The cumulative effect of race and ethnicity in juvenile court outcomes and why preadjudication detention matters." *Journal of Research in Crime and Delinquency*, 47(3), pp. 391–413.

Rogers, K. (2020). "Healthy Black kids die more often after surgery than White kids, study finds." June 20. *CNN News*. Available at: https://www.cnn.com/2020/07/20/health/black-children-surgery-death-risk-wellness/index.html

Ross, M. (2018). "The Institute for Municipal and Regional Policy Central Connecticut University Study by the Institute for Municipal & Regional Policy (IMRP) traffic stop data analysis and findings." State of Rhode Island Comprehensive Police–Community Relationship Act of 2015 (CCPRA). Institute for Municipal & Regional Policy. Available at: https://web.uri.edu/police/files/2016-Rhode-Island-Traffic-Stop-Study.pdf

Ross, S. L. and Turner, M. A. "Housing Discrimination in Metropolitan America: Explaining Changes between 1989 and 2000." *Social Problems*, 52(2), pp. 152–80. https://doi.org/10.1525/sp.2005.52.2.152

Rovner, J. (2014). *Disproportionate minority contact in the juvenile justice system*. Washington, DC: The Sentencing Project.

Rovner, J. (2016). *Racial disparities in youth commitments and arrests*. Washington, DC: The Sentencing Project.

Russell-Brown, K. (1998). *The color of crime: Racial hoaxes, White fear, Black protectionism, police harassment, and other macroaggressions*. New York, NY: New York University Press.

Sacks, T. K. (2019). *Invisible visits: Black middle-class women in the American healthcare system*. Oxford: Oxford University Press.

Saloner, B. and Le Cook, B. (2013). "Blacks and Hispanics are less likely than Whites to complete addiction treatment, largely due to socioeconomic factors." *Health Affairs*, 32(1), pp. 135–45.

Sampson, R. J. (1997). "Collective regulation of adolescent misbehavior: Validation results from eighty Chicago neighborhoods." *Journal of Adolescent Research*, 12(2), pp. 227–44.

Sampson, R. J., Raudenbush, S. W. and Earls, F. (1997). "Neighborhoods and violent crime: A multilevel study of collective efficacy." *Science*, 277(5328), pp. 918–24.

Schmid, C. H., Stijnen, T. and White, I. R. (2021). *Handbook of meta-analysis*. Boca Raton, FL: CRC Press.

SCHNEIDER, MIK Associated Press. (2019). "Probe: No bias by TSA supervisor, but profiling concerns." August 5. *ABC News*. Available at: https://abcnews.go.com/US/wireStory/probe-finds-evidence-discrimination-tsa-supervisor-64782462

Schreer, G. E., Smith, S. and Thomas, K. (2009). "'Shopping while Black': Examining racial discrimination in a retail setting." *Journal of Applied Social Psychology*, 39(6), pp. 1432–44.

Schuck, A. (2002). *Understanding the role of neighborhood in the long-term criminal consequences of childhood, final report*. Washington, DC: National Criminal Justice Reference Service.

Schumacher, M. and Kurz, G. A. (2000). *The 8% solution*. Thousand Oaks, CA: SAGE Publications.

Sealock, M. D. and Simpson, S. S. (1998). "Unraveling bias in arrest decisions: The role of juvenile offender type-scripts." *Justice Quarterly*, 15(3), pp. 427–57.

Sears, D. O., and Henry, P. J. (2003). "The origins of symbolic racism." *Journal of Personality and Social Psychology*, 85(2), pp. 259–275. https://doi.org/10.1037/0022-3514.85.2.259

Secret, P. E. and Johnson, J. B. (1997). "The effect of race on juvenile justice decision making in Nebraska: Detention, adjudication, and disposition, 1988–1993." *Justice Quarterly*, 14(3), pp. 445–78.

Sellin, T. (1931). "The basis of a crime index." *Journal of Criminal Law and Criminology*, 22(3), pp. 335–56.

The Sentencing Project. (2013). *Report of the Sentencing Project to the United Nations Human Rights Committee regarding racial disparities in the United States criminal justice system*. New York, NY: United Nations.

The Sentencing Project. (2016). "Racial disparities in youth commitments and arrests." Available at: https://www.sentencingproject.org/publications/racial-disparities-in-youth-commitments-and-arrests/

Shapiro, E. (2020). "Only 7 Black students got into Stuyvesant, N.Y.'s most selective high school, out of 895 spots." March 18. *New York Times*. Available at: https://www.nytimes.com/2019/03/18/nyregion/black-students-nyc-high-schools.html?smid=nytcore-ios-share

Sickmund, M. and Wan, Y. (2001). "Census of juveniles in residential placement databook." Available at: https://www.ojjdp.gov/ojstatbb/corrections/qa08201.asp

Sickmund, M., Snyder, H. N. and Poe-Yamagata, E. (1997). *Juvenile offenders and victims: 1997 update on violence*. Washington, DC: Office of Juvenile Justice and Delinquency Program, US Department of Justice.

Simoiu, C., Corbett-Davies, S. and Goel, S. (2017). "The problem of infra-marginality in outcome tests for discrimination." *Annals of Applied Statistics*, 11(3), pp. 1193–216.

Simpson, J. N., Goyal, M. K., Cohen, J. S., Badolato, G. M., McGuire, M., Ralph, A., Boyle, M. D., Hamburger, E. K., Gorman, K. C., Cora-Bramble, D. and Delaney, M. (2021). "Results of Testing Children for Severe Acute Respiratory Syndrome Coronavirus-2 Through a Community-based Testing Site." *The Journal of Pediatrics*, 231, pp. 157–161. https://doi.org/10.1016/j.jpeds.2020.12.030

Singer, S. (1996). *Recriminalizing delinquency: Violent juvenile crime and juvenile justice reform*. New York, NY: Cambridge University Press.

Smedley, B. D., Stith, A. Y. and Nelson, A. R. (2003) Institute of Medicine (US) Committee on Understanding and Eliminating Racial and Ethnic Disparities in Health Care. *Unequal Treatment: Confronting Racial and Ethnic Disparities in Health Care*. Washington, D.C.: National Academies.

Smith, T. B. G. (2020). "Pull over: Five things to remember when you see the blue lights." *Post and Courier*. Available at: https://www.postandcourier.com/archives/pull-over-five-things-to-remember-when-you-see-the/article_c898fb10-8905-5eba-ba01-7b2d15312fb4.html

Snyder, H. N. and Sickmund, M. (1999). *Juvenile offenders and victims: 1999 national report*. Washington, DC: Department of Justice, Office of Juvenile Justice Prevention and Delinquency Prevention.

Snyder, H. N. and Sickmund, M. (2006). *Juvenile offenders and victims: 2006 national report*. Washington, DC: US Department of Justice, Office of Justice Programs, Office of Juvenile Justice and Delinquency Prevention.

Son, E., Parish, S. and Igdalsky, L. (2017). "Disparities in health care quality among Asian children with special health care needs." *Health & Social Work*, 42(2), pp. 95–102.

Soss, J., Langbein, L. and Metelko, A. R. (2003). "Why do white Americans support the death penalty?" *Journal of Politics*, 65(2), pp. 397–421.

Stahl, A., Sickmund, M., Finnegan, T., Snyder, H., Poole, R. and Tierney, N. (1999). *Juvenile court statistics 1996*. Washington, DC: US Department of Justice, Office of Justice Programs, Office of Juvenile Justice and Delinquency Prevention.

Steffensmeier, D. and Demuth, S. (2000). "Ethnicity and sentencing outcomes in U.S. federal courts: Who is punished more harshly?" *American Sociological Review*, 65(5), pp. 705–29.

Stout, M. (2017). *Racial and ethnic disparities in traffic stops and stop outcomes in Springfield, Missouri*. Available at: https://www.springfieldmo.gov/DocumentCenter/View/45970/Racial-and-Ethnic-Disparity-in-Traffic-Stops-Report-2012-2016-

Strong, C., Lee, S., Tanaka, M. and Juon, H.-S. (2012). "Ethnic differences in prevalence and barriers of HBV screening and vaccination among Asian Americans." *Journal of Community Health*, 37(5), pp. 1071–80.

Styve, G. J., Layton MacKenzie, D., Gover, A. R. and Mitchell, O. (2000). "Perceived conditions of confinement: A national evaluation of juvenile boot camps and traditional facilities." *Law and Human Behavior*, 24(3), pp. 297–308.

Szklo, M. and Nieto, F. J. (2018). *Epidemiology: Beyond the basics*, 4th ed. Sudbury, MA: Jones and Bartlett Learning.

Taylor, L., Cowls, J., Schroeder, R., & Meyer, E. T. (2014). "Big Data and Positive Change in the Developing World." *Policy & Internet*, 6(4), 418–44. https://doi.org/10.1002/1944-2866.poi378

Texas Criminal Justice Coalition. (2020). "Ending the War on Drugs in Travis County: How Low-Level Drug Possession Arrests are Harmful and Ineffective." Available at: https://www.texascjc.org/system/files/publications/Ending%20the%20War%20on%20Drugs%20in%20Travis%20County.pdf

Texas Justice Initiative Home Page. (2020). Available at: https://texasjusticeinitiative.org/

Thernstrom, A. and Thernstrom, S. (2020). "Black progress: How far we've come, and how far we have to go." *Brookings*. Available at: https://www.brookings.edu/articles/black-progress-how-far-weve-come-and-how-far-we-have-to-go/

Thompson, D. (2020). "Report: California cops more likely to stop black drivers." January 3. *AP News*. Available at: https://apnews.com/article/138c163c8d46c6d86369fb41441d0bc0

Thornberry, T. P. and Krohn, M. D. (2000). "The self-report method for measuring delinquency and crime," in National Institute of Justice, *Measurement and Analysis of Crime and Justice*. Washington, DC: US Department of Justice, pp. 33–83.

Thornberry, T. P. and Krohn, M. D. (2003). "Comparison of self-report and official data for measuring crime," in National Research Council, Measurement Problems, *Criminal Justice Research: Workshop Summary*. Washington, DC: The National Academies Press, pp. 43–94.

Thornberry, T. P., Smith, C., Rivera, C., Huizinga, D. and Stouthamer-Loeber, M. (1999). *Family disruption and delinquency*. Washington, DC: US Department of Justice, Office of Justice Programs, Office of Juvenile Justice and Delinquency Prevention.

Thornberry, T. P., Lizotte, A. J., Krohn, M. D., Smith, C. A. and Porter, P. K. (2003). "Causes and consequences of delinquency," in Thornberry, T. P. and Krohn, M. D. (eds.), *Taking stock of delinquency*. New York, NY: Springer, pp. 11–45.

Tonry, M. (1994). "Racial politics, racial disparities, and the war on crime." *Crime and Delinquency*, 40(4), pp. 475–94.

US Bureau of Justice Statistics. (1985). *The National Survey of Crime Severity*. Washington, DC: US Department of Justice.

US Census Bureau. (2010). *Oklahoma population estimates, American Community Survey*. Washington, DC: US Census Bureau.

US Department of Health and Human Services. National Institutes of Health. National Institute on Drug Abuse. (1991). National Household Survey on Drug Abuse. Ann Arbor, MI: Inter-university Consortium for Political and Social Research. https://doi.org/10.3886/ICPSR06128.v3

US Department of Justice Civil Rights Division. (2015). *Investigation of the Ferguson Police Department*. Available at: https://www.justice.gov/sites/default/files/opa/press-releases/attachments/2015/03/04/ferguson_police_department_report.pdf

US Justice Department. (1993). *Arrests by offense, age, and race*. Available at: https://www.ojjdp.gov/ojstatbb/crime/ucr.asp?table_in=2

Valant, J. (2020). "The banality of racism in education." *Brookings*. Available at: https://www.brookings.edu/blog/brown-center-chalkboard/2020/06/04/the-banality-of-racism-in-education/

Villarosa, L. (2019). "How false beliefs in physical racial difference still live in medicine today." August 14. *New York Times*. Available at: https://www.nytimes.com/interactive/2019/08/14/magazine/racial-differences-doctors.html

Villarreal, D. (2020). "Body cam catches Boston cop bragging about running over Black Lives Matter protestors." *Raw Story*. Available at: https://www.rawstory.com/boston-police-body-cams/

Voigt, R., Camp, N. P., Prabhakaran, V., Hamilton, W. L., Hetey, R. C., Griffiths, C. M., Jurgens, D., Jurafsky, D. and Eberhardt, J. L. (2017). "Language from police body camera footage shows racial disparities in officer respect." *Proceedings of the National Academy of Sciences*, 114(25), pp. 6521–6526. https://doi.org/10.1073/pnas.1702413114

Wachsmuth, D. and Weisler, A. (2018). "Airbnb and the rent gap: Gentrification through the sharing economy." *Environment and Planning*, 50(6), pp. 1147–70.

Walsemann, K. M., & Bell, B. A. (2010). "Integrated schools, segregated curriculum: effects of within-school segregation on adolescent health behaviors and educational aspirations." *American Journal of Public Health*, 100(9), pp. 1687–1695. https://doi.org/10.2105/AJPH.2009.179424

Washington, K. (2020). "Racial equity in higher education starts in the admissions office." Urban Institute. Available at: https://www.urban.org/urban-wire/racial-equity-higher-education-starts-admissions-office

Wasserstein, R. L. and Lazar, N. A. (2016). "The ASA Statement on p-values: Context, process, and purpose." *American Statistician*, 70(2), pp. 129–33.

Wasserstein, R. L., Schirm, A. L, and Lazar, N. A. (2019). "Moving to a world beyond 'p < 0.05'." *American Statistician*, 73(sup1), pp. 1–19.

Welch, K. and Payne, A. A. (2010). "Racial threat and punitive school discipline." *Social Problems*, 57(1), pp. 25–48.

Western, B. and Pettit, B. (2005). "Black-white wage inequality, employment rates, and incarceration." *American Journal of Sociology*, 111(2), pp. 553–78.

Westervelt, E. (2021). "Off-duty police officers investigated, charged with participating in Capitol riot." January 15. *NPR*. Available at: https://www.npr.org/2021/01/15/956896923/police-officers-across-nation-face-federal-charges-for-involvement-in-capitol-ri

Wilbanks, W. (1987). *The myth of a racist criminal justice system*. Belmont, CA: Wadsworth.

Wilk, P., Maltby, A. and Phillips, J. (2018). "Unmet healthcare needs among indigenous peoples in Canada: Findings from the 2006 and 2012 Aboriginal Peoples Surveys." *Journal of Public Health*, 26(4), pp. 475–83.

Williams, J. D., Henderson, G. R. and Harris, A. (2001). "Consumer racial profiling: Bigotry goes to market." *New Crisis*, 108(6), pp. 22–4.

Wilson, J. Q. and Herrnstein, R. (1985). *Crime and human nature*. New York, NY: Simon & Schuster.

Wilson, M. R. and Eezzuduemhoi, D. R. (2005). "Ophthalmologic disorders in minority populations." *Medical Clinics of North America*, 89(4), pp. 795–804.

Winding, T. N. and Andersen, J. H. (2015). "Socioeconomic differences in school dropout among young adults: The role of social relations." *BMC Public Health*, 15(1054), pp. 1–11.

WISH TV 8. (2019). "Carmel's own data supports I-Team 8 investigation into police ticketing black drivers at higher rate." December 5. Available at: https://www.wishtv.com/news/carmels-own-data-supports-i-team-8-investigation/

Wolfgang, M., Figlio, R. and Sellin, T. (1972). *Delinquency in a birth cohort*. Chicago, IL: University of Chicago Press.

Wood, L. (2020). "Policing counter-protest." *Sociology Compass*, 14(11), pp. 1–10.

Woodward, C. and Oliver, D. (2020). "'Do you belong here?': Lawsuits allege Hilton, other hotels discriminated against Black guests." July 22. *USA Today*. Available at: https://eu.usatoday.com/story/travel/hotels/2020/07/21/hilton-discrimination-lawsuits-black-guests-allege-racism-hotels/5405270002/

Wordes, M. and Bynum, T. S. (1995). "Policing juveniles: Is there bias against youths of color?," in Kempf-Leonard, K., Pope, C. E. and Feyerherm, W. (eds.), *Minorities in juvenile justice*. Thousand Oaks, CA: SAGE Publications, pp. 47–65.

Wright, J. E. and Headley, A. M. (2020). "Police use of force interactions: Is race relevant or gender germane?" *American Review of Public Administration*, 50(8), pp. 851–64.

Wright, W. E. and Boun, S. (2011). "Southeast Asian American education 35 years after initial resettlement: Research report and policy recommendations." *Journal of Southeast Asian American Education and Advancement*, 6(1), pp. 1–92.

Young, B. (2011). "Police discretion in contemporary America." Master's Thesis. Georgetown University. Proquest.

Zane, S. N., Welsh, B. C. and Drakulich, K. M. (2016). "Assessing the impact of race on the juvenile waiver decision: A systematic review and meta-analysis." *Journal of Criminal Justice Volume*, 46(1), pp. 106–17.

Index

References to figures and photographs appear in *italic* type; those in **bold** type refer to tables. References to endnotes show both the page number and the note number (245n3).

A
abstract liberalism 147, 154, 155
Agnew, R. 21
Airbnb rentals 49
alcohol
  consumption **112–14**, 129
  D&A offenses 67, *67–9*, **83–5**
  treatment 48
American Airlines 49
Anderson, Elijah 22, 23, 144–5, 177
ANOVA tests 122n12
Asian Americans
  and Airbnb rentals 49
  in census data 35
  health and healthcare 47, 48
  and model minority myth 72n2
Asian juveniles
  juvenile justice system data 80, 143n16, 143n17
  juvenile self-report data 104–5, 121n8
  see also juvenile justice professionals; policing
assault **140**
attorneys 26, 76–7
  see also juvenile justice professionals
Austin, Texas 41

B
back-end decisions 55, 74
Ban Ki-moon 175
barrio neighbourhoods 161–4, **162**
Bauchner, Howard 47
Bernard, T. J. 8
Bias, Len 14
biological differences 7–8, 20
Bishop, D. M. 25
Blacks
  and Airbnb rentals 49
  in census data 34–5
  and driving 40–3

and drug arrests 44
and education 4–5, 50–4
health and healthcare 47–9
missing children 45
and parenting *see* parenting
and police use of force 43, 46
and shopping 50
and travel 49–50
Black juveniles
  and drug use 13–14, 44
  placement of offenders 24
  and racial profiling 25–6
  stereotypes and imagery 13–15, 26–7
  see also juvenile justice data; juvenile justice professionals; juvenile self-report data; policing
Black Lives Matter (BLM) 39, 43, 182
Bloomfield, New Jersey 43
Blumer, H. 154
Bonilla-Silva, E. 147, 150, 154, 155
Borowski, Susan 34
Boston Police Department 43, 44
Boyd, Rhea 49
boys *see* males
Brame, R. W. 120, 177, 183
breaking & entering **112–14**
breast cancer 47
Bridges, G. S. 24, 26, 27
Burlington, Vermont 41
Bush, George H. W. 14
Bynum, T. S 23, 24

C
California, traffic stops 41
Capitol, storming of 38–9
Carmel, Indiana 42
cases dismissed *92–3*, 93, 94–5, *95*, *98*, 137, **137**
census data 34–5

224

INDEX

Centers for Disease Control and Prevention 46
Chambliss, W. 14
Charleston, South Carolina 41, 43
Charlottesville, Virginia 40
Chetty, R. 153
childbirth 48
children 45, 48–9
 see also education
chronic offenders 145, 176–8
Cincinnati, Ohio 41
Clinton, Bill 14
Coates, T. 26
color-blind racism
 four frames of 147, 154–6
 unpacking 156–60
Columbus, Ohio 43
Community Intervention Centers (CIC) 57, 76
Connecticut, traffic stops 42
control theories 20–1
convictions in adult court 12, 92–3, *92–3*, 94, 97, *97–8*, 100n12, 100n15, **137**, 138–9, **139**
corporal punishment 151–2, 174
correction effect 181
court data 24–5, 37
 see also juvenile justice system data
court officials 24
 see also juvenile justice professionals
court supervision 78
court-ordered probation 78, *92–3*, 93–4, 95–6, *95*, *98*, 137–8, **137–8**, 181
COVID-19 46
criterion validity 125
cultural racism 147, 154, 155–6
culture of violence 161–4, **162**
curfew offenses 67, *67–9*, **140**
custody 78, 91–3, *92–3*, 96, *96*, *98*

D

"decent" people 144–5
declined cases 85–91, *86–7*, *89*, *91*, *98*
deferred decisions *see* informal probation
DeLuca, S. 37
diabetes 47
differential involvement 16–17, 19–23, 36–8, 176–7
differential selection 2
differential treatment
 and DMC (overview of findings) 2, 36–40, 176–80, *176*
 literature on 21, 23–5
 use and meaning of term 2, 17
Dilulio, John 14–15
disorderly conduct **140**
disproportionate minority contact (DMC)
 causes of (overview of findings) 2, 36–40, 176–80, *176*

future research 179, 183
recommendations for change 181–3
Disproportionate Minority Contact mandate 12
district attorneys (DAs) 76–8, 99n1, 180–1
diverted cases 85, 86, *86–7*, *98*
DMC *see* disproportionate minority contact
driving under the influence (DUI) 67, *67–9*
drugs
 arrests 13–14, 44, **140**
 crimes **134**
 D&A offenses 67, *67–9*, **83–5**
 dealers 14
 self-reported use 112, **112–14**
 treatments 48
D'Souza, D. 19
Du Bois, W. E. B. 58

E

education 3–5, 50–4
 see also schools
environmental factors 22–3

F

Facebook 150–1
family life *see* parenting
Feagin, J. 154
Federal Bureau of Investigation (FBI) 24, 25, 175
 National Crime Information Center (NCIC) database 45
Feld, B. C. 24
Feller, Bob 144
females
 and economic success 153
 in juvenile justice system 10, 44, 81, **81**
 physical violence 130–1, *131*
 in police reports 59
 and police use of force 43
 racial inequality in health 47
Ferguson, Missouri 42
foster care 45
Fraternal Order of Police unions (FOP) 182
Frazier, C. E. 25
Free, M. 25
front-end decisions 55, 74

G

gang membership **112–14**, 113–14, 142n11, 163, 164–71, **164–5**
general strain theory 21
ghetto neighbourhoods 161–4, **162**
girls *see* females
Goldwater, Barry 13
Gottfriedson, M. 21–2
Griggs, J. 141
gun violence 145

H

Harris County, Texas 6

225

health and healthcare 46–9
Hepatitis B virus 47
Hilton Properties 49
Hirschi, T. 20, 21–2
Hispanic *see* Latinx
HIV/AIDS 47
home life *see* parenting
homelessness 45
houses of refuge 9, 10

I
informal probation 77, 86, 88–90, *89*, *91*, 98, 99n2
intake dispositions 76
interlocal agreements 76

J
jails, adult 77
  see also sentencing in adult court
Jennings, W. G. 181
job applications 35
Johnson, Lyndon 13
Journal of the American Medical Association (JAMA) 46–7
judges 26–7, 77, 180–1
  see also juvenile justice professionals
juvenile courts
  court system in Oklahoma 76–8
  historical overview 9–11
  recommendations for change 181–2
  representation 26
juvenile detention facilities 6, 76, 77
  see also custody
Juvenile Justice and Delinquency Prevention Act 12
juvenile justice professionals 144–74, 179–80
  and bullying 173–4
  and color-blind racism 156–60
  on culture of violence 161–4
  on direct discrimination and DMC 171–3, **171**
  on existence of racism 171–3, **171**
  on gang membership 164–71, **164–5**
  interview methodology 145–7, 179, 190–5
  on parenting 148–54, **148**, 157–9, 163, 166, 180
  responses to miracle question 147–55, **148**, 156–7, 173–4
  on significance of prior record 169–71, **170**
juvenile justice system
  historical overview 8–12
  progression through *56*
juvenile justice system data 74–99
  characteristics of juveniles 80–2, **81**
  intake decisions 85–91, *86–7*, *89–91*, 97–9, *98*, 135–6, **135–6**, 140–1
  operation of justice system in Oklahoma 75–8

outcomes of court process 91–9, *92–3*, *95–8*, 136–9, **137–9**, 140–1
research methodology 79–80
types of offenses 82–5, **83–5**
juvenile self-report data 101–21
  characteristics of schools 106–9, **107–9**
  characteristics of study group 109–11, **110**
  comparison with school disciplinary data 125–31, **128**, *129–31*
  deviant and criminal behaviours 111–15, **112–15**, 120, **120**
  generalizability of data 132–40, **132**, **134–40**
  interactions with police 115–19, **116–17**, *118–19*
  research methodology 102–6, 125–7, 184–9
  conclusions 119–21, **120**

K
Kaba, M. 101
Kansas City 42
kappa (κ) statistic 127
Kempf-Leonard, K. 23
killing or injuring **112–14**
Kozol, J. 4
Krohn, M. D. 124
Kroll, Bob 55

L
Latinx, use of term 72n3
Latinx
  and Airbnb rentals 49
  in census data 34–5
  and driving 40–3
  and education 4–5, 50–4
  health and healthcare 47, 48
  and police use of force 43
  and racial profiling 24–5
  and travel 49–50
Latinx juveniles *see* juvenile justice data; juvenile justice professionals; juvenile self-report data; policing
law enforcement *see* policing
Lawton, Oklahoma 132–3, **132**, 142n13
lawyers *see* attorneys
literature review 19–27
Livingston, Edward 46–7
log binomial regression models 68, 73n6 n. 6–7
logistic regression model 73n7
Lombroso, Cesare 8
Los Angeles Police Department (LAPD) 5–6, 41, 44
Los Angeles Unified School District 3–5
Lowery, Robert 45

M
males
  and economic success 153

INDEX

in juvenile justice system 81, **81**
physical violence 130–1, *131*
in police reports **59**
and police use of force 43
Martin, John McCullough 1
Martinez, Ramiro, Jr. 22, 23, 177
media reporting 45, 153
meta-analyses 143n19
methodology *see* research methodology
micro-aggressions 40
minimization of racism 147, 154, 155–6
missing children 45
model minority myth 72n2
Moynihan, Daniel Patrick 22
Moynihan Report 13

N

National Academy of Sciences 43
National Association for the Advancement of Colored People 49
Native American, terminology 72n1
Native American juveniles *see* juvenile justice data; juvenile justice professionals; juvenile self-report data; policing
Native Americans
 in census data 35
 and education 4–5, 50–4
 health and healthcare 47–8
 and parenting *see* parenting
naturalization 147, 154, 155
New York City 49
Newsweek 12–13
non-White, use of term 2, 58
North Carolina, traffic stops 41

O

Occam's Razor 34
Office of Juvenile Justice and Delinquency Prevention (OJJDP) 15, 23, 24, 25
Oklahoma
 statewide data 132–40, **132**, **134–40**
 see also juvenile justice data
Oklahoma, University of 52–4, 178–9
Oklahoma City
 juvenile self-report data *see* juvenile self-report data
 law enforcement contact with juveniles *see under* policing
 views of juvenile justice professionals *see* juvenile justice professionals
Oklahoma Office of Juvenile Affairs (OJA) 23, 75–6, 99n4
 custody of juveniles 78, 91–3, *92–3*, 96, *96*, *98*, **137–8**
 Juvenile On-Line Tracking System (JOLTS) 79, 133
 severity score 100n9
Oklahoma State Department of Education (OSDE) 102–3, **103**, 121n2

O'Neill, Tip 14
Orange County, California 145
Oregon, traffic stops 41, 42
"out-of-place" doctrine *see* racial profiling

P

Pager, Devah 35
parens patriae 9, 10
parenting 21–3, 26–7, 153
 views of juvenile justice professionals 148–54, **148**, 157–9, 163, 166, 180
Peck, J. H. 181
person offenses and crimes 99n8
 in juvenile self-report data 112, **112–14**, **134**
 in police data 67, *67–9*, **83–5**
 see also assault; gun violence; physical violence
petitions for court involvement 86–7, 90, *90–1*, *98*
Philadelphia 144–5
physical violence 112, **112–14**, *129–31*, 130–1
Piquero, A. R. 36, 38, 120, 177, 183
policing 55–72
 discretion employed 56–7, 76
 felony arrests 101–2
 law enforcement contact with juveniles 55–72
  characteristics of juveniles 58–62, **59**, **61–2**
  importance of findings 70–2
  juvenile self-report data 115–19, **116–17**, *118–19*
  outcome of contact 62–6, *63–5*, *69–70*, *98*, 132–3, **132**, 139–40, **140**
  research methodology 57–8, 63
  types of offenses 66–70, *67–8*
 of marches versus riots 38–40, 182
 police report data 22, 37, 57–8, 124, 178–9
 police searches 5–6
 and racial stereotypes/profiling 24, 25–6
 recommendations for change 182–3
 traffic stops 40–3
 treatment of missing children 45
 use of force incidents 43, 46
 see also juvenile justice professionals
prison data 124
probation
 court-ordered 78, *92–3*, 93–4, 95–6, *95*, *98*, 137–8, **137–8**, 181
 informal 77, 86, 88–90, *89*, *91*, *98*, 99n2
 in Progressive Era 10
probation officers 27
Progressive movement 8–9, 10
property offenses and crimes
 arrest rate ratios **140**
 in juvenile self-report data 112, **112–14**, **134**

227

in police data 67, *67–9*, **83–5**, 99n7
  see also theft
Proud Boys 38–9, 155
psychiatric care facilities 100n14
public defenders 26, 76–7
public order offenses and crimes 67–8, *69*, **83–5, 112–14, 134**

R
racial profiling 24, 25–6, 50
Ray, Rashawn 46
Reagan, Ronald 14
Reno, Janet 74
research methodology
  overview 16–18, *17*, 27
  interviews with juvenile justice professionals 145–7, 179, 190–5
  juvenile justice system data 79–80
  juvenile self-report data 102–6, 125–7, 184–9
  law enforcement contact with juveniles 57–8, 63
residential treatment facilities 6
Rhode Island 42
risk ratios, reading of 65, 66, 73n10, 88, 100n15, 100n10 n. 10–11
Rovner, J. 141
Russell, Kathryn 25–6

S
San Francisco 44
schools
  demographic data 106–9, **107–9**
  disciplinary data 126–31, **128**, *129–31*
  rural school 102, **107**, 108–9, **109**
  suburban school 102, 106–7, **108**
  Title I high schools 3–5, 50, 53–4
  urban school 102, 106
self-control theory 21–2
self-report data, reliability of 124–5
Sellin, Thorsten 124
sentencing in adult court 12, 92–3, *92–3*, 94, 97, *97–8*, 100n12, 100n15, **137**, 138–9, **139**
The Sentencing Project 60
severity scores 88, 100n9
sex crimes **83–5**, **134**
shopping 50
single-parent families *see* parenting
smoking, quitting 47
  see also tobacco
social bonding theory 20
social media use 150–1
South Bend, Indiana 44
Springfield, Missouri 43
St. Louis County, Missouri 42
status offenses 12, 77, **83–5**, 99n5, **134**
  see also curfew offenses; tobacco
stealing 112, **112–14**, *129*
Steen, S. 24, 26, 27

STEM programs 53
stereotypes, racial and ethnic 13–15, 21, 24, 26–7, 50
strain theory 21
"street" people 144–5

T
technical violations **83–5**, 99n5, **134**
Texas, use of force 43
theft **112–14**, *129*
Thornberry, T. P. 124
Time magazine 13, 39
tobacco
  offenses 67–8, *67*, *68*, *69*
  use by juveniles 112, **112–14**, 129–30, *129*
Tonry, M. 14
traffic offenses 67, *67–9*, 68
traffic stops 40–3
Transportation Security Administration 49–50
travel 49–50
Travis County, Texas 44
tribal-run juvenile facilities 76
Trump, Donald 39
Tukey HSD test 122n13
Tulsa, Oklahoma 132–3, **132**

V
vandalism **112–14**
violent crime **140**
Violent Predator Act 11
visual impairment 47

W
"war on crime" 12–13
"war on drugs" 13–14
warrant offenses *67–9*, 68
Washington, DC 41
weapons
  in juvenile self-report data 112, **112–14**, *129*
  offenses and crimes *67–9*, 68, **83–5**, **134**, **140**
Whites
  and Airbnb rentals 49
  in census data 35
  and driving 40–3
  and education 4
White juveniles
  and drug use 13–14, 44
  placement of offenders 24
  see also juvenile justice data; juvenile justice professionals; juvenile self-report data; policing
Wilbanks, W. 16
Wilson, Natalie 45
Wilson, William Julius 153
Wordes, M. 23, 24

Y
youthful offender designation 100n13

www.ingramcontent.com/pod-product-compliance
Lightning Source LLC
Chambersburg PA
CBHW070921030426
42336CB00014BA/2487